'The literature on decline and survival of the handloom sector in India in the nineteenth century had been ideological, focusing on the British policies of deliberate destruction of the industry. This book, based on data and quantitative estimation rather than preconceived assertions, is a much-needed contribution to the literature. A leading contributor to Indian economic history, Roy more than anybody else is well positioned to write this narrative.'

Bishnupriya Gupta, *Professor of Economics, University of Warwick, UK*

'Given the continued importance of artisanship generally and handloom weaving particularly, both in cultural and economic terms, the book would be likely to find a wide audience among development workers, those interested in cultural heritage, as well as anyone interested in economic history more broadly.'

Abigail McGowan, *Associate Professor of History & Associate Dean of the College of Arts and Sciences, University of Vermont, USA*

THE CRAFTS AND CAPITALISM

This book presents a comprehensive history of the handloom weaving industry in India to challenge and revise the view that competition from machine-produced textiles destroyed the country's handicrafts as claimed by historians until recently. It shows that skill-intensive handmade textiles survived the competition on a large scale and that handmade goods and high-quality manual labour played a positive role in the making of modern India. Rich in archival material, *The Crafts and Capitalism* explores themes such as the historiography of craft technologies; statistical work on nineteenth-century cotton cloth production trends; narratives of merchants, the social leaders, the factory-owners; tools and techniques; and the shift from handloom to power loom. The book argues that changes in the handloom industry were central to the consolidation of new forms of capitalism in India.

An important intervention in Indian economic history, this book will be useful to scholars and researchers of Indian history, economic history, colonial history, modern history, political history, labour history, and political economy. It will also interest nongovernmental organizations, textile historians, and design specialists.

Tirthankar Roy is Professor of Economic History, London School of Economics and Political Science, UK, where he teaches South Asia and global history. He is the author of *India in the World Economy: From Antiquity to the Present* (2012), *Law and the Economy in Colonial India* (with Anand V. Swamy, 2016), and *The Economy of South Asia from 1950 to the Present* (2017). His research interests are history and development of South Asia, global history, empires, and environmental history.

THE CRAFTS AND CAPITALISM

Handloom Weaving Industry in Colonial India

Tirthankar Roy

Routledge
Taylor & Francis Group
LONDON AND NEW YORK

First published 2020 by Routledge

2 Park Square, Milton Park, Abingdon, Oxon OX14 4RN
605 Third Avenue, New York, NY 10017

Routledge is an imprint of the Taylor & Francis Group, an informa business

First issued in paperback 2021

Publisher's Note

The publisher has gone to great lengths to ensure the quality of this reprint but points out that some imperfections in the original copies may be apparent.

British Library Cataloguing-in-Publication Data
A catalogue record for this book is available from the British Library

Library of Congress Cataloging-in-Publication Data
A catalog record for this book has been requested

ISBN: 978-0-367-36528-8 (hbk)
ISBN: 978-1-03-217516-4 (pbk)
DOI: 10.4324/9780429346835

Typeset in Sabon
by Apex CoVantage, LLC

FOR ASOK AND SYAMALI DAS

CONTENTS

FIGURES

MAPS

TABLES

PREFACE

In 1993, I published a book called *Artisans and Industrialization: Indian Weaving in the Twentieth Century*, which was the first attempt to write a systematic economic history of handloom weaving. To date, it remains the only monograph on the subject. Since its publication, the scholarship on topics related to it has processed a lot more evidence than that which the book had dealt with. I have played a part in that enterprise. A new book has become necessary that can synthesize this material.

Why is such a book needed? It is needed because the research conducted in the last 25 years has completely changed the narrative about the industry, but popular debates and discussions on history are yet to register that change. Popular history books and the hundreds of internet blogs that describe the tragic legacies of British rule in India recycle an essentially obsolete story about the crafts, which said that the British Industrial Revolution and the free trade policy of British colonial rule in India had a profoundly destructive effect on Indian artisanal weaving. That story cannot be right, because the crafts, including handloom weaving, continued in large scale well into the twentieth century.

The alternative narrative developed in the book starts from the premise that handloom weaving was a differentiated bundle of skills so that the effects of British industrialization and free trade on it was differentiated too. One of the main markers of differentiation was design skill that added some dimension of quality to the finished cloth. Consumers understood and valued quality. Those handloom weavers who had the skills that the consumers valued gained from the same processes – free trade and British industrialization – which threw their colleagues into unemployment. Where they could use design capability efficiently, merchants and master-weavers made more money and invested more money than before, increasing inequality within the industry.

As this statement shows, the main drivers of change in the industry, according to the book, were internal to the handlooms rather than the external competition of mechanized cloth producers of England or India. That is how the alternative narrative has changed the scholarship. It invites us to write the economic history of handlooms by paying close attention to its capability and how that capability needed to adapt to changing patterns of demand for traditional goods, rather than just assume that machines made that capability so redundant that we need not study it at all.

Besides my own writing, a few publications have significantly advanced our understanding of the history in the last 25 years. The most relevant for the project is Douglas Haynes's *Small Town Capitalism in Western India: Artisans, Merchants, and the Making of the Informal Economy, 1870–1960* (2012), along with several of his writings published in the 1990s and not incorporated fully in *Small Town Capitalism*. Although Haynes's main interest is in small-scale powerloom weaving, there are areas of overlap and compatibility between *Small Town Capitalism* and that part of the book which shows how handloom weaving became a field for new types of business enterprise. Haynes makes the argument in a comparative historical framework, which my book will do too, only differently. There is rather less overlap on most other points.

In the years between the first statement of the thesis and this updated and stronger statement, friendship, discussions, and collaboration with Haynes enriched my thinking on textile history. When I began my career around 1990, Dharma Kumar, the maverick historian, saw the significance of my intellectual project more clearly than I did. She thought (I suspect) that *Artisans and Industrialization* had underestimated the significance. This is an appropriate occasion to remember her role in my decision to write this book. Many others also contributed to the shaping of the project, whom I have acknowledged elsewhere.

Finally, I wish to thank two anonymous referees for their positive assessment of the project, and thank Mrinmoyee Roy for the excellent glossary and invaluable help in preparing the biographical sketches that appear at the end of the book.

1
INTRODUCTION

Until the end of the 1980s, making cloth on hand-powered looms, or handloom weaving, was the largest industry in India measured in employment. The standard historical narrative about the industry during British colonial rule in the region (c. 1765–1947) said that the British Industrial Revolution and the free trade policy followed by the colonial rulers had a profoundly destructive effect on the industry. That narrative did not sit well with the extensive presence of the industry in postcolonial India. In the last 25 years, a literature emerged to offer an alternative account of history. The book restates and illustrates that alternative account.

The reinterpretation consists of several propositions. The most important of these is that handloom weaving was a differentiated bundle of skills so that the effects of British industrialization and free trade on it was differentiated too. One of the main markers of differentiation was the design skill that made a difference in the quality of the cloth. If the advantage of mechanized weaving was to increase the speed of production, '[t]he technology involved in designs,' I said in an earlier work, 'was . . . to the advantage' of the handloom.[1] Every weaver did not command skill, but many did.

Other propositions follow from this. Consumers of cloth minded quality. Some handloom weavers possessed the skills that the consumers valued. Surviving artisans gained from the same processes – free trade and British industrialization – which threw their less-skilled colleagues into unemployment. And these conditions consolidated capitalism; that is, they helped merchants to sell more and factory owners who were making handmade cloth to earn more money and invest more money than before. That process, in turn, encouraged technological change and increased inequality within the weaving industry.

The rest of the chapter summarizes the interpretation that I believe fits the evidence better. Before that, it is necessary to engage with the conceptual tools and arguments used to explain the long-term tendencies in artisanal industries. A good place to begin is the set of two terms – 'deindustrialization' and 'protoindustrialization' – commonly used in comparative economic history to understand the historical experience of the textile artisan since the nineteenth century. How relevant are these concepts to Indian history?

Deindustrialization

Around 1750, India is believed to have supplied a quarter of the world's industrial output. On the Indian Ocean littoral, during the 250 years following Vasco da Gama's discovery of the sea route between Europe and India (1497–8), cotton textiles procured by the European merchants in Gujarat, Bengal, and the Coromandel Coast dominated world trade, eventually shaping consumer preference in the West.[2] According to some historians, Indian textiles induced import-substituting industrialization in Britain.[3]

Such prominence reflected the Indians' extraordinary proficiency with a whole range of technologies that went into the making of cloth. The most important element in the basket of skills was the weaver's ability to operate the handloom to make a wide variety of products, from coarse cloth to superfine muslins, cotton to silk, plain cloth to cloth designed on the loom or delivered to the printer, dyer, painter, and embroiderer. Deep knowledge of materials, from cotton to silk to wild silk to organic dyeing agents and gold thread, complemented that ability.

Given how successful Indian handmade cloth was as a traded good, what then happened to it in the nineteenth century must have been a very great shock. Between 1820 and 1880, the Indian weaver's prominence in the world's cloth trade and industry declined, as British machine-made yarn and cloth started trading widely. India's decline together with the rise of the cotton textile industry in Britain led to the narrative that the rich artisan tradition in the region suffered a catastrophic shock in the nineteenth century after imported European manufacturers began to flood Indian markets.

Until the 1990s, there was near-total agreement among historians about the shock, its source, the scale, and its aftereffects. 'Artisans,' wrote S.J. Patel, 'especially weavers and tanners, were faced with the ruination of their occupations by the increasing competition of industrial goods.'[4] In the process of this ruination, the self-sufficient village economy was destroyed, and a wage-dependent labour force emerged when none had existed before, according to Patel. '[E]vidence does suggest,' writes Amiya Kumar Bagchi, 'the working of a general process of de-industrialization in India over much of the nineteenth century, caused mainly by the decline of the traditional cotton-weaving and spinning.'[5] Irfan Habib calls the catastrophe the 'eclipse of the handloom.'[6] 'Traditional industry,' writes Aditya Mukherjee, 'was destroyed.'[7] Many scholars have measured the extent of the decline and found it of significant order. One of these works concludes, 'total handicraft textile employment fell absolutely over the entire century.'[8]

These claims confirm a proposition the Indian nationalists had made around 1900, that the free trade policy the British Empire had imposed on India took a heavy toll on Indian livelihood.[9] 'The destruction of indigenous handicrafts,' the nationalists claimed, 'had created unemployment for millions, forcing them to fall back . . . upon agriculture.'[10] In the historiography of economic change in colonial India (1765–1947), this account has become known as the 'deindustrialization' thesis.[11]

If the fact of a decline in handloom weaving is well established, so is the theory that explains it. What happened to handlooms in India was the inevitable outcome of the British Industrial Revolution, that is, the outcome of the invention of a loom that ran eight times faster than the handloom and the emergence of the factory system enabling its wider use. This was a global process. British industrialization caused an industrial decline in the rest of the world on an enormous scale. 'The ruin, sooner or later, of the old-style craftsmen,' wrote Daniel Thorner, 'was as integral a part of the Industrial Revolution as the coming of the factory system.'[12] The third world paid the price for Britain's economic emergence. To quote Bagchi again, 'adjustments to technological change in the advanced capitalist countries took place overseas.'[13]

Economists treat this theory of asymmetric adjustment as a vital piece in the economic history of the world in the nineteenth century. The economist Jeffery Williamson has written articles and books suggesting that industrialization in the western world generated deindustrialization in the rest of the world via changes in relative prices, and, in turn, caused international economic inequality to increase between 1820 and 1950. 'Britain's productivity gains in manufacturing,' he writes, 'led to declining world textile and metal product prices, making their production in India less and less profitable.'[14]

India's deindustrialization, in this way, becomes a crucial example in a bigger story about the economic history of the modern world. That story is about the origins of international economic inequality in the world from 1820 until 1950. Contributors to this literature hold, usually based on unreliable datasets, that Asians were once better off than the Europeans before modern economic growth ushered in a dramatic reversal of status. The decline of the artisanal textile industry was one of the main reasons and symptoms of the fall of Asia. India enters world economic history as a tragedy largely because of the misfortune of its handloom weavers.

For someone who is mainly interested in knowing what happened to the Indian handloom weaver, this narrative will appear unsatisfactory for two reasons. First, it denies the non-West any worthwhile industrial history. Starting with Karl Marx in the 1850s, arguments in world economic history usually treat the 'rise of the western world' as the benchmark narrative and deduce what happened to the rest of the world from what happened in the western world. Following this tradition, economists more recently have used a variety of theories of economic growth to explain the rise of the West. The regions outside Western Europe and North America – the rest of the world – enter the causal theory as regions where the factors causing economic growth were missing. The deindustrialization argument does exactly that. It identifies British industrialization as the thing to be explained and deduces change in India as an effect of British industrialization. Indian economic history is an inference drawn from studying British economic history. The premise is that Britain changed and India did not change and therefore suffered. But if India did not change, why study India at all? Deindustrialization as a theoretical construction makes it unnecessary to conduct a serious investigation into Indian textile history. Everyone knows what happened to the Indian artisans. They were the victims of the invention of machinery. Why study them, then?

The second problem is theory-fetishism. Causal models of long-term economic growth concentrate on the cause, not the region and its specific history. If Indian textile history is derived from a theory of world inequality, it is worthwhile to concentrate on the theory and not on India. An example of theory-fetishism is Jeffery Williamson's book *Trade and Poverty*. The book explains deindustrialization with a theory of relative price changes. Like any economics book, *Trade and Poverty* takes its theory seriously, so seriously that it fails to notice that the textile history of India had rejected the fact that the theory wants to explain.[15]

That brings us to the question: what fact should we be explaining? The next chapter delivers a fuller answer to the question. I select one set of statistics from the chapter to make a quick point. Consider Figure 1.1. Estimates of the consumption of handmade cloth in India confirm that there was a decline in the nineteenth century. *The trend then reversed.* From about 1880, there was a rise in the consumption of handloom cloth, sustained until the end of the data series, 1940. Not only was there a turnaround, but there was also a significant growth in productivity in the industry in the early twentieth century. Between 1900 and 1930, the volume of handloom cloth production about doubled, even as the number of workers and looms did not change (Chapter 5, Table 5.1). As far as we can measure, real wages in hand-weaving held steady, which would mean that profits in the industry increased. Handloom weaving in the early twentieth century was becoming a profitable business.

The turnaround as such is not a new finding. 'At a certain stage,' wrote D.R. Gadgil in 1928, 'a point of equilibrium was reached' in the competition between handloom weaving and machine weaving.[16] Gadgil did not discover this fact but quoted provincial officers like Alfred Chatterton of Madras, C.A. Silberrad of the United Provinces, and Abdul Latifi of Punjab, to restate the fact. These officers and others like them had already produced a significant body of writings on local weaving industries (see also 'monographs' in the Glossary and the 'Selected biographies' at the end of the book). They showed that in most parts of India, the industry was becoming differentiated. That is, one part of it continued to decline, whereas another part was stable, even growing. Figure 1.1 shows that between 1880 and

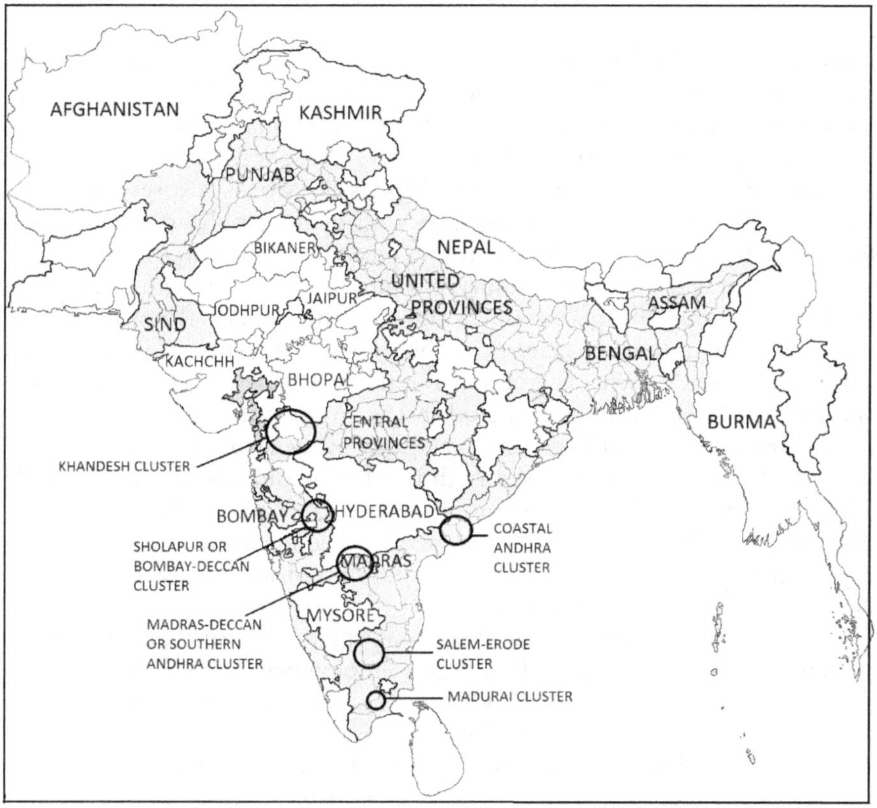

Map 1.1 India around 1940, showing major political divisions and concentrations of urban handloom weaving

Source: Author

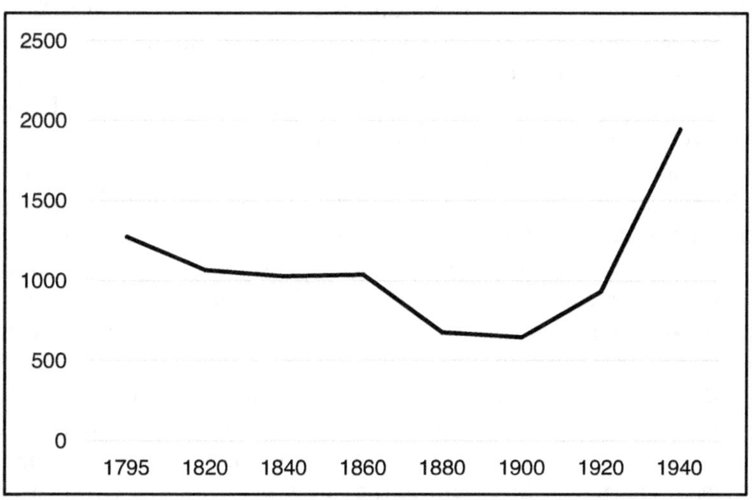

Figure 1.1 Consumption of handmade cloth (million square yards), 1795–1940

Source: Based on Tirthankar Roy, 'Consumption of Cotton Cloth in India, 1795–1940,' *Australian Economic History Review*, 52(1), 2012, 61–84. See also Chapter 2.

1900, growth and decline balanced one another, and after 1900, the growth outweighed the decline. Neither Gadgil nor these officers offered useful generalizations on either the reversal or the differentiation. The paradigm of obsolescence, therefore, met with no effective challenge.

In the 1960s, an American scholar, Morris D. Morris, expressed puzzle over the historians' morbid fascination with deindustrialization (the term was not yet popular when he wrote the piece in 1963). He observed that the handloom weaving industry survived into the mid-twentieth century. In 1901, handlooms engaged about a third of the industrial workforce of 13 million. The proportion came down but was still large in the late-twentieth century.[17] Morris's own explanation for the survival was incomplete. He said that the huge fall in cotton cloth prices in the nineteenth century had an 'income effect' on Indian consumers; that is, believing they were better off overall, consumers purchased both handloom and machine-made cloth in bigger quantities. But why would they do that if the costlier handmade cloth and the cheaper machine-made cloth were identical in quality? The argument makes sense only if we accept that the consumers saw these goods as distinct; this needs to be shown.

After Morris, economists and historians spent a lot of their energy on measuring the extent of the fall in textile employment in India in the nineteenth century (see discussion in Chapter 2). This exercise ran into diminishing returns quickly. Scholars who took part in this exercise behaved as if those who had pointed out the reversal also denied the earlier decline. The new scholarship tried to prove the deindustrialization deniers wrong. Morris was one of the main targets. His critics painstakingly showed that a decline did happen.

The critics missed the point. The point is not whether deindustrialization happened or not. Rather, it was that a turnaround demands of us an analytical narrative on the textile industry that does not yet exist. Whether, in the earlier times, five weavers lost jobs or five million did, the story of technological obsolescence does not change. The story is that, since machine-weaving was eight times faster than the hand-powered loom, the hand-weavers would sooner or later suffer a fall. But precisely because machine-weaving was eight times faster, even if one handloom weaver survived the rise of machines, there is a puzzle to explain. If millions of such weavers survived, as they did in India, the dark and tragic account of the history of the weavers collapses completely and another account becomes necessary. That account must show why the handlooms might have an advantage over machine-weaving. Measuring how many people lost jobs will not supply that account.

Beyond inspiring measurements to prove him wrong, Morris had another effect on economic history. From the 1980s, some scholars mainly using regional experiences as evidence wrote on the industry, suggesting that handloom weaving appeared resilient in the late nineteenth and early twentieth century.[18] Almost invariably, they cited Morris, though the idea had much older roots, as I have shown.

One of these works, mine, claimed this to be the case for India overall. Collectively, however, these works did not quite deliver a coherent alternative to deindustrialization. These works seemed to agree that product differentiation with machine-made cloth was partly responsible for the survival of handlooms. But they did not offer useful generalizations about how this might work and often contradicted each other. For example, whereas several scholars suggest that handlooms survived by shifting into lower-skilled coarse weaving, my work stressed the application of quality and skill to a greater extent. While suggesting a revision, therefore, these studies did not lead to a paradigm of transition in weaving that could become an alternative to deindustrialization. They did not partly because of their regional focus and partly because macroeconomic data spanning the entire nineteenth century and beyond did not yet exist. Figure 1.1 changes that.

To sum up, observers of the crafts – from Gadgil and his sources in the early 1900s to the historians of the 1990s – saw correctly that handloom weaving had seen a reversal and that the reversal called for a new historiography of the handlooms, but they did not offer a persuasive new narrative on Indian textiles that would account for both the earlier decline and the later reversal within the same analytical framework. The old model of technological obsolescence based on divergent loom speed fails because it does not explain the reversal. If we stick to the idea that the British machines made Indian artisans obsolete, we would need to show that the survival and the rise had owed to technological catch-up. There were indeed numerous improvements in technical and operational efficiency in the handloom in these years, but they do not add up to anything like catch-up. It was still a far slower machine. Obsolescence is just not the right ingredient to construct a new narrative on the textile artisans.

If deindustrialization is unfit as an explanation for the long-term trend in handloom weaving, can protoindustrialization explain it?

Protoindustrialization

Survival of artisans on a significant scale did not happen only in India. In continental Europe and Japan, crafts (like silk in Japan) were the forerunner of factories and machine-using industrialization. Current research on textile history in Asia and Africa continue to discover numerous local cloth-producing clusters that survived British industrialization and trade. Even when trade did destroy the local industry, it did not necessarily displace local merchants, who understood consumer preference, became mobile, and reorganized commerce. Often, they met local tastes by procuring cloth from India or Japan rather than from Britain.[19]

These experiences have led to an alternative and more optimistic story of how the crafts fit modern economic growth. Variously called 'protoindustrialization,' 'labour-intensive industrialization,' and 'industrious revolution,' the narrative suggests that the crafts can grow by drawing on certain strengths.[20] For example, the availability of cheap part-time peasant family labour can make the rural industry competitive. Or the desire to consume a variety of consumer goods can motivate rural artisans to work harder.

The problem with protoindustrialization is, partly, that it is again derived from the European experience. Industrialization driven by mass production and technological change in the West remains the benchmark model of world development; everything else must fit into it as a derivative, as a 'de' or a 'proto.' Such an approach directly or indirectly biases the mind against believing that craft textiles in any region could draw on a distinct advantage against the machines.

In fact, the Indian case of survival of hand-weavers does not fit protoindustrialization very well. Protoindustrialization does not explain why any producer operating an inferior technology should carry on for a long time. In the presence of technological change of the kind the nineteenth century witnessed in textiles, the peasant weaver should and did disappear in many places. The Indian weaver did not disappear.

Indian nationalists did claim, or at least hint, that the 'hand-looms still survive in India to some extent' thanks to a symbiosis between agriculture and industry. In an earlier and happier time, '[t]he various industries of the country,' said Romesh Dutt, 'were carried on by humble artisans in their own villages and huts.'[21] Dutt did not elaborate on the compatibility between agriculture and industry and supplied no evidence to support the claim. Later works, such as a widely cited essay by the economist Surendra Patel, suggested that the artisans had been part of a village community that foreign rule and foreign textiles destroyed; by extension, any survival had owed to the reliance of the village barter system. The nationalist leader M.K. Gandhi (1869–1948, see also Chapter 8), saw the village exchange system as an ideal state of society that was under threat due to economic modernization and needed to be restored. Extensive literature now exists that shows that the village community in this sense was a myth. Chapter 7 discusses evidence to suggest that, in the growing clusters of weaving in western and southern India, the industry was urbanizing rapidly. That is, contrary to what Dutt, Patel, and Gandhi believed, survival happened more in the towns and not in the villages.

The protoindustrial weaver was much more than a weaver who was the neighbour of the peasant. He or she was sometimes a peasant and a weaver combined. The Indian story does accommodate the peasant weaver. Weaving was a relatively rural industry in Bengal for a long time. In 1804, a survey of economic conditions in Bengal said, 'no apology can be offered for the peasants indifferently quitting the plough to use the loom and the loom to resume the plough. Industry cannot be worse directed.'[22] More than a century later, the percentage of part-time weavers was relatively high at 25–40 in eastern India. In the extensive handloom-weaving enterprise of Assam, women of peasant families wove on the side. After the Green Revolution of the 1960s and the 1970s, in some pockets of south India, peasants took up textile production.

But such part-timers were not the main institutional type. The percentage of part-time weavers was considerably smaller in the growing handloom hubs, 12–15 in western and southern India. Part-timers would consist of both peasant-cum-weaving households as well as women in any household. 'Weaving among the Assamese,' a 1904 article said, 'forms part of a girl's education.'[23] Not a lot of the production of Assam in this time entered the cloth market, however, which the specialist weaving castes served. The case of north-eastern India, of which Assam is a part, therefore, does not fit protoindustrialization. Even the Bengal data is unclear. In 1897, Nitya Gopal Mukerji found some landowning silk weavers in middle Bengal around 1900. But most such people and one would assume those whom H.T. Colebrook had observed in 1804, were weavers by caste who owned some land on the side. By and large, peasants rarely wove, and weavers rarely cultivated land in India.[24] The peasant-weaver was an exception rather than the rule.

To sum up, deindustrialization is flawed because it rests on the assumption that all handmade technology is unskilled and inferior. Protoindustrialization is flawed because it does not tell us how crafts can continue against machines. Scattered within Indian and world history one can find statements that producers bound by strong cooperative communities can withstand crises better, or that nationalist politics of the interwar period in India helped the crafts face competition, or that the state stepped in to help them.

How believable are these other theories that credit either institutional strengths or external agency as the saviour of the crafts?

Institutions, nationalism, and state aid

When discussing how people overcome obstacles or adversity of any sort, economic historians often look for state intervention or the agency of institutions. Neither of these two subjects will figure in my book in a significant way. State and institutions were not missing nor unimportant in India, but they were not the key factors. The key factors were commercialization and the deployment of skills and techniques to meet changing markets, not the activist state or cooperative institutions.

An institution is an expansive term, and, in one generic sense, it does figure in the book, which is an industrial organization. There is usually another specific sense in which discourses about the Indian artisan sometimes bring in institutions. When challenged with a puzzle about Indian history, Europeanists as a matter of habit ask, 'what about caste?' Surely some sort of socially inherited ability to cooperate and combine would help a livelihood in trouble cope better? I do not deny that this factor was occasionally important. Caste ties helped information-sharing among capitalists, or as Douglas Haynes suggests, to keep industrial relations peaceful. Mattison Mines suggests that in the formation of industrial cooperatives in Tamil Nadu, caste affiliations played a role.[25] There is extensive discussion on caste and community, and for a reason, in some of the sources on which the scholarship draws.

Still, the use of caste as a business instrument appeared in certain contexts, and we must explain why they appeared in those contexts.[26] Overall, caste played no necessary role, or necessarily a benign role, in history. Many weavers were not Hindus to begin with. In weaving towns, caste sympathies did not necessarily diffuse intra-caste inequality, which was growing all the time. Growing inequality could break up cohesion easily. Caste does not play either a simple or a large part in the history of handloom weavers.

Indianist historians sometimes claim that a rising nationalist spirit in the early twentieth century explained the turnaround in weaving. The keyword is 'swadeshi,' literally translating into 'our country.' In practice, it was a campaign to boycott imported goods and promote the purchase of homemade articles of consumption. The swadeshi ideology did not specifically favour the artisan, and I shall soon argue that it discriminated against the artisan. That some historians believed otherwise had more to do with sentiment than evidence. The chief inspiration behind the textile policy of post-independence India, Gandhi, had no doubt that 'hand spinning and handweaving are steadily increasing' as a result of his successful campaign for swadeshi.[27] Citing Bagchi, Irfan Habib writes that the twentieth-century revival of the handlooms was due to 'not the least, the Swadeshi movement.'[28]

Besides the narrow emphasis on the boycott of imports, which political swadeshi was all about, nationalism had a cultural renaissance dimension to it that did favour the craft goods. There is now a large amount of literature on nationalism and the accent that contributors to the ideology placed upon the handicrafts.[29] That sort of interest again led to a range of initiatives on craft revival, of which a significant example is the poet Rabindranath Tagore's Sriniketan experiment (see Glossary). However, the impact of such initiatives was limited and local.

As for the boycott campaign, it was unhelpful at best and damaging at worst for the handloom weaver. First, it is implausible that the nationalist campaign changed mass consumption habits and persuaded poor people to buy costlier cloth on a scale that could produce the turnaround shown in Figure 1.1. That would amount to an extreme simplification of history and has no evidence to support it. Second, the campaign to boycott imports went against the interest of successful commercial crafts like the handlooms.

Weavers relied heavily on imported inputs, from yarn to dyes to gold thread to rayon. A campaign against imports was not in their interest. In fact, as the nationalist movement became stronger, some of these materials rose in price, and handloom weaving did worse, according to the data available.

The ideological campaign around the crafts was largely a male discourse, whereas the biggest field of handloom production was women's wear. That the movement could persuade women, who were extremely scarce in the political platforms, to change habits, adjust budgets, and buy more expensive handloom cloth simply because it was made by the politically correct producer, and do this all over India, is an absurd notion. When the spirit of swadeshi took on a more aggressive attitude in the new leader Gandhi's insistence that his followers should wear coarse white clothing made of handspun yarn, the instruction upset the women among his followers. Some of them read it as an outright misogynist order, which it was in effect (see also Chapter 8). Swadeshi, in short, harmed rather than helped the handloom weaver.

The state did not help much either. That the artisans could do better with some help from the state was stressed from time to time in administrative circles. The idea became a campaign point around 1900 when officers of the provincial service dealing with the crafts and like-minded writers impressed by the arts-and-crafts movement of England suggested that the Indian crafts were under threat from modernization. The threat came not from machines but from chaotic commercialization and too much experimentation. In the process, a rich and complex knowledge system, they believed, was degrading fast.

Whether there was truth in this view or not, the governments in the provinces commissioned a series of fact-finding enquiries on the crafts. The reports of the enquiries were published between 1895 and 1905 and were called monographs. Collectively, the material contains the most systematically collected and detailed database on production, consumption, technology, and the people involved in these industries. But little more followed from the government. Crafts were a subject for the provincial governments, which were permanently short of money within a state that collected one of the smallest tax receipts per head in the whole world. The British Indian state, in other words, was a platform for building discourses but did not have the money to create action plans to follow.

This dismissive assessment of the state should be qualified. There were a few areas where the state did try to make a difference and which did leave a legacy. One of these was the promotion of cooperative credit to help poorer artisans invest in the industry or a collectively owned central yarn depot to supply the yarn. The cooperative movement did not progress much in colonial times. It took off from around 1910. In the 1930s, the percentage of weavers in cooperatives was still small and the mortality of societies high. In many societies, the members were ill-equipped to deal with production.

Defaults were crippling. A major survey of handlooms conducted in 1942 concluded that 'in spite of the efforts undertaken for over three decades the co-operative movement was a failure in most parts of India.'[30] The report attributed the failure to the same factor that made private enterprise flexible and innovative, 'leadership.' The people who managed the societies, if they were capitalists by background, would be competent but have a conflict of interest. And if they were not capitalists, they were not competent to manage the business.

Despite all of these problems, the idea and some of the infrastructure had taken root by 1947. After independence in 1947, provinces with many weavers, such as Tamil Nadu, rebuilt the cooperatives and used these as partners of the state in a more ambitious handicraft regeneration policy. Through interventions like these, the institution turned into a not-too-efficient bureaucratic office sheltered from competition.

Technical instruction was a second area where the government left a legacy. A series of unofficial industrial conferences in the first decade of the twentieth century laid great stress on training and discussed a suitable administrative structure for organizing technical education. Those who took part in these discussions included crafts experts in the employ of provincial governments, especially Madras, and discussed proposals that came from master weavers. They discussed how to aid the diffusion of new tools and the correct handling of tools (like synthetic dyeing agents). Although schools were set up to serve these needs, they were too few and too under-funded to be effective.

World War I changed the government's attitude towards industrial promotion from one of indifference to engagement. One of the new areas of emphasis was industrial training. Ironically, the government was going bankrupt at the same time. Schools grew in number but were starved of staff and money. And yet, this side of the government's action did have some effect when leading weavers in a community joined such campaigns. Where such partnerships existed, successful diffusion occurred. A few examples of such intervention will be discussed in the chapter on technology (Chapter 6).

To sum up, the revival of handlooms cannot be attributed to technological catch-up, nor to the cheapness of peasant labour, nor to institutions like caste and community, nor to an external agency like the state, nor to the nationalist movement and the spirit of swadeshi. In this book, the explanation builds on the idea that the handlooms possessed a technological advantage against machines, which made the handloom cloth qualitatively distinct from machine-made cloth. Skill and quality are the essential keywords for the thesis, which I now state more fully.

Skill as capital

In this book, the accent falls on the advantage of the artisan cloth producer, which I shall call skill, as a convenient shorthand. Handloom weaving survived competition not because it could access cheap labour but because hand-weaving was better at producing complex patterns on cloth.

In the theory of the history of handloom weaving that I develop in this book, there were two drivers of change, external and internal. British industrialization, mass production, and the free trade policy of the colonial state in India together formed the externally induced driver. The adverse effect of import was more severe in the production of standardized quality goods, raw materials, and intermediate goods, like cotton yarn or grey cloth of medium fineness, than in final-consumption goods like designed cloth where consumers minded product differences and the quality of the articles that they purchased. The former part of handloom textiles was of generic quality and price-sensitive, which machine-made cloth displaced between 1820 and 1880. There is no denying that the shock was large, though it was not necessarily a destructive type of shock. Industrialization in Europe also offered options to the Indian weavers that lowered their costs or improved their capability.

The latter part of handloom output was quality-sensitive and embodied skill. This part withstood competition or was not too susceptible to it. This part then started growing. The growth gained from the trade regime, but that was an incidental advantage. Whatever drove this growth was internal to the industry. Machines had little direct agency. To see this driver of change better, we need to study consumption more closely. The consumption of handloom cloth was protected by the quality it could deliver to the consumers. We still need to show what the word means in this context. And since quality was not an unchanging factor, we also need to show how the meaning changed.

Clothes embodying skill usually means clothes containing very fine or expensive yarn which requires care in weaving or complex looms. Or it can mean clothes embodying designs. Designs on cloth can be either woven on the loom or performed by outside sources, such as printers, dyers, and embroiderers. If woven on the loom, the weaving process involves either weft-manipulation or warp-manipulation. In the past, these techniques, and especially weft-manipulation, slowed down weaving so much as to make it uneconomical for the mechanized looms to try to weave these. The key advantage of a powerloom is speed and using attachments to manipulate warp or weft will reduce the speed. Most machine-made cloth in the nineteenth century tended to be plain cloth or greys that were sent for dyeing and bleaching. Most bordered sarees, on the other hand, were made on the handloom because these were designed on the loom. Machines could technically make these but not at a lower price.

The machine-artisan competition, therefore, had a lot to do with costume styles, which, of course, differed between men and women. In colonial India, what the men wore changed in a manner consistent with mechanization and mass production. Men's wear was more standardized, was plainer in appearance, contained more workwear, and was usually tailored cloth, which required the fabric to be of a standardized mass-produced type. In tailored garments, machine-made fabrics were more commonly used. What the women usually wore was a draped garment, the saree. Each piece of a draped garment was a finished piece. The saree is a draped cloth, usually with a strong border on three sides, which serves to differentiate each product and add value to the appearance. By their shape, the rectangular garment offered a good field for the application of woven designs.

In making sarees, the handlooms did better. The top-end of the saree market featured sarees with borders that were woven using the weft-manipulation techniques. Handlooms were especially economical in doing that. The highest quality of such goods was/is expensive to buy, whether in the past or in the present. Whether poorer and middle-class women afforded these goods or not, it is a plausible assumption that they understood what quality meant. I cannot put this assumption to test, nor can I accept a narrative that does not start with a reasonable assumption about women's choice and knowledge of quality in a saree. To write this book, I must assume that there was that knowledge, and, because there was, the weaver could innovate on border designs (Chapter 3).

None of the advantages of the handloom sheltered them from the forces of competition. Machines tried hard to break into new fields, consumers wanted different designs and quality, migration and urban wage-work standardized tastes, especially among the men, and whereas hand-weavers experimented to meet new demands, these experiments sometimes failed. When the design was added outside the weaving shop, the weaving did not need to be skilled. Usually, it was skilled because printing, dyeing, and embroidering added a lot of value to the cloth and demanded that the cloth be valuable too. For this reason, in earlier times, printers, dyers, and weavers often clustered in the same towns. The discovery of mineral dyes, however, snapped the bond between weaving and dyeing because now anybody could dye cloth; therefore, dyeing did not need to be concentrated in towns where specialist dyers and their material could be found. Dyeing moved into the cities and closer to the mills, even inside the mills.

Weavers who overcame these challenges did so partly because they had gained from the same globalization process that threw other weavers into unemployment. They could gain from foreign trade by obtaining access to imported raw materials. The railways brought distant markets closer to them. A lot of useful knowledge was transferred from Europe to India because the empire kept borders open to transactions in people and in tools. Knowledge spillover was embodied in tools, machines, and processes, and reduced costs of production increased productivity and enhanced economies of scope. Nearly all of the most important tools and processes adopted by the weavers in late-colonial India, such as the fly-shuttle slay, the frame-mounted loom, the Jacquard, dobby, drop-box, and synthetic dyes, had been invented in Europe. Globalization and colonial trading connections brought them within the easy reach of handloom weavers.

But this is only part of the story. The successful weaver also made innovations on quality. A significant part of the innovation that the weavers did to make their products more attractive involved weaving designs on the loom.

Design innovation in handmade textiles

Innovation in handmade cloth is a difficult subject to write about. The subject remains almost completely unresearched. Economists who study textile history do not take design seriously. Economics journals and economic history journals do not publish articles on textile designs. Perhaps in the macho scholarly world of economists, design is deemed too feminine a subject to merit a paper. Unfortunately, in journals that publish articles on designs, there is a parallel and profound oversight on economic history. Squeezed between the two types of amnesia, textile scholars have forgotten to write a good economic history of one of the most significant costume types of the world, the saree of India.

As Chapter 3 shows in more detail, throughout the twentieth century, high-quality sarees simplified the design, traded more widely, established brand names, and introduced variety. Increasingly in the twentieth century, merchants of handloom sarees operated in an all-India market connected through political unification of a vast territory and the railways. That process made the market for high-grade handloom cloth a pan-Indian one and encouraged trade. It also encouraged branding of the saree border. Many types of technical change were tied to the commercialization of the saree border and associated innovation. Innovations on the saree border had a dynamic independent of competition from machinery.

To understand that dynamic better, we need to engage with the historiography of consumption. The idea that objects acquire value from the context of their use has long been a canon in the social sciences, especially within Marxist discourses on commodity fetishism and those on Thorstein Veblen's prestige goods. But these constructions explain value in reference to relationships among people, among men to be more precise, which is an awkward starting point for a study on the saree. They overlook the specific aspects of the commodities consumed and do not tell us how producers innovate on the product, seeing how the context of use changes.

Historians have reacted to these rigid ideas by showing how objects and artifacts became a component in the self-definition of middle-class consumers in the nineteenth century, as wage-work, industrialization, and mass production threatened their individuality.[31] A large historical scholarship on 'commodity culture' in Britain explores themes like these. Crafted objects had a special ability to serve this need, each unit being differentiated from others and all embodying a rare skill. Economists tell us that income induces consumption. Economic historians of Britain reverse the causality between consumption and work. Starting from consumption of Asian goods and new goods in the early modern times, they show how, in the eighteenth century, 'the desire, most graphically expressed by women, for special items of personal or household adornment in distinctive materials and styles which would give them individuality,' could encourage industriousness.[32]

These general propositions are useful in understanding why Indian consumers might become more sensitive to craft goods and saree designs from the nineteenth century. During much of the twentieth century, women left rather than joined the paid workforce, so that drawing a connection between consumption and work is difficult. It is still plausible that women's wardrobes had more variety than those of the men at all levels of income. At the very least, variety became a positive value. A reduction in trade costs encouraged the mass market of affordable designs. Morris's income effect argument should have validity for women. Handloom weavers saw these possibilities and responded creatively.

In high-quality handmade textiles, skills embodied in the person of the weaver were a form of capital. This capital, just like money capital and, if sensibly deployed, led to the accumulation of more capital. In this way, handloom weaving became a part of the emerging industrial capitalism in colonial India.

From crafts to capitalism

Until the 1990s, the history of artisans and the history of capitalism (or business history) remained two parallel discourses that did not meet. When discussing the capitalist in the handicrafts, historians tended to draw a sharp line separating the producer, the poor exploited weaver, from the rich exploiting merchants and moneylenders who held the weavers in their iron grip. The intellectual support for the cooperatives in the crafts drew inspiration from that picture. This trademark Marxist picture of a polarized society misreads the character of artisan industries by ignoring that some artisans possess something like a skill capital. Accumulation of capital and concentrated application of skill were interdependent processes, and weavers were engaged in doing both.

In the twentieth century, long-distance trade in handloom sarees induced a variety of responses that needed money, information, and market access. Accumulation of these resources and their wider use – an extension of capitalism – intensified inequality. Just as there were different types of cloth, so were there different types of weavers. Some had more money than others, some had more saleable skills than others, and some were more fortunately located nearer markets and merchants. Therefore, even in the same line of production, weavers could face dissimilar experiences. At one end, we see the emergence of relatively large trading or manufacturing firms, and at another more migrants desperately seeking jobs. Both processes were present in the handloom-weaving industry.

In the process of these changes, handloom weaving saw its business side develop. Merchants and factory owners could make more money and invest more money than before, and in the process increase inequality within the handloom weaving industry. Even when mechanization of cotton cloth production did destroy local industry here or there, it did not necessarily displace merchants or the industry at large because handloom merchants understood certain types of consumer preference better than did the merchant trading in factory-made goods.

In 1998, an article of mine on the Sourashtra weavers of Madurai town in south India introduced the concept of the 'artisan-capitalist' to suggest the need to bring the crafts and capitalism into a compatible relationship. As a community, the Sourashtra weavers of Madurai town in south India were exceptionally skilled handloom weavers and dyers, as well as merchants in yarns, dyes, cloth, and other textile raw materials, and owners of dyehouses. They were weavers and capitalists. Being artisanal in root, their entrepreneurship carried certain distinct features: rootedness in textiles, preference for the non-corporate organization, reliance on informal finance, and reliance on the community in making contracts and arranging collaborations. I suggested that these features should be the markers of 'artisan-capitalists,' examples of which could be found in other growing craft towns in the interwar period.

About the same time that this article on the Sourashtras was published, writings and then-ongoing research by Douglas Haynes used the phrase 'weaver-capitalist' to claim that artisans shaped capitalism. Haynes developed an argument about capitalism based on a study of the small-scale textile industry in western India that lent itself to comparative history especially well. Arguing that the belief in the inevitability of the decline of the crafts stems from an understanding of industrialization derived from European history, or the experience of the port cities, his book 'centres an understanding of industrial capitalism squarely in the history of the broader structures of the regional economy rather than in Europe or the colonial ports of India.'[33] The key sites were small towns from western India, the fieldwork region for the study, like Sholapur, Ahmadnagar, Malegaon, and Ichalkaranji, and the key actors the skilled migrant handloom weavers who formed settlements here. These towns were 'small' in comparison with the centres of factory industry, such as Ahmedabad or Bombay, but they grew rapidly in the late twentieth century partly upon a livelihood-base of which handloom weaving was the core. The 'small town' in the book, in other words, represents a distinct form of regional capitalism.

Haynes offers a particularly useful description of the weaver-capitalist as an emerging body of relatively wealthy employers who led the transition to powerloom factory, a small weaving workshop run on electric power.

Handloom weavers initially started many of these. The factories they operated were quite different from the factories of Bombay and Calcutta. They hired fellow community members, made use of paternalistic relations, and used the idioms of caste and community to create a family-like atmosphere in the work site. And yet, by the logic of capitalist development, inequality increased, living standards of migrant workers fell behind those of employers and traders, and all of that inevitably encouraged labour mobilization and disturbed industrial peace. Whereas Haynes's work focuses on the mid-twentieth century power-using weaving factories or 'powerloom' factories, I narrate broadly similar tendencies over a longer time span and for the handlooms.

Finally, an explanatory note on the sources used in this study is in order.

A note on sources

Because artisans were a low-priority subject for the state, there is little material on them in the government archives. On the other hand, considerable non-official and semi-official material on these industries was produced between 1880 and 1940 because they were so important for local and regional economies, especially the economy of the smaller towns in the interior, as opposed to the port city. These publications form the main resource for the study. These materials are uneven in the level of detail or the type of detail reported. My strategy is to bunch these into four temporal clusters so that a chronological account can emerge from this diverse material. On each topic, I try to use this material on a chronological scale, moving from one cluster to the next.

The appointment of Lord Ripon (George Robinson, 1827–1909) as the Viceroy of India in 1880 marked the start of a period of serious official interest in the crafts. Besides serving vaguely defined commercial objectives, the official policy also made a concession to the arts-and-crafts movement. In any case, the concrete outcome of that policy was a series of fact-finding publications that appeared in quick succession. Works published in the last quarter of the nineteenth century form the first of the four clusters. Around then, several Gazetteers and an important survey of northern India (by William Hoey) supply good material on the handloom weavers. The second cluster appeared between 1895 and 1905, including a set of craft monographs (see 'monographs' in the Glossary). Two provincial surveys, by Atul Chatterjee on the United Provinces and a report prepared for the Central Provinces, belonged in this time and were a part of the same programme to build an information base.

There is rather little material available between 1905 and 1925. In the next twelve years, another set of provincial reports, the Banking Enquiry Commission reports, and two important scholarly works (by N.G. Ranga and K.S. Venkatraman) were created, forming the third cluster.[34] The last milestone in this information project was a landmark enquiry report called

Fact-finding Committee. Handlooms and Mills, produced in 1942. No survey quite as detailed, as systematic, and as historical in outlook had been conducted on the textile industry until then, or since this report. The committee tried to identify the long-term pattern of change through interviews and statistical data, an agenda that this book shares. However, whereas the committee drew on its own data, the book synthesizes information taken from a wide variety of sources.

Plan of the book

The rest of the book has seven chapters. Chapter 2 offers a long-range and partly quantitative account of trends in the industry based on a set of cloth consumption data covering the period 1795–1940. The attempt restricts itself mainly to cotton cloth production in handlooms. But the chapter ends with a discussion of the composition of clothing in the 1930s, for which time we have good data to measure the production of cloth of all types. Chapter 3 discusses market and consumption; Chapter 4, capital, labour, and inequality; Chapter 5, technology; Chapter 6, towns and regions; and Chapter 7 studies the origins of the powerloom weaving factory from a foundation of the handloom-weaving business. The concluding chapter offers a brief overview of the history of the handloom-weaving industry in post-independence India (1947 to the present).

Notes

1 Tirthankar Roy, *Artisans and Industrialization: Indian Weaving in the Twentieth Century*, New Delhi: Oxford University Press, 1993, 111. This accent on design, or quality of cloth, more generally, as a benchmark in consumer choice and an instrument of competition is now commonplace in global textile history. It was not when the statement was made.

2 See essays in Pedro Machado, Sarah Fee, and Gwyn Campbell, eds., *Textile Trades, Consumer Cultures, and the Material Worlds of the Indian Ocean: An Ocean of Cloth*, London: Palgrave, 2018; Giorgio Riello and Tirthankar Roy, eds., *How India Clothed the World*, Leiden: Brill, 2009; Giorgio Riello and Prasannan Parthasarathi, eds., *The Spinning World: A Global History of Cotton Textiles, 1200–1850*, Oxford: Oxford University Press, 2008.

3 Business and textile history recognize the role of Indian products in shaping the British textile industry, see S.D. Chapman, 'David Evans & Co. The Last of the Old London Textile Printers,' *Textile History*, 14(1), 1983, 29–56; or on Macclesfield weaving, Brenda M. King, *Silk and Empire*, Manchester: Manchester University Press, 2005. The topic became mainstream in arguments about global economic transition more recently, Prasannan Parthasarathi, *Why Europe Grew Rich and Asia Did Not*, Cambridge: Cambridge University Press, 2011.

4 S.J. Patel, *Agricultural Labourers in Modern India and Pakistan*, Bombay: Current, 1952, 15.

5 A.K. Bagchi, 'De-Industrialization in India in the Nineteenth Century: Some Theoretical Implications,' *Journal of Development Studies*, 12(2), 1976, 135–64, cited text in p. 145.

6 Irfan Habib, 'Studying a Colonial Economy: Without Perceiving Colonialism,' *Modern Asian Studies*, 19(3), 1985, 355–81, cited text in p. 364.
7 Aditya Mukherjee, 'The Return of the Colonial in Indian Economic History: The Last Phase of Colonialism in India,' *Social Scientist*, 36(3/4), 2008, 3–44, cited text in p. 9.
8 M.J. Twomey, 'Employment in Nineteenth Century Indian Textiles,' *Explorations in Economic History*, 20(1), 1983, 37–57, cited text in p. 55.
9 See Bipan Chandra, *The Rise and Growth of Economic Nationalism in India*, New Delhi: People's Publishing House, 1966.
10 Bipan Chandra, 'Colonial India: British versus Indian Views of Development,' *Review (Fernand Braudel Center)*, 14(1), 1991, 81–167, cited text in p. 85.
11 On the etymology of the word and its various uses in economic history, see Indrajit Ray, 'The Myth and Reality of Deindustrialisation in Early Modern India,' in Latika Chaudhary, Bishnupriya Gupta, Tirthankar Roy, and Anand V. Swamy, eds., *A New Economic History of Colonial India*, London: Routledge, 2015, 52–66.
12 Daniel Thorner, *Land and Labour in India*, Bombay: Asia, 1962, 70.
13 'Deindustrialization,' cited text in p. 153.
14 J.G. Williamson, *Trade and Poverty: How the Third World Fell Behind*, Cambridge, MA: MIT Press, 2013, 75. In an article co-authored with David Clingingsmith, Williamson offers a slightly different explanation for India's industrial decline (see Chapter 2), but this twist in the story need not concern us here.
15 Williamson, *Trade and Poverty*.
16 D.R. Gadgil, *The Industrial Evolution of India*, London: Oxford University Press, 1928, 174.
17 Morris D. Morris, 'Towards a Reinterpretation of Nineteenth Century Indian Economic History,' *Journal of Economic History*, 23(4), 1963, 607–18.
18 C.J. Baker, *An Indian Rural Economy 1880–1955: The Tamilnad Countryside*, New Delhi: Oxford University Press, 1984; Konrad Specker, 'Madras Handlooms in the Nineteenth Century,' *Indian Economic and Social History Review*, 26(2), 1989, 131–66; Sumit Guha, 'The Handloom Industry of Central India: 1825–1950,' *Indian Economic and Social History Review*, 26(3), 1989, 297–318; Peter Harnetty, 'Deindustrialization Revisited: The Handloom Weavers of the Central Provinces of India, c. 1800–1947,' *Modern Asian Studies*, 25(3), 1991, 455–510; Haruka Yanagisawa, 'The Handloom Industry and Its Market Structure: The Case of the Madras Presidency in the First Half of the Twentieth Century,' *Indian Economic and Social History Review*, 30(1), 1993, 1–27. My book, *Artisans and Industrialization*, was the published version of a doctoral thesis of Centre for Development Studies, Trivandrum, 1988.
19 See essays in Machado, Fee, Campbell, eds., *Textile Trades*.
20 Gareth Austin and Kaoru Sugihara, eds., *Labour-Intensive Industrialization in Global History*, Abingdon and New York: Routledge, 2012; Akira Hayami, *Japan's Industrious Revolution: Economic and Social Transformations in the Early Modern Period*, Tokyo and London: Springer, 2016; Jan de Vries, *The Industrious Revolution: Consumer Behavior and the Household Economy, 1650 to the Present*, Cambridge: Cambridge University Press, 2008.
21 Romesh C. Dutt, *The Economic History of India*, vol. 2, London: Kegan Paul, 1903, 389.
22 H.T. Colebrook, *Remarks on the Husbandry and Internal Commerce of Bengal*, Calcutta, 1804, 11.
23 H.F. Samman, 'The Cotton Fabrics of Assam,' *Journal of Indian Art*, 10, 1904, 21–4.

24 N.G. Mukerji, *A Monograph on the Silk Fabrics of Bengal*, Calcutta: Government Press, 1903.
25 Mattison Mines, *The Warrior Merchants: Textiles, Trade and Territory in South India*, Cambridge: Cambridge University Press, 1984, 107–20.
26 For more discussion, see Tirthankar Roy, *Company of Kinsmen: Enterprise and Community in South Asia 1600–1950*, New Delhi: Oxford University Press, Second Ed., 2017.
27 M.K. Gandhi, *The Wheel of Fortune*, Madras: Ganesh and Co., 1922, 19.
28 Habib, 'Studying a Colonial Economy,' 85.
29 See C.A. Bayly, 'The Origins of Swadeshi (Home Industry): Cloth and Indian Society, 1700–1930,' in A. Appadurai, ed., *The Social Life of Things*, Cambridge: Cambridge University Press, 1986, 285–322; Emma Tarlo, *Clothing Matters: Dress and Its Symbolism in Modern India*, Chicago: University of Chicago Press, 1996; Abigail McGowan, *Crafting the Nation in Colonial India*, London: Palgrave, 2009; and Kaamya Sharma, 'The Orientalisation of the Sari – Sartorial Praxis and Womanhood in Colonial and Post-Colonial India,' *South Asia: Journal of South Asian Studies*, 42(2), 2019, 219–36.
30 India, *Fact-Finding Committee: Handlooms and Mills*, Calcutta: Government Press, 1942, 182.
31 See the review essay on a set of books using mainly literature as a source, Jennifer Sattaur, 'Thinking Objectively: An Overview of "Thing Theory" in Victorian Studies,' *Victorian Literature and Culture*, 40(1), 2012, 347–57.
32 Maxine Berg, 'Women's Consumption and the Industrial Classes of Eighteenth-Century England,' *Journal of Social History*, 30(2), 1996, 415–34.
33 Douglas E. Haynes, *Small Town Capitalism in Western India: Artisans, Merchants, and the Making of the Informal Economy, 1870–1960*, Cambridge: Cambridge University Press, 2012, 6.
34 On Ranga, see entry in 'Selected biographies' at the end of the book. Venkatraman was a professor in a Pune college.

2

SCALE AND COMPOSITION, 1795–1940

India was a major exporter of cotton cloth in the world in the mid-eighteenth century. From around 1820, cheaper British cloth started coming to India, and soon imports grew to become an enormous trade. What happened to the textile industry, especially handloom weaving? Drawing on my 2012 statistical work on nineteenth-century cotton cloth production trends, the chapter answers the question.[1] I show that there was a decline between 1820 and 1880 and a revival between 1880 and 1935, after which a series of minor shocks hit the industry.

The first half of the chapter deals with cotton cloth. This is easier to measure. But the measure is biased because, until recently, handlooms also wove a variety of non-cotton fabrics like wool, mulberry silk, wild silk, mixed-fibre fabrics (one type of thread in the warp and another in the weft), and rayon. Later in the chapter, the definition of the cloth is expanded to include other fibres.

This attempt to measure the scale of the textile handicrafts since the nineteenth century is not the first of its kind. I discuss these other measures to show why a new one is necessary.

Previous estimates of scale

Previous estimates of the scale of nineteenth-century Indian textiles have been made with the purpose of measuring the effects of industrialization, colonization, and trade on the handicraft industry. The default hypothesis is that the effects were serious and adverse, happened in the nineteenth century, and followed from three causes: a decline in aristocratic consumption with the rise of colonial power, which reduced the consumption of finer textiles like muslins (roughly 1765 onward), a decline in the export of Indian cloth (1790 onward), and importation of machine-made yarn and cloth from Britain to India (1820 onward).

How much decline was there? The interest of present-day historians in aggregate textile data began from an article by Morris D. Morris, which I cite in Chapter 1.[2] Import of cheaper British goods substituted handloom cloth. But the underlying reason (a big fall in cloth prices), Morris suggested, could have a positive income effect too. Further, increasing income in the commercializing agricultural activities could lead to a growth in the demand for traditional clothing. If the positive effect was sufficiently strong, the handicraft textiles could gain in the net. In either case, consumption should increase, tempered perhaps by job loss and therefore a fall in demand for consumer goods in the craft sector.[3]

If a negative and a positive effect do combine, what was the net effect of technological change in cotton textiles on the artisan cloth producer? One paper answered that the net effect was negative.[4] The paper used employment data drawn from two sources. Employment data have problems, the most serious one being that it usually includes both part-timers and full-timers, and the proportion of part-timers was especially large in textiles because many women worked in the industry alongside performing family duties.[5] If, for some reason, the proportion of part-timers falls and women exit the industry, we should see a fall in employment, which would not necessarily mean a fall in production.

Another statistical work approached the measurement issue from a different angle.[6] This paper compiled trade data for the early and the late nineteenth century and read off production and consumption in 1850 from a demand equation. The demand equation itself used data that pertained to a later period, incorporated national income statistics of an earlier and now largely discarded vintage, and for a proxy of relative prices, deflated import price by a consumer price index that is unlikely to have included handloom cloth. The production figure for the early nineteenth century was then converted into notional employment using a method and parameters developed in another study.[7] Again, the finding was that a large job loss did happen. A recent paper approached the subject with different methods and showed that the job loss in one major region, Bengal, was possibly of a smaller order than the range implied by earlier calculations.[8] Finally, an unpublished article used a method somewhat similar to the one I use a little later and estimated cotton cloth production from raw cotton statistics.[9] The main finding was again that a large fall happened in the local production of textiles.[10]

The fact of a decline in domestic textiles is neither disputable nor surprising. The timing remains obscure. The early statements of the episode of a decline used impressionistic data and timed it in the first half of the nineteenth century.[11] The earlier timing has one virtue. It is consistent with the belief that there was a general economic depression in the Deccan region in the 1820s because of the tax policy of early British rule in the region.[12] But there is little solid evidence from the textiles side to confirm that deindustrialization had any role in this episode. Census data (1872–1931) suggest a fall in craft employment in the last quarter of the nineteenth century and the first half of the twentieth century. Based on these findings, some authors locate deindustrialization from the late-nineteenth century.[13] The correct reading of the census data is a debated issue because the censuses changed the definition of a worker often.

What factors led to the decline? Here again, there is much uncertainty because the factors potentially at work were at work at different times. Mechanical inventions were the most important factor causing a fall in craft textiles. But it was not the only one. There was also a fall in export demand and in elite consumption. A recent paper adds to these factors adverse climatic and political conditions of the eighteenth century that might have affected the supply conditions of Indian textiles.[14] The evidence is speculative. But it is a plausible thesis. The textile history scholarship overlooks the effects of disorder and warfare of the eighteenth century on internal trade, cultivation of cotton, and local industry. These factors do deserve attention.

To sum up, then, most measures restrict themselves to showing that a net decline happened. But the decline could not simply continue forever because then we would have nothing left to discuss when we come to the twentieth century. In fact, millions of weavers carried on and expanded their production in the twentieth century. Any measure of cloth consumption, production, and market-share that we develop must be able to generate the revival and show how the revival fits the earlier decline.

I now move to that task. The next section is all about datasets relating to cotton cloth consumption and production, how to fill those gaps, and the best ways to use them. Those readers not keen on numbers can skip the section and move straight to the section called 'results.'

A new measure of consumption, production, and market-share, 1795–1940

Of all the datasets so far used in this scholarship, cotton cultivation data is perhaps the most promising and available for a long span of time. It is also the least utilized. I adapt my method to be able to use this data.

By definition,

Total consumption of cloth = Production + Net import.

There are trade statistics of good quality for the early nineteenth century. Production can be approximated by the following identity:

Production of cloth = [(Cotton acreage x yield of cleaned cotton per acre – export of cleaned cotton) × (proportion of output of cleaned cotton used in textile uses) × (1- proportion of cotton lost in conversion to yarn) – (net import of yarn)] × (cloth/yarn conversion).

Many of the elements entering the expression are ratios that are structural or technical in nature and should not change quickly. Still, the values of the conversion ratios represent some openness. A brief discussion of the elements is in order.

The first reliable official statistics on acreage under cultivation did not become available before 1880. However, a series of parliamentary enquiries on the state of cotton cultivation in India, in the wake of the American civil war and cotton export boom in India, led to a compilation of data on acreage under cotton cultivation for the 1860s based on returns submitted by district collectors.[15] I have totalled the numbers that are available for the year 1860. These numbers are shown in Table 2.1. It is immediately clear that the numbers for 1860 are too low, even when we account for a large increase in cultivation in the next quarter of a century in response to the cotton famine. The differences between 1860 and 1885 are especially large for central and southern India. It is unnecessary to go into the details of why there might be a large discrepancy for these provinces.[16] In the absence of any other basis for correcting the data, I raise the acreage figures of these two large cotton-growing provinces by using the ratio of 1885 and 1865 acreage for the other main provinces, excluding Punjab. Punjab is excluded because in this region new canal projects raised the cultivable land frontier substantially. The revision is shown in the 1860 (revised) column.

Acreage did not change much between 1840 and 1860.[17] For the cotton-growing Gujarat and Bombay districts Broach, Surat, Kaira, and Khandesh, there was no change at all in the acreage under cotton between 1840 and 1860. In the case of Ahmedabad, there was a small increase, but the levels

Table 2.1 Cotton acreage, 1860–1885, millions

	1860 (before revision)	*1860 (revised)*	*1885 (used for 1880)*
Madras	0.31	0.82	1.36
Bombay	1.37	1.37	2.22
Northwestern Provinces, Agra and Oudh	0.96	0.96	1.66
Punjab	0.42	0.42	1.03
Central Provinces and Berar	0.38	1.47	2.45
Other	0	0	0.02
Total	3.44	5.04	8.74

Source: India, *Statistical Abstracts for British India*, for 1885, and British Parliamentary Papers, *Cotton Goods. Return of the quantities of cotton goods exported to the British East Indies, and the quantities of cotton imported from the British East Indies, in each year, from 1855 to 1861*, London: HMSO, 1861; British Parliamentary Papers, *Calicoes, &c. Return of the quantity and value of calicoes, muslins, and cotton goods and cotton yarn exported from, and imported into, India, in each year, from 1833 to 1852; also, similar return for the United Kingdom, for the same* period, London: HMSO, 1852–3. For the revision, see text.

were low for this district in both years. If these regions, which are easily accessible from Bombay port and located close to clusters of old spinning industries, did not experience a large shift in overall production, it is unlikely that any of the other regions in India did either.[18]

Inferring the 1820 figure requires cautious speculation. In the second quarter of the nineteenth century, land was abundant and agriculture in most parts of India was labour-constrained. Expansion in cultivation, then, should entail either population growth or migration. Neither of these changes occurred to a significant extent. A fall in cultivation or a shift from cotton to grain production is possible because the derived demand for cotton from spinners would have fallen due to the import of yarn, and possibly the import of cloth as well. The ground for a large shift is not strong because the relative price of cotton and grain in the domestic market did not change at all. On these grounds, I assume the absence of a major shift in cotton acreage, except to the extent of the area equivalent of the additional import of yarn, which is a little more than 200,000 acres. I add this number to the 1840 figure to get the 1820 figure.[19]

The productivity of cleaned cotton per acre varied across space and according to what kind of seeds was taken. The problem of adopting an average yield is that cotton yields were notoriously variable and unpredictable. In the period in question, much experimentation was going on with foreign varieties, especially Bourbon or Mauritius, Sea Island, and most importantly, Georgia and New Orleans. While the official interest in the project and the voluminous documentation that it produced might lead us to believe that it was successful, in fact, the diffusion was limited.

Even though the new varieties did not change the average yield much, they added to the dispersion. An 1840's survey found per-acre yields in one district in Bundelkhand to range from as low as 50 lbs/acre to 150 lbs/acre.[20] In one influential opinion, these variations owed to the effect that soil and moisture exerted on the local varieties of seeds, leaving little scope to human labour, knowledge, or biological inputs to alter the yield.[21] The indigenous varieties did not usually fail but on average produced a poor crop. The higher figures came from the American, Mexican, and Mauritian varieties. These seeds were poorly adapted to the Indian environment and susceptible to pest attack and too much heat as well as too much rain when commercially cultivated.[22] Any average we adopt, therefore, is subject to a margin of error produced by the huge variations and the increase in the overall risk. On the other hand, on the plausible assumption that cotton yields were determined by the environment, the average yield should change little in the long run, so that it is possible to confirm the earlier values with reference to later and more reliable survey-based values.

A previous scholarly work considered an average of 75 lbs/acre, a reasonable number for the Bombay Presidency in 1850.[23] I have found many numbers from the experimental farms started in the 1830s, which usually placed the yield of Indian varieties at above this figure.[24] The American and Mauritian seeds produced between 90 and 100 lbs of clean cotton, sometimes higher. Although susceptible to failure, these seeds did define an upper end of the range of yields. That upper end was somewhere above 100 lbs. Parliamentary committees on Indian cotton placed the overall average yield for Punjab at 91 lbs/acre and that for United Provinces at 103 lbs/acre in the 1840s.[25] But they also placed Bombay yields at considerably less than the 75 lbs assumed in the study cited previously. That the Bombay yields were on average smaller than the Indian average seems to be confirmed by another work that reported estimates for 1868–1940.[26] The Royal Commission on Agriculture collected more reliable averages for a later period (1914–27), which figures show many variations from year to year and place to place and a modal number of 90 lbs/acre of cleaned cotton. I adopt this number.[27]

I have used a rough benchmark proportion of 10 percent to account for cotton that went into non-textile uses and hold it constant. This is not much more than a guess; surely the textile use of cotton was far more lucrative than cotton going into items like quilts so that the non-textile proportion should be low, and because quilts were a matter of utility rather than fashion, the proportion should change little. The extent of loss involved in the conversion of cotton into yarn is based on the results of experiments made in Lancashire with Broach cotton, which showed that a pound of Gujarat cotton converted into 0.75 lbs weight of yarn on average.[28] I use this proportion.

The ratio of harvested to cleaned cotton is ignored. This is based on the following reasoning. A long-time grievance of Lancashire about India was the high admixture of dirt and seeds in the cotton exported. Cotton production deviated by as much as 25 percent from the weight of the cotton usable by the mills. A great deal of cleaning in the mid-eighteenth century was performed by manual methods, single rollers usually operated by village women or double rollers and the string method operated by a specialist team of two men. The former method produced the cleanest cotton it was possible to make by hand but was exceedingly labour-intensive. No sizeable cotton trader could possibly wait for the whole cargo to be cleaned by this method. The second method worked faster but wasted much cotton. The Whitney saw gin took a long time to become generally acceptable and was accepted eventually in locally adapted variations. The problem of dirt, therefore, was quite a serious one. Precisely because it was a serious matter, most yield figures used, as far as I can ascertain, were stated in terms of cleaned cotton.

The last ratio, which transforms yarn into cloth, is extremely variable between apparels and countries. One cotton enthusiast, a Major Briggs, brought a bundle of cotton cloth before a parliamentary committee as evidence of the wardrobes of Indian families. Briggs's bundle contained 32.5 square yards of clothing for an adult male and female and weighed 5 lbs.

Briggs was possibly working from a normative measure. What about the quality of the bundle that he had submitted? Almost a century later, a major government committee assumed an average cloth-yarn conversion of 4 yards/lb for 1900–1930, adjusting it upward slightly to 4.6 for the 1930s, in acknowledgment of an increase in the average counts spun in the Indian mills after tariffs rose on the finer counts.[29] It is plausible that the average fineness of cotton yarn in the 1830s was above the levels a century later. There was still a considerable domestic and export demand for muslins and persistence of production of the cotton varieties that led to these goods. Elsewhere the figure of 5.2 square yards per pound was used as a conversion ratio between the weight of yarn and the length of cloth for the 1930s (for handloom cloth only), and the committee's and other contemporary estimates were criticized for not being very mindful of the sensitivity of this ratio to time.[30] We can assume that the average ratio, which is mainly sensitive to yarn counts, fell between 1800 and 1920, but the rate of fall slowed owing to the tariffs after that. Accordingly, Briggs's implicit conversion ratio, 6.5 yards/lb, is adopted for 1820–1840; 5.2 yards/lb is adopted for 1860–1920, and the committee's 4.6 yards/lb is taken for 1940.

A good test of the reliability of any new procedure in measurement is to compare the old and the new measures for one benchmark year. I perform this test for 1900 and compare the 1900 cloth production derived from cotton data with an alternative measure available for 1900 derived from yarn production data. A 1942 survey used the second method to create a dataset on cloth production for 1900–1939.[31] This alternative involves dividing the yarn production by Indian mills into three parts: 'retained,' or converted into cloth by the mills; yarn exported; and 'free' yarn, or the part sold to the handloom weavers. These datasets, combined with trade data, have long been used for the measurement of production, consumption, and market shares. For one year, 1900, my approach yields aggregate numbers (yarn production 330 million lbs; and cloth production 1284 million yards) that are close to those registered by the second method (yarn 353 million lbs; cloth 1347 million yards). The proximity between the two sets of numbers should assure us of the reliability of the nineteenth-century estimates in this chapter.

The correspondence breaks down in the interwar period. The results we get with the cotton cultivation method, and those we obtain by using yarn production statistics, begin to diverge. They differ far too much for 1940, if not 1920. I have not been able to identify the exact reason behind a growing discrepancy. There is a crucial printing error in the official statistics for cotton export in the 1930s, but the discrepancy remains after appropriate corrections. The obvious answer is that some of the parameters assumed constant began to change. But which ones changed value?

Three hypotheses suggest themselves. First, a long run of exceptionally good weather and the newly established government laboratories and extension work succeeded in raising the average yield of cotton (a rise by a third, from 90 to 120 lbs/acre, eliminates the discrepancy).[32] Second, the desperate 'rationalization' drive in interwar Bombay, as well as the new mills that started in the smaller towns, managed to improve the cotton-to-yarn conversion ratio (a 5 percent improvement in the ratio adds 40 million lbs to the output). Third, a controversial argument advanced by Alan Heston, that the official agricultural statistics in the interwar period displayed a cumulative downward bias in yield, merits a serious look.[33] Fortunately, we have the option of switching to the yarn dataset from 1920 onwards.

For population data, I rely on one study that used an indirect procedure to infer population between 1801 and 1871.[34] This study worked from the first census in 1872 backward, adjusting for under-enumeration, under-coverage, and the presence of 'disturbing factors' in the nineteenth century. The figures show a small but positive growth rate of population in the nineteenth century and somewhat larger population totals than those customarily used. This is the only systematic attempt to create a series for the period in question and, therefore, the best resource for the purpose.

It is necessary to comment on the 1795 figures. Cotton cultivation statistics are unavailable for 1795, when much of the Indian land area did not belong to one political unit. We do have reasonably good data on trade. It would be logical to test the waters by making assumptions on the extent of cotton cultivation. One assumption is that production remained constant between 1820 and 1795. This is reasonable because the population, the main variable resource in the cultivation of land, remained unchanged between these years. This assumption gives us an upper bound on the extent of cultivation.

On the other hand, there are reasons to consider that the extent of cultivation was smaller in 1795. The major areas of cotton production in 1795 formed parts of the Maratha territories that faced a collapse of state power, warfare, and reshuffling of territories. This was the case all over the Deccan plateau. The major north-south and east-west roads had armies and bullock caravans carrying military provisions pass often enough to disrupt commercial traffic. Cotton export regions outside of Deccan, the Narmada Valley and Berar, for example, were in disarray under the tottering rule of the Holkar and Bhonsla chiefs. Reports of contemporary travellers, who were stopped every few miles by local landlords seeking tolls, suggest that the trade routes connecting Nagpur, and possibly Hoshangabad, with northern and southern India, were as good as cut off.[35] In northern India, the Awadh territory yielded small and unstable revenues, suggesting anarchic agricultural conditions. Taking these disruptions into consideration, I assume constant average consumption of cotton cloth between 1795 and 1820, which places the extent of cultivation at a level of 25 percent smaller than that in 1820.

The results: size of the market

The results of the exercise are set out in Tables 2.2 and 2.3. The tables show that the average consumption of cotton cloth about trebled between 1795 and 1940. There was a decline of 20 percent in the domestic production of cloth. But the decline was outweighed by the increase in import. Much of the imported cloth, in other words, added to consumption rather than displacing local production.

Even as there was a decline in hand-spinning, it had little impact on the economy of cotton. Cotton cultivation and production registered growth between 1840 and 1880. The extra output was destined for the export market. But the output that entered domestic markets held steady. Descriptions

Table 2.2 Cotton yarn, 1795–1900 (million lbs)

	Domestic production	*Export*	*Import*	*Net import*
1795	170–221	0	0	0
1820	161	0	3	3
1840	142	1	17	16
1860	168	0	31	31
1880	188	67	33	-34
1900	330	118	35	-83

Source: Based on data taken from a range of sources, as described in the text.

Table 2.3 Consumption of cotton cloth, 1795–1940 (square yards)

	Domestic production, million	*Net import, million*	*Total consumption, million*	*Population (million)*	*Per head consumption*
1795	1102–1437	-22	1080–1415	200	5.4–7.0
1820	1065	-23	1042	205	5.1
1840	1026	173	1199	212	5.7
1860	1035	825	1860	232	8.0
1880	799	1334	2084	254	8.2
1900	1284	1935	3220	294	10.9
1920	2985	1314	4299	319	13.5
1940	5620	358	5978	400	15.2

Notes: 1820–1900: third and sixth columns in Table 2.2 × conversion ratio. 1920–1940: based on yarn production and trade data. The 1795 figure is based on the following information: 'Imports into the United Kingdom during the ten years 1791–1800 of calicos and muslins averaged 2.2 million pieces of about ten sq yds. each per annum.' R. Robson, *The Cotton Industry in Britain*, London: Macmillan, 1957, 1. Other trade data from sources cited in Table 2.1. Population data come from P.C. Mahalanobis and D. Bhattacharya, 'Growth of population in India and Pakistan, 1801–1961,' *Artha Vijnana*, 18, 1976, 1–10; and India, *Statistical Abstracts*, later years.

of agriculture in these times rarely say that the deindustrialization badly affected the peasants growing cotton. There was an agrarian depression in the Deccan in the early nineteenth century, but it occurred before the acceleration in yarn and cloth imports.

Domestic cotton availability appears less responsive to the decline in textile production because the decline was of a moderate extent. Textile history of the nineteenth century notes with surprise the tenacity of hand-spinning in the face of the rising import of yarn. The hand-spinning industry was not dealt a mortal blow by Lancashire yarn, which came in particular counts and was of moderate extent. The high cost of internal transportation of the pre-railway era joined with the overseas trade costs before the Suez Canal (1869) to shelter hand-spinners. The decline of hand-spinning accelerated after 1860 as a result of the combined effect of the railways, the fall in trade costs, and the Indian mills. Therefore, as far as the cotton-growing peasant was concerned, the fall in hand-spinning was almost immediately compensated for by the rise of factory production of yarn.

Finally, we come to the topic of most interest to this book – the artisans, the hand-spinners, and handloom weavers. The revised set of numbers shows the contrasting experiences of the craft and mechanized methods of textile production. Tables 2.4 and 2.5 present the results. There are four major findings. First, as mentioned previously, the timing of the decline in hand-spinning was later than is usually thought to be the case.[36] Second, cloth production in handlooms fell to a relatively moderate extent and revived to exceed the early nineteenth century levels. The turnaround happened in the 1880s. Third, the fall in hand-spinning was more than offset by the rise in mill spinning, thanks to export markets and the emerging

Table 2.4 Production of yarn by origin, 1795–1940 (million lbs)

	Hand-spun yarn	*Indian mill yarn*	*Imported yarn*
1795	170–221	0	0
1820	161	0	3
1840	142	0	17
1860	168	0	31
1880	107	81	33
1900	0	353	33
1920	0	660	47
1940	30	1235	41

Column 3 in Table 2.2 minus Indian mill yarn.

Sources: M.P. Gandhi, *The Indian Cotton Textile Industry*, Calcutta: The Book Company, 1930, 53, for 1880, India, Fact-finding Committee: Handlooms and Mills, Calcutta: Government Press, 1942, remaining years.

Table 2.5 Production of cloth by origin, 1795–1940 (million yards)

	Handloom cloth	*Indian mill cloth*	*Imported cloth*
1795	1102–1437	0	0
1820	1065	0	26
1840	1026	0	199
1860	1035	0	825
1880	677	122	1334
1900	646	421	2005
1920	931	1563	1511
1940	1945	3905	579

Note: 1795–1860: Domestic production of yarn (Table 2.4) converted. 1880–1940: Based on free yarn data; for sources see text.

handloom market. And, fourth, when all sources were combined, consumption was protected.

How bad was the effect of the decline of textile exports from India on the handloom weaver? The exercise yields a set of numbers showing the percentage of export in the production of cotton cloth. Cotton cloth was the largest export of early modern India. In 1795, the percentage of export in total production fell in the range of 1–2 percent, which was much smaller than the proportions in the late nineteenth century, 5–6 percent between 1880 and 1900. The percentage fell in the interwar period only to rise again during World War II. In 1700, the total textile import by all European companies from India amounted to 25–35 million square yards. Based on data on bullion supplies, we can surmise that the scale of the business increased slightly in the middle of the century to decline again. If we assume the roughly constant scale of cotton cultivation in the century, the export-production ratio for 1750 should be higher than those at the beginning or the end of the century, but perhaps not by more than one or two percentage points. These calculations imply that the early-modern Indo-European trade was largely irrelevant to both producers and consumers on the subcontinent. Textile export was not a big deal. Therefore, its fall was not a big deal either.

A further useful byproduct of this exercise is a set of price data for different types of cloth. Table 2.6 shows the results. I draw attention to the relative price, which gives us a clue to one part of the whole story – the decline between 1820 and 1880. It does not explain the other part – continuance and revival. Purchases of handloom and imported cloth responded negatively to changes in relative prices, shown in the last column of the table. However, the price elasticity of demand for handloom cloth was negative and insignificant (-.14), whereas that for imported cloth was negative and large (–1.46).[37] The result explains why handloom cloth production changed the way it did at the turn of the twentieth century. Demand for cloth had a large

Table 2.6 Prices, 1795–1900

	Price of handloom cloth (1820=100)	*Price of imported cloth (1820=100)*	*Relative price (handloom cloth to imported cloth)*
1795	96		
1820	100	100	1.00
1830	62	114	0.54
1840	80	34	2.31
1850	106	31	3.42
1860	154	30	5.12
1870	251	42	6.04
1880	258	30	8.62
1890	314	32	9.84
1900	226	21	10.52

Note: Derived as an average of prices of cotton and mill yarn, weighted by the proportion of handspun and mill yarn used in handloom production. All other prices are from sources on trade statistics cited next, Tables 2.3 and 2.4.

fixed component in which handloom cloth dominated. Substitution happened within a relatively small price-sensitive component. But even here, the income effect of cloth prices may have been the dominant influence rather than substitution.

These findings suggest the hypotheses I shall explore more fully in Chapter 3, that consumers of handmade and machine-made cloths responded to different kinds of stimuli. The demand for handloom cloth was especially sensitive to quality, as well as ritual, status, occasion, and the gender of the wearer. With such segmented preferences, handloom cloth could retain a market for itself, though on a diminished scale, whereas mechanized cotton cloth took over only those segments where quality (as the buyers understood the term) and ritual, status, occasion, and gender mattered less than the cheapness of the cloth. Women's clothing dominated the former set, men's the latter.

Let me now discuss in a little more detail the second phase in this history, the post-1880 stabilization and revival.

1880–1940: re-industrialization, production, wages, profits

Hard statistics on prices, wages, and incomes in the major segments of the handloom industry become more easily available after 1880 and allow us to create a fuller picture of the revival. For the industry in the twentieth century, four general propositions can be made, as I show in the rest of this section. First, there was no significant change in employment or looms between

1900 and 1940 (Table 5.1). Second, the physical output increased, implying a significant rise in physical productivity (Table 5.1). Third, the composition of output, employment, and looms changed towards higher-value products (see next in this section). And fourth, profitability was stable and probably increased between 1924 and 1940.[38] For periods before 1924, price and cost data are incomplete. There are some data on wages and profits, and these suggest that the last point may be generalizable. The transition in the industry benefited capital more than the wage earners. This point will be illustrated with different kinds of evidence throughout the book.

Estimated handloom output was growing between 1900 and 1939. It is, however, a series that fluctuated far more than did the series of mill cloth output in the same period. One such episode occurred during World War I due to the shortage and high prices of imported yarn. Nevertheless, the market grew, as did long-distance trade in handloom cloth and in the raw materials used. There is no direct estimate of increasing distance or volume of trade in handloom cloth. There is, however, indirect evidence. For example, descriptions of trade in major handloom saree brands and descriptions of regional trade networks suggest growth in these networks.[39] The conditions of supply of four major raw materials, cotton yarn, dyes, gold thread, and silk, changed greatly from the mid-nineteenth century. Cotton yarn, earlier made locally by hand, was either imported or manufactured in mill towns and distributed in handloom towns and villages by merchants specializing in these trades. Dyes, gold thread, and silk yarn had earlier been obtained locally and were now imported to a varying extent. The railways and urbanization brought down the real costs of migration considerably.

Overall, there was a transition from localized exchange to trade based in market towns that were also increasingly sites of the settlement of migrant handloom weavers. This whole movement towards more market transactions we can call 'commercialization.'

These tendencies translated into increased profits. Discussions about incomes in weaving tend to be preoccupied with wages. Real wages, usually piece-rates converted into hourly wage rates, were at best stable in the first half of the twentieth century. S. Sivasubramonian concludes that weavers' money wages 'declined from a high level [in 1900] to low levels by the end of the thirties.'[40] Data I have collected and reconstructed show that there was some increase in the interwar period but a reversal in the years after the Great Depression. Major official sources were generally pessimistic about wages. Stagnant wages should not surprise us. The existence of surplus labour and unemployment predicts such a trend in wages.

There is a great deal of survey data on merchant profits not previously used in these assessments of income. Unlike the estimates cited above, these data have the virtue of including a wide variety of clothes. Most samples were from regions and products in which new tools were being installed. These data show that the rates of profit were high in the 1920s. Profits were also relatively stable. Profits fell somewhat in the post-depression period but did not decline to the same extent as money wages.

An interesting feature of this dataset is the scarcity of observations for the prewar period. Prices and earnings data are not rare around 1900, but these usually refer to weavers who hawked their products and sold directly to consumers. Merchant profit as a category and merchants themselves became more visible (in the sources on the industry) in the interwar period because they set up more processing shops or frame looms or contracted with larger numbers of weavers.

In the nineteenth century, the average cotton weaver's earnings and the extent of demand for cloth were unstable. Instability arose mainly from the agrarian origin of a large part of the demand for handloom cloth. Weavers were the first to be reduced to starvation at the onset of famine and the first to migrate. It is significant that after 1900, British India did not face the threat of famines. While that may have reduced serious risks to life, large parts of rural weaving and weaving located in semi-arid areas continued to suffer from dependence on the monsoon rains and unsteady agricultural demand. This dependence was substantially less in the major textile towns; some of them grew rapidly in the twentieth century.

In the 1930s, another shock occurred. Yarn was in serious shortage, partly because protectionist policies erected barriers to import of higher-grade cotton yarn from Manchester to India. Growth stopped, and real wages fell. Profits were squeezed too but did not fall to the extent the wages did. Money wage rates and yarn prices fell somewhat faster than product prices. Profits were protected, and yet the industry was in trouble. Weavers reacted by shifting money to non-cotton yarn and powerlooms. An endogenous form of creative destruction happened as one segment of the handloom industry invested in mechanized weaving.

The story so far has focused on cotton. Handlooms also wove wool and silk, and some of these other fibres, especially silk and silk-substitutes, added a lot of value to handloom production. Usually, the weaving of each type of fibre existed as a separate industry. We have rather thin data to show how these other industries evolved in colonial times. Based on what material there is, I can offer some estimates of the scale of all forms of non-cotton weaving for the 1930s. The findings are interesting.

Composition of cloth production in the 1930s

Except for cotton, all other important types of yarn – wool, mulberry silk, wild silk, a variety of mixed fabrics (cotton warp and silk weft) and increasingly in the twentieth-century, viscose fibres – were woven by the handlooms until about 1920. Mills did not weave these fibres because most mills that wove any cloth at all were composite mills, that is, integrated a spinning mill, a weaving mill, and a processing shop in the same site. To weave

Table 2.7 Handloom market shares in the 1930s

	The proportion of non-cotton cloth in handloom production (% of value)	*The proportion of handloom cloth in total cloth production*	
		% of quantity	*% of value*
1931–2	29	33	48
1932–3	28	33	49
1933–4	26	33	48
1934–5	31	30	45
1935–6	26	32	47
1936–7	33	30	45
1937–8	45	31	49

Note: For details of the calculation, see Tirthankar Roy, 'Size and Structure of Handloom Weaving in the mid-1930s,' *Indian Economic and Social History Review*, 25(1), 1988, 1–24.

a non-cotton cloth would amount to underutilizing spinning and processing capacity. These boundaries were shifting in the interwar period because a group of pure weaving factories started weaving non-cotton yarns on powerlooms. This trend would seem to spell death for the handloom performing this line of work, except that some of these factories had been started by the handloom weavers themselves.

Partly because of these tendencies, the fullest data to reconstruct the volume and value of production by fibre type can be found only for the 1930s. I have used this data for this purpose, and the results show that the combined handloom-powerloom units were dominant within a segment of the market. If we convert physical volumes into values, the cotton mills of Bombay and Manchester were not the main players in the Indian textile market in late-colonial India. Small firms using manual and semi-manual technology were.

That is not the end of the story. When we convert these into market shares, handlooms look to be a large supplier of non-cotton cloth. However, its share was not rising and was about to fall. These tendencies occur too late in the period of interest to merit a detailed discussion here. But they do illustrate a point made before and one that will reappear in Chapter 3, that the specialization patterns were unstable, especially after the rise of pure weaving factories in the 1930s.

Conclusion

The chapter suggests two sets of lessons.

The first set concerns consumption. As Morris had predicted, in the long run, the average consumption of clothing increased significantly in India. Cessation of exports, deindustrialization, and the fall in aristocratic fortunes had little or no effect on the long-term trend in consumption. The loss of the weavers' purchasing power did not slow down the growth in average cloth consumption. The Morris conjecture, that a fall in the global price of cotton cloth increased the purchase of handmade cloth in India, was right.

The second set of findings concerns the artisan producer of cloth. Handloom weaving declined between 1820 and 1880, and after a gap, was revived. The first phase of decline shows the effect of a fall in cloth prices on the price-sensitive segment of handloom production. From 1880, a new era began in which the more quality-sensitive component in handloom demand played a larger role. It sustained the handloom market and enabled it to grow. In this phase, the increase in the consumption of clothing accelerated, which aided textile-based industrialization in India in which both handlooms and mills played similar and positive roles.

If specialization protected a large part of the handloom market, in the interwar period, it was an unreliable cushion at best, as we will see next.

Notes

1 Tirthankar Roy, 'Consumption of Cotton Cloth in India, 1795–1940,' *Australian Economic History Review*, 52(1), 2012, 61–84.
2 Morris D. Morris, 'Towards a Reinterpretation of Nineteenth Century Indian Economic History,' *Journal of Economic History*, 23(4), 1963, 607–18.
3 The magnitude is sensitive to the strength of the substitution and income effects. A partial test found the demand for imported cloth to be price elastic, but the test neither included the relative prices between handmade and machine-made cloth, nor could it use a reliable income. Meghnad Desai, 'Demand for Cotton Textiles in Nineteenth Century India,' *Indian Economic and Social History Review*, 8(4), 1970, 337–61.
4 A.K. Bagchi, 'De-Industrialization in India in the Nineteenth Century: Some Theoretical Implications,' *Journal of Development Studies*, 12(2), 1976, 135–64.
5 Daniel Thorner, '"Deindustrialization" in India, 1881–1931,' in D. Thorner and A. Thorner, eds., *Land and Labour in India*, New York: Asia, 1962. See also Marika Vicziany, 'The De-Industrialisation of India in the Nineteenth Century: A Methodological Critique of Amiya Kumar Bagchi,' *Indian Economic and Social History Review*, 16(2), 1979, 105–46.
6 M.J. Twomey, 'Employment in Nineteenth Century Indian Textiles,' *Explorations in Economic History*, 20(1), 1983, 37–57.
7 Om Prakash, 'Bullion for Goods: International Trade and the Economy of Early Eighteenth Century Bengal,' *Indian Economic and Social History Review*, 13(2), 1976, 159–86.
8 Indrajit Ray, 'Identifying the Woes of the Cotton Textile Industry in Bengal: Tales of the Nineteenth Century,' *Economic History Review*, 62(4), 2009, 857–92. An earlier study also contains useful discussion of the Bengal region, Ruma Chatterjee, 'Cotton Handloom Manufactures of Bengal, 1870–1921,' *Economic and Political Weekly*, 22(25), 1987, 988–97.
9 Amalendu Guha, 'The Decline of India's Cotton Handicrafts: 1800–1905: A Quantitative Macro-Study,' in *Occasional Paper No. 117*, Calcutta: Centre for Studies in Social Sciences, 1989.
10 The extent of the fall, however, was overstated in the paper. The acreage under cotton, for example, was assumed to be improbably large; the yield per acre

assumed to have fallen; and the conversion of cotton to yarn was done under an unrealistically low ratio of conversion loss. The overall result suggested exceedingly high levels of handicraft activity in 1850, and, therefore, a far-too-rapid decline in the next half century.

11 The pre-1970 historical scholarship on craft unemployment usually dealt with the early nineteenth century. The important authors were Romesh Dutt, A. Sarada Raju, R.D. Choksey, H.R. Ghosal, and A.V. Raman Rao. These older studies are discussed more fully in Tirthankar Roy, *The Economic History of India 1857–1947*, New Delhi: Oxford University Press, Third Ed., 2011, 59.

12 See P.J. Thomas and B. Natarajan, 'Economic Depression in the Madras Presidency (1825–54),' *Economic History Review*, 7(1), 1936, 67–75.

13 S.J. Patel, *Agricultural Labourers in Modern India and Pakistan*, Bombay: Current, 1952; Raghabendra Chattopadhyay, 'De-Industrialisation in India Reconsidered,' *Economic and Political Weekly*, 10(12), 1975, 523–31.

14 David Clingingsmith and Jeffrey Williamson, 'Deindustrialization in 18th and 19th Century India: Mughal Decline, Climate Shocks and British Industrial Ascent,' *Explorations in Economic History*, 45(3), 2008, 209–34. I have not seen enough evidence in the sources either for or against this thesis to form an opinion. However, trade historians might raise the objection that the formation of the East India Company state and consequent political control on terms of trade could potentially offset the effects of climate on productivity that this paper considers important.

15 See under Table 2.1, and J. Forbes Royle, *On the Culture and Commerce of Cotton in India and Elsewhere*, London: Smith Elder, 1851; J. Talboys Wheeler, *Hand-Book to the Cotton Cultivation in the Madras Presidency*, Madras: Higginbotham, 1862; J.G. Medlicott, *Cotton Handbook of Bengal*, Calcutta: Bengal Printing, 1862.

16 One possibility is that the railways, which connected the cotton districts of the Deccan Plateau with Bombay only in the 1870s, had a disproportionately large effect on the cotton trade and production in this region, where pre-railway overland transportation was expensive. It is unlikely, however, that cotton acreage increased by a factor of 5–8, as suggested in the parliamentary enquiries. My revision will still leave a large expansion in acreage but of a more credible magnitude.

17 I base this conclusion mainly upon one careful survey of cotton cultivation in the biggest cotton-producing province, Bombay Presidency. The survey compiled district statistics. W.R. Cassels, *Cotton: An Account of Its Culture in the Bombay Presidency Prepared from Government Records and Other Authentic Sources in Accordance with a Resolution of the Government of India*, Bombay: Government Press, 1861. As one author observes, during the Civil War, when India supplied over half of the demand for cotton in Lancashire, 'the bulk of India's cotton was cultivated in Western India and within a radius of three hundred miles of Bombay,' F. Logan, 'India's Loss of the British Cotton Market after 1865,' *Journal of Southern History*, 31(1), 1965, 40–50.

18 A later work reckoned that in 1851, cotton acreage was four million in Bombay and Gujarat, which I find improbable considering that the acreage in these regions in the earliest reliable official measure, for 1885, was placed at 2.2 million. Amalendu Guha, 'Raw Cotton of Western India: 1750–1850,' *Indian Economic Social History Review*, 9(1), 1972, 1–41.

19 My assumed figure of roughly three million acres between 1820 and 1840 receives indirect support from contemporary informed discourse. The Secretary to the United States Treasury had placed the cotton crop of India in 1834 at 185

million lbs. The number translates into an area a little over two million acres. A careful discussion of this number rejected it for being too low and inconsistent with export trade volumes. Forbes Royle, *Culture and Commerce*, 18.

20 Forbes Royle, *Culture and Commerce*, 285.

21 The view that the yield of Indian cotton varied greatly by location, and that it was, therefore, influenced more by soil and climate than by cultivation practices originated in the opinions of the nineteenth-century cotton planters in India. See, for example, the discussion in Forbes Royle, *Culture and Commerce*, 168–87.

22 In the nineteenth century, a number of experimental farms modelled after the indigo plantations of Bengal and owned or managed by American 'practical men' tried these seeds, and with some exceptions, failed to make a profitable business out of them.

23 Guha, 'Raw cotton.'

24 Mr. Hughes 'was well content with one hundred pounds per acre, of fine clean cotton.' Forbes Royle, *Culture and Commerce*, 220. See also, 285–6 for yield figures pertaining to Bundelkhand and Rohilkhand districts.

25 British Parliamentary Papers, *Cotton (India): A Return of the Quantity of Cotton Wool Exported from the British Possessions in India, in Each Year during Which the Accounts Have Been Kept; Stating the Ports of Shipment, Quantity Shipped, Countries to Which Exported, and Shipment to Each Country*, London: HMSO, 1847.

26 Sumit Guha, *The Agrarian Economy of Bombay-Deccan*, New Delhi: Oxford University Press, 1985, 105–6, 110.

27 India, *Royal Commission on Labour in India*, vol. 11, Supplementary, London: HMSO, 1931, 76.

28 Forbes Royle, *Culture and Commerce*, 24.

29 India, *Fact-Finding Committee: Handlooms and Mills*, Calcutta: Government Press, 1942.

30 Tirthankar Roy, 'Size and Structure of Handloom Weaving in the Mid-Thirties,' *Indian Economic and Social History Review*, 28(1), 1988, 1–28.

31 India, *Fact-Finding Committee.*

32 On evidence of a rise in Bombay yield, see Guha, *Agrarian Economy*, 110.

33 Heston, 'National income,' in Dharma Kumar, ed., *The Cambridge Economic History of India*, vol. 2, Cambridge: Cambridge University Press, 1983, 376–462.

34 P.C. Mahalanobis and D. Bhattacharya, 'Growth of Population in India and Pakistan, 1801–1961,' *Artha Vijnana*, 18, 1976, 1–10.

35 See Tirthankar Roy, *Economic History of Early Modern India*, London: Routledge, 2013.

36 Commercial hand-spinning had a mild revival in 1940. India, *Fact-Finding Committee*, measured the extent of production, a number cited in Table 2.4.

37 Desai, 'Demand for Cotton Textiles,' and Twomey, 'Employment,' also find import demand to be price elastic.

38 No contemporary attempt was made to estimate trends in prices and costs of handloom cloth. However, the early twentieth century saw many descriptive reports that produced quite a large database on prices, weavers' wages, and merchants' profits for different regions, times, and types of product. This database can be used in three ways to make broad inferences about incomes in the industry. First, in his work on national income statistics, S. Sivasubramonian gathered much of the available data on wages of artisans to produce a series on incomes from small-scale industry between 1900 and 1946, *National Income of India in the Twentieth Century*, New Delhi: Oxford University Press, 2000, 264–77. Where weavers are concerned, the raw data in almost all cases refer to 'wages,'

or income of a weaver working for a merchant. Second, from prices and cost data, Roy estimated a composition of value-added for a standard product for the period 1924–39, previous version of this book. This is the dataset referred to in point 4. The third dataset is that of Table 2.3 (see below).

39 On the development of a regional trade network with reference to handlooms, see D. Haynes, 'Market Formation in Khandesh, c. 1820–1930,' *Indian Economic and Social History Review*, 36(3), 1999, 275–302.

40 Sivasubramonian, *National Income of India*, 282. This work nevertheless finds a rising trend in real income per worker in small-scale industry driven by a trend in income of a generic category, 'skilled artisan.'

3

CONSUMPTION AND MARKET

The chapter illustrates a central argument of the book – that handmade cloth competed against machine-made cloth not because it was cheaper or could be made cheaper but because handmade cloth embodied qualities that consumers valued and that machines could not deliver except at a high cost. Consumers like these included most Indian women around 1900.

Weaving, therefore, was subject to processes of change that were largely endogenous to the handloom market. I show in this chapter that as the cloth market grew in scale it also changed in types of costumes, materials, and designs that were consumed. In part, the latter change came from a fall in the costs of trade and integration of markets, which enabled the buyers to compare styles more than before. The chapter shows that along with many specific ways that handloom weavers responded to these changes, two big processes stand out: withdrawal from men's wear and innovation in women's wear.

In telling the story, we should also acknowledge that competition with machines was ever present on the margins even of such clothes where quality and brand image protected the handlooms to some extent. The border between what machines could do and what handlooms could do was constantly shifting. Quality did not mean a fixed thing. If consumer tastes changed enough to accept a type of saree border that the machine could deliver, handlooms would have to retreat from that line of work. And yet, whereas shifts in consumer preferences threatened the weavers, these also offered them opportunities to develop new products and conduct experiments.

I first try to define the boundary between mechanized and handmade cloth on quality as the boundary stood around 1880–1900. I will then move on to discussing changes in quality; and finally, adaptations to these changes. From this chapter onward, the text will frequently refer to towns with a significant presence of weavers; Maps 3.1, 3.2, and 3.3 may be helpful as a reference.

What was 'quality' in handmade cloth?

What was that 'quality' in cloth that hand technology could deliver but machines could not? To understand quality in cloth, we should first distinguish three dimensions of quality: fineness of the fibre material, the fibre type, and design. These distinctions are useful to explain not only market shares at certain points in time but also how the borderlines changed in the long run. Table 3.1 breaks up quality into three benchmarks and shows how crafts and machines delivered quality by these benchmarks.

Contemporaries, and some later historians, speculated that most Manchester cloth being of medium counts, handlooms lost the market in medium-count cotton, concentrating in coarse and fine types of yarn. This is broadly correct. Around 1900, handlooms tended to specialize in coarse and fine cotton weaving, like 10s and above 40s, whereas the Indian factories of Bombay and Ahmedabad specialized in the low-to-medium range, like 20s and 30s, and Manchester mills supplied medium-range and finer cotton cloth. Machines in India spun mainly short-staple cotton and therefore wove coarse-to-medium cloth. Machines in Britain used cotton imported from all over the world and therefore had a wider range.

Coarse cotton cloth survived in certain pockets. The weaving of below-10s count of cotton yarn was more common in the countryside of Punjab, United Provinces, and Bihar. In the interwar period, these regions responded relatively more to M.K. Gandhi's campaign to revive handspun yarn.[1] Coarse weavers were often peasants and agricultural labourers. The weaving itself did not need much skill or specialization or sophisticated equipment and

Table 3.1 Handmade and machine-made cloth compared on quality, c. 1880–1900

	Hand	*Machines*
Fineness of cotton	Coarse (below 10s), associated with hand-spinning Fine (above 40s) and muslins (very fine)	Medium (20s-40s)
Design	Supplied to printing, embroidery Woven on the loom by manipulating weft-thread (manual change of shuttles or the drop-box) or by manipulating warp-thread (manually or by Jacquard and dobby)	Plain or grey in the nineteenth century Dobby or geometrical patterns after 1850
Material	Cotton Silk Rayon	Cotton – the captive spinning constraint of composite mills (see text)

Note: Based on general data about textile production.

was well suited as a part-time pursuit of the peasant household.[2] Peasants were the main buyers of these goods too. The dispersed location of the market suited the family-based production system well and gave it some shelter from foreign cloth.[3] The material generally used in such cloth was spun locally, more in the cotton-growing tracts than elsewhere. Therefore, local production and decentralized production had an added advantage.[4] On the other hand, machines were unlikely to get into this range of cloth. It would be a waste of their economies to engage in a line of work that delivered a cheap and small output and led to too-frequent breaks and stops in operation.

While coarse weaving carried on in a limited way, nowhere did it represent an elite form of weaving. The opposite was the case. In southern and central India, the coarse-cloth weaver was usually a member of the labouring caste, not an artisan but a village servant. There were few merchants and capitalists among them, and elite weaving castes would not associate with them. Facing similar pressure, the more skilled weavers would migrate nearer to the market and take over marketing; the coarse weaver would more likely become a general labourer or, to use the generic colonial term, a cooly.[5]

Data on the fineness of yarn going into textiles suggest that there was a slow and steady rise in the share of the finer cloth, implying that the rural industry in handlooms was in stress whereas the urban weaving was not (Table 3.2). But regional differences continued, decided by local preferences and costs of trade. The rise was more visible in the hinterlands of the port enclaves, regions where mills came up, including Bombay, Ahmedabad, Bengal, Bihar, and Orissa. Eastern India was the largest market for imported grey cloth. On the other hand, in Punjab, cloth made of the handspun yarn continued. In parts of the Central Provinces, coastal Andhra and

Table 3.2 Cotton cloth by counts (percentages of column), 1906–1940

Counts	*1906*			*1931–2*		*1940*	
	Mill	*Hand*	*Import*	*Mill*	*Hand*	*Mill*	*Hand*
≤ 20s	10	55	12	39	65	57	54
21–30s	83	9	44	48	8	26	20
31–40s	7	27	30	8	18	12	14
40s≤	..	9	14	5	9	5	12

Notes: Based on Raoji B. Patel, 'Handloom Weaving in India' in Proceedings of the Industrial Conference at Baroda, Madras, 1906, 83–92; G.S. Hardy, *Report on the Import Tariff on Cotton Piecegoods and on External Competition in the Cotton Piecegoods Trade*, Calcutta: Government Press, 1929; India, *Fact-finding Committee: Handlooms and Mills*, Calcutta: Government Press, 1942. Patel's count-classes are slightly different, 6–16, 20–26, 26–40 and above 40.

Mysore, coarse weaving persisted too but not necessarily using handspun yarn.[6] Demand for clothes made of handspun yarn was relatively strong in the north where winters were colder, and thick and durable cotton garments were in demand as winter wear.

The weaving of fine counts of cotton yarn was quite a different story. Muslins (superfine, usually above 80s counts, plain cotton cloth) were once a successful export from India, especially eastern India in the eighteenth century. Before the rise of machine spinning, cotton suitable for muslin did grow on a limited scale in parts of India. Muslin was an established industry in the lower Bengal Delta, though confined to a few pockets.[7] On a small scale, muslins carried on in the United Province and central India. These were rarely plain white cotton cloth as the Dhaka muslins had been in the time of East India Company trade and were often embroidered or otherwise decorated.

I have discussed the fineness of cotton. Next, consider designs or technologies to impart designs on cloth. Decorations on the cloth could use three types of technology – external application of colour via printing, dyeing or painting, embroidering, and weaving patterns on the loom. Before the introduction of mineral dyes in the 1860s, an extensive industry existed in India in dyeing and printing. Indian artisans had great proficiency in dyeing and printing thanks to advances in handling organic dyes and mordanting. When cloth was dyed or printed, the artisan did not need to procure a high-quality cloth. But since printing and painting were labour-intensive processes and therefore the products were expensive, it made sense to use the finer cloth as the base. A weaving industry usually existed in those towns that had a brand name for printing and dyeing. The same logic led to a bond between weaving and embroidering as well.

Weaving patterns on the loom required either manipulation of the warp thread or manipulation of the weft thread or both. Warp-manipulation can be done with the Jacquard, a perforated card panel attached overhead. This was invented in 1804 in France. The Jacquard allowed manipulation of individual warp threads. On the other hand, the dobby (earlier known as the draw-boy) and the tappet were attachments that worked by moving whole shafts through which the warp threads passed. Using these, simple geometric patterns can be woven on the loom. The dobby was used in Manchester in the late nineteenth century. Weft-manipulation would mean the use of several shuttles each carrying a thread of one colour or material different from the warp colour and material. Moving these shuttles by hand added an enormous quantity of labour to the production of the cloth. The drop-box, a device that held several shuttles, reduced that labour somewhat, but it was not suitable for many types of design that were woven on typical Indian garments like the saree.

Designs woven on the loom had a closer association with handmade cloth and designs printed or embroidered with the machine-made cloth. This was so because handmade cloth, thanks to the shorter warps and facility with warp- and weft-manipulation, could more easily implement designs woven on the loom. Printing and dyeing, on the other hand, did not need the weaver and was slowly taken over by systems of production outside weaving. Embroidering similarly existed as a profession apart from weaving and became more distant from it.

Not all of these techniques worked equally well on all types of apparel. There was a correlation between basic shapes and designs of clothing. The distinction between tailored and draped garments is useful to understand this correlation.

When English cloth arrived in India about the 1820s, two sorts of costumes were in existence.[8] Some apparels were wrapped or draped around the body, and some were bought as fabrics, stitched, and tailored. These types did not always co-exist in the same household. Rather, they represented different social worlds. Tailored garments, for example, were probably more common in northern and western India, among Muslims and among men. In 1858, Edward Balfour's *Encyclopedia Asiatica* mentioned a common belief that the Hindus did not know or have a word for needle-made dresses. At 1800, the typical attire of a Bengali Hindu male was a dhoti and a chaddar, both wrapped around the body, and the urban Muslim would wear kurta and pyjama, both tailored garments. Tailoring as a craft had a strong association with Muslim artisan tradition. The Hindu gods and goddesses were (and are) shown in nothing but the most authentic draped clothes (that is, the goddesses avoided stitched breast clothes). The divide was so striking that in the nineteenth century, when European observers began to be interested in the Indian market, there was a debate on whether this was a matter of comfort and climate or religious prescription.[9] In the north, where winters are severe, upper garments were more generally stitched. In the south, where summers are sultry, draped garments were more common for both Hindus and Muslims.

Between 1850 and 1900, machines had taken over the fabric going into tailored garments. But handlooms ruled in draped garments, mainly the sort that the women wore. The former type was more suited to mechanization because the cloth going to be tailored was a mass-produced intermediate good. In men's clothing, the tendency was towards homogenization and a shift to tailored apparel, like shirts and trousers. Machine-made fabrics suited that tendency. Buyers bought a piece of cloth and tailored it into a garment. The tailor may give it some individuality, but the fabric itself only needed to be durable and cheap, not unique in any other way. Draped garments, on the other hand, suited handmade cloth better because each piece of a draped garment was distinctive, usually by the way it looked. Handlooms had the skill to impart that distinctiveness on the loom. The most important draped garment was the universal women's apparel, the saree.

Draped clothes, being geometrically shaped, lend themselves more readily to designs woven on the loom. On a rectangular surface, linear and symmetric motifs could be naturally introduced, typically occurring on the sides of the cloth, the lower and end borders of a saree, for instance. The strict separation of borders and field heightened the design. The border itself rigidly defined each piece of cloth as a singular entity. If each saree were to represent a non-standard unique type of identity, the producer would have to use a technique that lent itself to making such differentiation. Mass production systems would be able to do that to a limited extent. Handloom weaving could impart that differentiation more economically and in greater variety. Handlooms added uniqueness to sarees via border designs woven on the loom.

Machines were good at weaving long sheets of similar quality because these could be woven at a high speed and with long stretches of warp. Changing warp and weft is costly with any high-speed loom. But when we come to sarees, each saree of 6–9 yards of warp length could become a self-contained dress if the loom could handle a shorter warp length and more frequent changes of the shuttle. Handlooms had a natural advantage in such clothes. To deliver a border on a saree required the simultaneous handling of many weft threads involving multiple shuttles. This was something at which the handlooms were better. A change of shuttles or warp at that rate would slow down weaving so much as to make the mechanized loom uneconomical to work.

Finally, consider material. Among the high-quality fabrics that had a close association with handloom weaving, silk was somewhat unique. Until the mid-twentieth century, silk was almost exclusively woven by the handloom. Handlooms faced little competition from the cotton mills in silk. Most mills were 'composite,' that is, contained a spinning, weaving, and processing shop in the same compound. The mills did not produce silk yarn and therefore had no reason to weave it.

These boundaries were unstable. How were they unstable?

Unstable boundaries between machines and handlooms

First, the Indian mills diversified into finer counts of yarn and finer cloths between 1906 and 1940 (Table 3.2). Protective tariffs on imported yarn, introduced on a significant scale in the 1920s, were higher on the finer counts. Second, the mills decided that they would enter the women's clothing market by producing printed sarees. According to the Fact-finding Committee report (1942), mill-made sarees introduced a break in the pattern of market-sharing after the mid-1920s. Not all big mills could move into this new area with equal facility, however. As mentioned before, the composite mills could not switch product lines owing to their captive spinning capacity and the quality of raw cotton available. A few

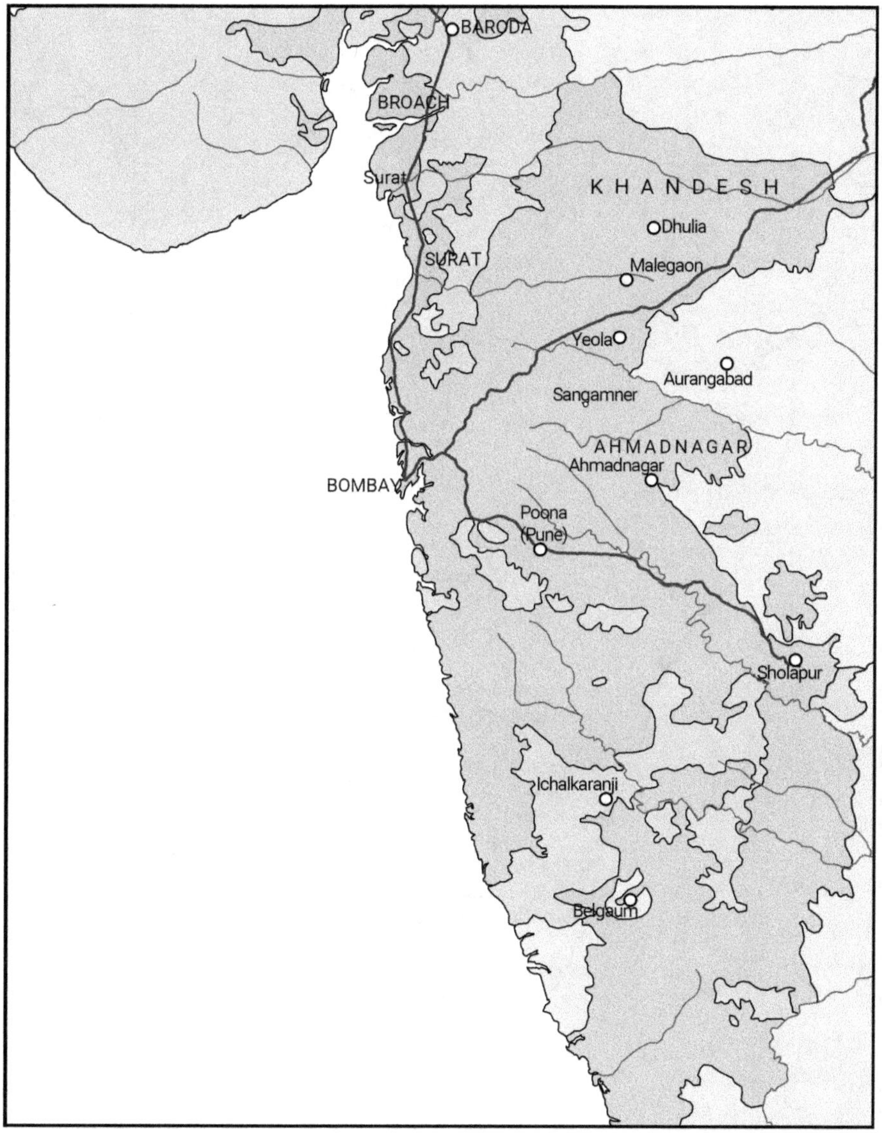

Map 3.1 Weaving towns in Bombay Presidency around 1940

Source: Author

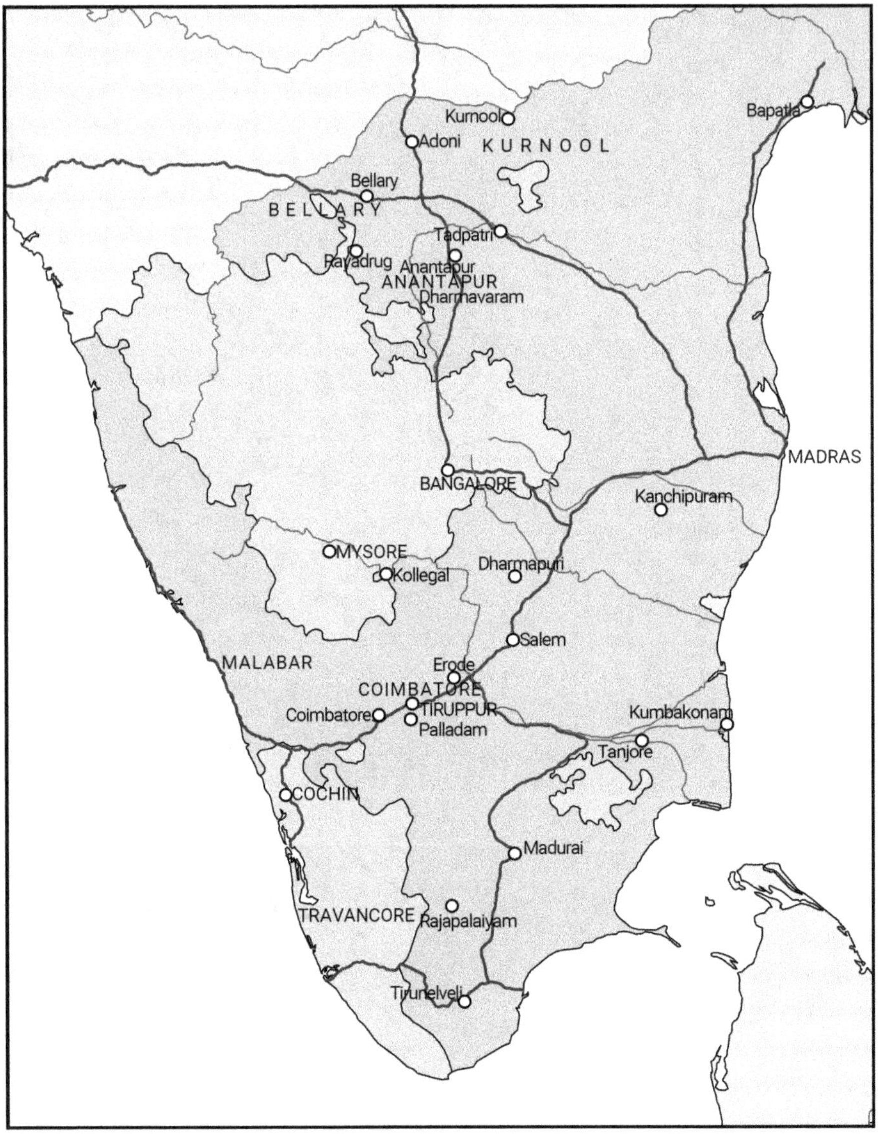

Map 3.2 Weaving towns in Madras Presidency around 1940

Source: Author

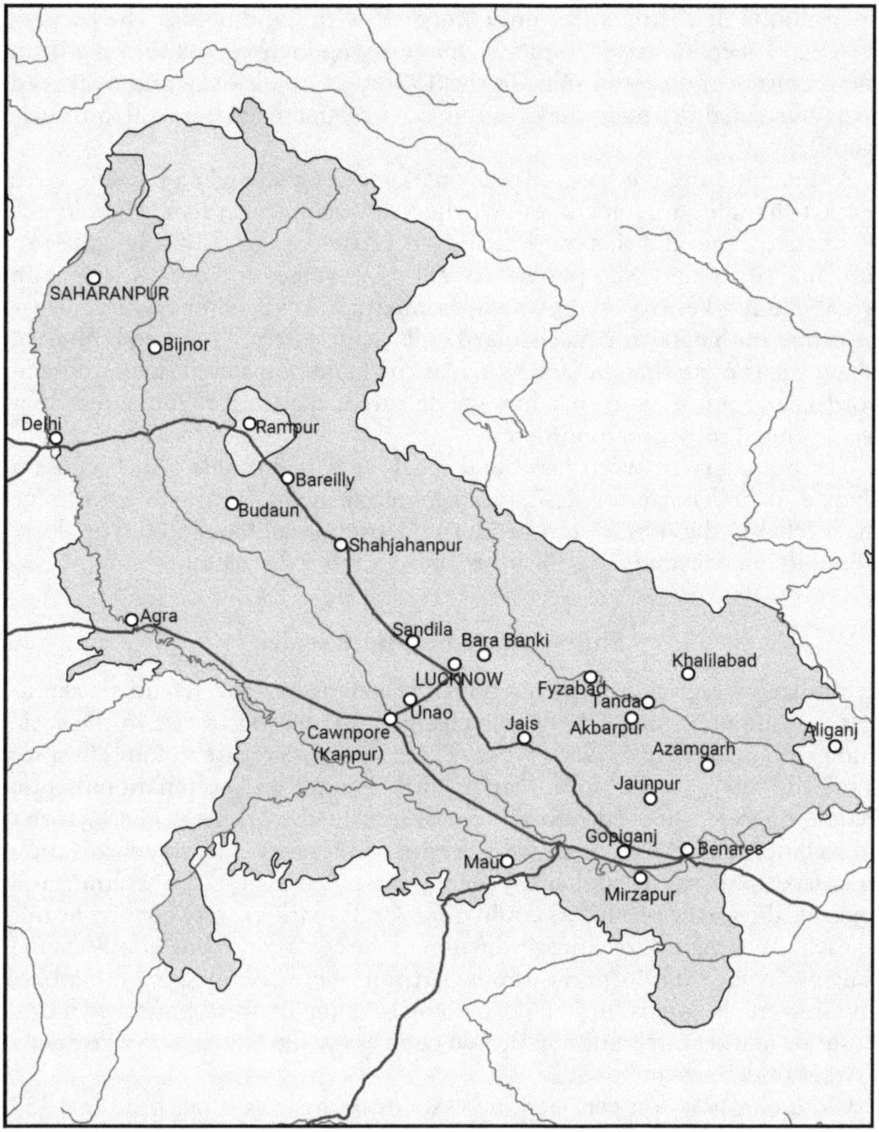

Map 3.3 Weaving towns in the United Provinces around 1940

Source: Author

mills that only had looms were less burdened. These mills were mainly based in Ahmedabad with looms between 200 and 400 in number though many units in Surat and Baroda worked with fewer looms. They wove finer counts of cotton yarn and competed with handlooms. The owners were yarn merchants of Bombay. One weaving factory was set up within the premises of a cotton mill. In the 1920s, as inefficiency and overhead costs burdened the big mills of Bombay, these factories gained from their trouble.[10]

As the mills and mechanized weaving factories encroached into the saree market, handlooms sometimes switched to non-cotton yarns. Handlooms of western India did this more readily because they usually sold sarees to the same consumers who purchased mill-made sarees and because the main wholesale market for rayon was in Bombay. A 1948 Bombay survey suggests that both hand and mechanized mills made sarees.[11] Further, both used rayon yarns more than before. Whereas the handlooms used rayon more in borders of cotton cloth, machine-made sarees made all-rayon sarees that were printed rather than bordered.

The boundary between hand and machine was unstable also because a change in preference for design and material might eventually encourage the mechanized looms to start producing a traditional handloom type cloth. The shifts in consumption, therefore, need a fuller discussion.

Shifts in consumption: scale

In the larger region, and throughout the nineteenth and twentieth centuries, consumption of clothing was changing. There was a rise in the scale and greater diversity of cloth types. There was an increase in long-distance trade and integration of local markets into regional and even national ones. People migrated, moved into the cities, into new work sites like factories and plantations where there were greater uniformity and standardization in everyday attire. Technological change expanded the range of colours and textures the textile producers could offer. Craft markets were coming nearer to each other thanks to a huge reduction in the costs of moving goods via the railways being built from the 1860s. Artisans were becoming more mobile, and so were the goods they made. Designs and quality were compared more. In short, market integration increased choices for the buyers and activated a market in designs and quality.

Cloth consumption per head increased from five yards per head in 1820 to 15 yards in 1940 (Chapter 2). The range of goods used in a middle-class Indian household expanded. Clothing purchases diversified similarly. Consumers bought more coloured cloth than before. Consumers of fine cotton cloth bought more rayon cloth or cloth that looked like silk and yet was cheaper than silk. Descriptions of the market for handloom cloth around the turn of the century suggest an increased preference for better quality and more variety in designs. Handloom cloth traded more widely, enabling more comparison between regional design styles.

The joint process of technological change and market integration affected men's and women's clothing quite differently. In men's wear, there was a shift in costume style as well as more standardization. In women's wear, both changes were slow at the most, whereas the usage of a wider variety of coloured yarn and cheaper yarn induced more experiments with designs.

Shifts in consumption: standardization in men's clothing and differentiation in women's clothing

No matter where the division between draped and stitched apparels came from or why it existed, in the colonial period, there was a convergence between the two types of clothing in the same household. It happened in this way – men took more readily to stitched garments. Women's preferences, however, changed more slowly. This was so not because women were more conservative and men more colour-blind, but mainly because women worked in public places and paid work much less than men. Those women who did may have switched to dyed sarees more readily.

'Among men throughout India,' a survey done in 1942 concluded, 'the use of turbans has greatly diminished, shirts and kurtas have come into common use and . . . the demand for chadars and angavastrams has fallen. Among women, generally, the use of blouses has become common throughout India. In the north, the saree has largely replaced the traditional Hindu (lehnga or ghaghra, and kurta) and Musalman (salwar, kurta or dupatta) forms of dress.'[12] Each of these large examples of change involved an alteration of the design idea and sometimes the design technique. There was, in the process, a drive to simplify designs. Head-dress, perhaps, illustrates the move from complexity to simplicity the best. 'The partial substitution of rumals and caps for head-dress on the part of Hindus strike a blow at [the turban weaving, patterning and dyeing industries].'[13] The wrapped men's garment called dhoti (in 1942) contained an ever-smaller proportion of the heavy-bordered varieties like the ones still being made in small quantities in large weaving hubs like Salem, Kanchipuram, Serampur or Srirampur, and Umrer.

The intellectuals and officers who prepared the monographs around 1900 (see 'monographs' in Glossary) attributed the change in men's clothing habits to changes in livelihood. Edgar Thurston said that the 'jungle tribesman' working in the planters' estates does not seem happy with a country-made loincloth anymore, but must appear, on high days and holidays, in a turban and woven coat of English cut. The mildly racist language notwithstanding, the statement points to a wider tendency. Migration and work sites containing thousands of workers made the worker (and employers) in the modern enterprises more sensitive to fashion and standardization and more willing to express the new identity as a city-dweller through the choice of clothing. Western-influenced tailored attire answered that need better than draped garments worn at home. Factories and the plantations did insist on dress codes, and the workers in these enterprises were mainly men. Therefore, wage-employment, the rise of new work sites, and male dress preference were interconnected. All changed together.

In women's clothing, the homogenizing tendency was weaker because women worked for wages less and migrated in fewer numbers. The most important draped garment was the saree. At the top-end of the class of bordered sarees, the handloom also used other methods to add value to the cloth. Where value was added by craftsmanship, the value would be enhanced if the material was special, too, such as silk or muslin. Therefore, for some of the finest works made by the loom, handlooms preferred to use silk (and later rayon or mixed cotton and silk) cloth. Draped garments like sarees used up more cloth than stitched for each corresponding unit. The quality of the cloth mattered more for a saree than for a men's shirt. In short, sarees were more likely to use silk or synthetic threads for that reason too. In some types of cotton weaving, the method used to size yarn – as an adjunct to the hand-weaving industry (see Chapters 4 and 5) – also added to the durability and strength of the fabric.

In southern and western India, the weaver's saree advantage was stronger. Handloom designs here were more often loom-woven, whereas in the north, the United Provinces, Rajasthan, Punjab, and Gujarat, Persian influence had established prints and embroidery as the main decorative traditions. North Indian women wore more stitched clothing. Non-wearing items like blankets, carpets, and hangings were more common articles in the north. By contrast, product structure in the major southern towns rarely went beyond the bordered saree, dhoti, and turban. The southern products, in other words, entered a less segmented but bigger market.

How do we illustrate and prove what was happening to the saree border since the nineteenth century?

The saree border and bordered sarees

The saree border changed in the twentieth century. The story of how it changed and how that change related to marketing, technology, and innovation is quite a central one for this chapter and perhaps the hardest one to write. It is difficult to write that story because the consumers, women, left little written record to show how they made choices. Moreover, neither the tools of analysis nor the sample is easy to determine. I will nevertheless suggest a story in this section. It forms a set of informed hypotheses that future work using better tools may well qualify.

My strategy is to compare John Forbes Watson's book, the two volumes on women's garments, and contrast what we see there (c. 1860) with what

I know (and will discuss later) on the pattern of saree consumption in the present days.[14] Three sets of hypotheses are developed on that basis relating to marketing (increasing branding of borders), technology (increasing use of mineral dyes, the frame loom, and the drop-box that together broadened the range of border designs and simplified the process of weaving), and innovation (a new expressionist sensibility led to more experimentation with borders).

First, let me discuss the branding of borders. Browsing Forbes Watson's collected pieces, we should be struck by the fact that they are classified by the source town or region but rarely by the design type associated with that town. The two sample books contain about 20–22 pieces that are likely to be sarees, about 3–4 of silk and mixed silk and cotton. These sarees, if they are sarees, came from Kumbakonam, Kanchipuram, Benares, and Central India. None except for the Kumbakonam one has a distinctive border. A modern buyer of sarees when looking at these books will be bewildered by the randomness of the design and the absence of any apparent association between place of origin and design style.

The obscurity of the saree border as a brand continues into the monograph on silk that Edgar Thurston published in 1899. Two years before, E.B. Havell had toured the major production centres in southern India. Both acknowledge that bordered clothes were widely woven, but between them mention only one place, Dharmabharam, where the border was distinctively identifiable with the place. Things were a little different in the 1920s. A 1929 report on textile markets wrote that in women's wear 'borders and headings are of great importance and exert a much greater influence on price.'[15] In the present times, no high-quality saree will sell in a city market that does not have a geographical brand attached to it. Each saree at the top end of the market for quality is identified with a unique place name (Kanchipuram, Dharmavaram, Paithan, Pochampally, Patan, or Baluchar) and a unique design style (Patola of Patan, Baluchari of Baluchar). The provenance of these sarees is not necessarily fixed anymore. They are woven in many places, though usually still rooted in the original regions. I am, of course, talking here about traditional sarees and not the growing market for designer sarees identified with an individual or collective.

Where am I going with this? I am suggesting that the so-called traditional saree defined by a border style is a modern twentieth-century invention. The major saree border names by which buyers recognize and differentiate high-quality sarees today emerged as trade names through a process of market integration and market creation. Sarees traded over long distances. Railways reduced trade costs and made markets more comparable. Weavers and merchants became more mobile, moved into the cities, and invested in retail sale. This is a twentieth-century process that culminated in the high-street saree shops in metropolitan cities of the late-twentieth century that offered the buyer a range of design types identified by a brand name that was also the name of a town. The basic concept or skill that went into that border design may have taken shape in the past. But they became part of a national market in the twentieth century.

The testimony of Nalli Kuppuswami Chetti, grandson of the founder of possibly the biggest silk saree trading firm Nalli, hints at the kind of innovation and reflection that went into the invention of a branded border in a silk saree. The origin of the bordered silk saree in Kanchipuram was a relatively recent one. In the late nineteenth century, Kanchipuram weavers switched to making silk sarees in competition with Benares sarees. Banares' silk sarees then, as now, made heavy use of gold thread on a silk body. It was not distinguished for the use of colour combinations. Kanchipuram weavers, rather a few pioneer designers, simplified the saree to use more coloured yarn, introduced a starker contrast between the body and the border, and possibly reduced the usage of gold thread in comparison with Benares.[16]

Second, the technology associated with design changed, which simplified the process of weaving designs and at the same time made it possible to add a lot more variety. Again, the modern viewer of Forbes Watson's books will be struck by the limited range of colours in use in the coloured sarees. The basic shades are few – madder red, indigo blue, or turmeric yellow – and to add variety to it, weavers tended to add gold thread and woven designs on the body of the saree often. If we add the dyeing labour and the weaving labour of such a saree together, the labour that would go into the making of one such saree would be staggeringly large. There would not be a mass market for such a product, and there was not. From the 1870s, mineral dyes expanded the range of combinations possible, and, in turn, enabled a simpler plainer body for the saree. Frame looms, like the 'naksha' or figure loom of Murshidabad (Figure 5.2) made the process of weaving the border much simpler, directly and by enabling the use of attachments. These changes made the saree a more portable and affordable product.

Thirdly, the design sensibility changed, that of the buyers and of the makers of sarees. Of course, buyers would love variety and colour, and the weavers could deliver that. The top-end sarees now use less gold thread on the body of the cloth than before but a wider range of coloured threads. With more variety possible, the border could be more identifiable as distinctive than before. Contemporaries observed that the demand for heavy borders with metal threads had declined, and lighter borders and a greater variety of colours such as could be provided by dyed yarn were preferred.[17]

Along with these expected forms of innovation, there was something else too. Offbeat weavers and merchants turned into designers. The nineteenth-century example that we know something about was the weaver Dubraj and the Baluchari saree type that he is said to have pioneered (see Chapter 1 and Figures 3.1 and 3.2). The old designs followed traditional motifs, whereas the new ones drew pictures on the loom. The fact that urban buyers loved these experiments suggests that others must have tried similar experiments.

Figure 3.1 Baluchar sari border, traditional, c. 1900

Source: N.G. Mukerji, *A Monograph on the Silk Fabrics of Bengal*, Calcutta: Government Press, 1903.

What they were and how successful they were remains to be studied in a systematic way.

While these changes carried on, merchants and provincial officials worried over a certain relaxation of norms. The use of coloured yarn exposed handlooms to competition from prints. Bad work accompanied, as with dyed and printed cloth, relaxation of preferences. Various forms of adulteration were added to 'lack of uniformity in texture, inexactness regarding dimension, lack of finish.'[18]

One special source of anxiety was the quality of dyeing.

Figure 3.2 Baluchar sari border, experimental, c. 1900

Source: N.G. Mukerji, *A Monograph on the Silk Fabrics of Bengal*, Calcutta: Government Press, 1903.

Dyeing and printing or how colour-use affected handloom weavers

Designs woven on the loom were not the only kind of textile designs, nor the main kind. But the other main technologies had a less systematic link with handloom weaving. This link was becoming weaker in the twentieth century. Men's clothing preference had something to do with this.

Men were not condemned to live a life without colour. If draped clothes had a regular shape to allow the border to dominate, the tailored cloth did not have such geometric regularity, and designs here could display a freer, less rigid character, often randomly spread out all over the surface in most tailored clothes. Some geometric designs were woven on the loom using a dobby. But the dobby was rarely used in the early twentieth century. Designs for tailored garments were not usually woven on the loom. Designs were instead printed, embroidered, or just replaced by bright dyes.

In the eighteenth century, printing in India was 'technically far in advance of anything produced in Europe.'[19] The secret was in mordanting or making colours stick, the mordant media being available in abundance throughout India. Europe was yet to discover fast dyes and depended, in decoration, mainly on embroidery. The initial advantage had matured into several distinct methods: block-printing, painting, and resist-dyeing of which one variant was tie-dyeing.[20] The basic colours were few.[21] The choice was constrained by the raw materials available. Cultivation of the plant, preparation of the dye, mordanting, and the actual dyeing were labour-intensive and knowledge-intensive processes so that inherited local skills and knowledge mattered a lot to successful dyeing and printing. The production of a mixed shade out of three basic colours, for example, involved three separate processes, successive immersion, and boiling off, instead of just one. With all of these problems, the organic dyes retained a distinctness. Admirers marveled at the 'freshness' of the colours of Masulipatnam 'chintz,' their being 'brighter after washing than before,' harmony in 'the most prismatic colours' achieved in Kota and Alwar muslins. One feature often cited was the absence of 'pure' shades, uniformly replaced by compound tints and a subdued appearance which derived from the darker tints of the mordants.[22]

A former connection between local dyeing (and dyeing substances) and a local textile tradition became significantly weaker due to two technological shocks: wider availability of machine-made fabrics from the 1830s and the discovery of the coal-tar dyes and their wider diffusion from the 1870s. After the first of the two shocks, the block-printer could, in theory, choose to print a mill-made cloth. In practice, the choice was less common than one may think; the reason was that the printer was still constrained to use colouring substances and knowledge available locally, could not easily migrate closer to the towns containing big cloth markets, and therefore often retained ties with the local handloom weaving industry.

But when the second shock occurred, the two sides fell apart. Now, mills could print and dye on their premises. And printers could make their colours. So could the weavers in their yards. The facility increased the options of the printer over where to get their fabric from, and it increased the options of the weaver over how to get the dyeing and printing done. One side did not need the other as badly as they did before.

These processes affected the quality of the application of colour on cloth or yarn. The change led to the near-extinction of indigenous dyeing systems. Indirectly, the decline of local dyeing brought down some printing hubs as well. The actual extent of displacement in printing remains uncertain. The industry probably relocated itself in fewer towns.[23] In Burhanpur and Ellichpur of central India, a large and ancient handloom weaving, dependent on a printing tradition, declined.[24] Other instances of decay, Masulipatnam chintz or Punjab prints, were more complex, usually involving a decay in the quality of work. The painted cloth of the Andhra coast, once a staple export to Europe, suffered due to unstable demand. In Mysore, decline of hand printing had more to do with poverty of the court elite.

By the first decade of the twentieth century, cotton yarn was dyed mainly by the weavers themselves, although printers carried on their old profession in many places. Local dyeing absorbed foreign material readily wherever handloom cloth was coloured. Availability of a vast range of basic shades and the possibility of making mixed shades by adding colours instead of adding processes were advantages so great that they made the professional dyer and the knowledge of local substances that the dyer embodied redundant.[25]

That the assimilation was far from perfect comes out vividly from contemporary accounts. There was an outburst of demand for brighter and newer shades.[26] The 'passion for bright, raw and fleeting colours of the imported aniline dyes' expanded the market for coloured cloth. The new dyes made wearing colours more affordable.[27] But it made fastness, a distinction of Indian handmade coloured cloth, a rarity.[28] Sometimes, dyes damaged the fabric. And often, the Indian product became too similar to the European copies of oriental clothing. Some of these were products where 'the European dyers know how to turn the tar products to good account.'[29] In some cases, as with woven or knotted carpets, it was the British carpet dealers who changed the old Indian system of using 'soft' combinations and introduced hard combinations. Under the rule of the design-book, colours were recommended at the same time as patterns. The dealers' notion of colours had, however, less relation to the Indian dyer's repertoire than it had with the German dye-makers' catalogue. Carpets of Mirzapur and Warangal, silks of Tanjore and Hyderabad, prints of Punjab and Gujarat, dyed cotton of Benares, Madras handkerchiefs, were but a few examples in which decline in weaving owed to the 'miserable aniline dyes.'[30]

In 1918, a dyeing adviser to the Madras government explained why this difference emerged. The Indian weaver 'has learnt how to use the imported materials, but in a majority of cases it is only through the medium of a "recipe" and not with any understanding of the nature of the materials or of the process.' The recipes were then 'improved upon' to obtain 'secret' processes. Unsuccessful experiments, in turn, encouraged the search for new secrets even more jealously guarded.[31]

What was going on here? While making the job of dyeing far simpler, less labour-intensive, and much cheaper, the chemical dyes required a knowledge system that took time to learn. The usage of new dyes, therefore, was not efficient and led to a lot of complaints about fading and running of colours. Complaints were rife also about the aesthetic quality of these colours. 'Their principal defect is that the resulting colours are often harsh and glaring and soon fade into hideousness.' These hazards were, however, due to inadequate treatment of the cloth with soaps and salts before dyeing. In 1896, in the bazaars in the textile towns of Bombay Presidency, two sets of dyes were usually available, the prices varying in the ratio of 1:8, depending on whether kutcha (fleeting but bright) or pucca (fast, reliable) colours were wanted.[32] The huge price gap shows the extent of the problem.

The vegetable dyes were not perfect, of course, and most of them (with exceptions like lac and indigo) were quite fleeting unless mordants were carefully applied. Technically, the new dyes represented an altogether superior material in terms of creative possibilities and firmness. But they were easy to use and therefore easy to use badly. 'So handy is the insidious aniline dye, that one needs not long experience to handle it; one may oneself colour the silk, and save the wage of the hereditary dyer.'[33] The new dyes, furthermore, induced changes in colour combinations and therefore designs.

If in dyeing the trade in colouring agents increased, something rather similar happened in printing too. In block printing, wooden blocks were once the focus of innovation. Wooden blocks for textile printing, mica-etchings for brocade designs, even drawings on paper in carpets were known to exist from the early days of European trade in these goods. Some of them were old when rediscovered by the nineteenth-century observers. One example of such a re-discovery was a large repository of Arcot wood blocks found in weavers' homes in about 1890, which were believed to have come from Persia centuries ago. Some of these were reproduced in an 1899 book.[34] But these were simply tools of production, not traded goods as far as one can see.

A pattern-book was a different matter. It embodied the knowledge of both the producer and the merchant's perceptions of what the producer should do. That complicated the delivery of designs on clothing.

Commercialization of designs and anxiety over commercialization

Printed books containing patterns and designs became common from the nineteenth century. It turned variety into a tool for commerce. East India Company employees used to keep books containing drawings of textiles sent from Bengal, though few of these survived. These books informed the British manufacturer what the Indian artisan could do. Indian textiles, and especially textile design, became a constitutive element in an emerging

British design sensibility and design production in the nineteenth century. Exhibitions, schools, pamphlets, pattern-books, and collections appeared in an attempt to adapt Indian design ideas to British consumer tastes and the capability of the British printing industry or that of the design-weaving looms of recent vintage.[35] An annotated sample book called, *The Textile Manufactures and the Costumes of the People of India*, prepared by John Forbes Watson, was the most famous and systematic compilation of its kind (see 'Selected biographies').[36]

In the original home of such designs, the pattern-book was used to show the Indian artisan what he should do. In the complex textiles such as Benares' kinkhab, the ancient mica etchings became relics.[37] What took their place? One weaver produced a book containing English wallpaper designs that he had discovered while window-shopping in London, where he had gone to participate in an exhibition. A comparable example would be the artisan furniture maker collecting IKEA catalogues for inspiration, as many Indian carpenters now do in fact.

From the late-nineteenth century, observers of the Indian crafts expressed the worry that modernization of tastes, merchant agency, and reckless adaptation made the Indian artisan more careless in the application of design skills. Who were these scholars and what were they trying to say?

A key example was George Birdwood (1832–1917), an officer of the India Office, author of the classic *Industrial Arts of India* (1880), and a major figure in the organization of international exhibitions featuring Indian and colonial products between 1857 and 1901. Another example was Ernest Havell (1861–1934), principal of first Madras and then Calcutta Schools of Art and author of books on Indian architecture, art teaching, and the crafts. His belief that art teaching in India must look for ideas in Indian cultural roots both inspired and troubled Indian students in Calcutta. Percy Brown was curator of Lahore Museum and author of a two-volume book on Indian architecture, which is still widely consulted. The Indian colleagues of this group of senior officers produced some of the most detailed field investigation reports. Nitya Gopal Mukerji's 1903 monograph on the silk industry in Bengal remains unrivalled after a century in the level of technical detail on the industry. Trailokyanath Mukharji, a Bengali litterateur known for his fantastic and satirical writings, wrote a major book on the artisan industries (see 'Selected biographies'). The Industrial Conferences of the turn of the century drew together a wide section of the intellectual community, including some of the contributors in this literature. At least some of these writers carried on their project in their non-official output as well. Along that margin, this scholarship seamlessly merged with a vernacular 'nationalist' discourse on the crafts.[38]

These writers popularized the idea that the artisans knew what the best work was but did not deliver it thanks to the agency of traders and buyers. What was the point in designing a complex good when the middle-class buyers were happy to buy a cheaper but simpler version? These observers fretted at what they thought was the progressive loss of a rich tradition, a de-skilling that threatened artisanal livelihoods more than did machine-made alternatives.

To some extent, this scholarship reflected a mood of the times that westernization had spoilt an Indianness, which the real nationalists now must recover. A generation later, M.K. Gandhi repackaged the same sentiment to serve a political purpose (Chapter 8). In England, the distinction between the authentic and the imitation in designs corresponded to social distinctions, that between peoples who had refined tastes and those who had newly acquired tastes.[39] It was a sentiment no doubt but not entirely a sentiment. Their accounts discussed many stories of experiments that went wrong. We need to understand the risks that experiments entailed.

The backdrop to the weavers' experiments and the activists' anxieties was a slowly emerging trans-local and national market for quality in handloom cloth. Despite the many pitfalls, the response from the weavers took the industry in a positive direction.

Patterns of response

As we have seen, handlooms steadily withdrew from weaving sheets of medium-count cloth that went into tailored garments, mostly used by men. This was no doubt the general tendency, but locally, weavers often experimented. More such experiments involved noncotton fibres.

Early instances of handlooms adapting to the popularity of stitched clothes are available from the silk towns. Benares weavers introduced 'Kashi silk,' cheap plain sheets suitable for stitched garments. Surat weavers also diversified into long sheets or piece goods. On a larger scale, noncotton piece goods were being made somewhat later in Ahmedabad, Bombay, and Punjab. The early history of handloom factories and powerlooms, especially in western India and in the Malabar, is associated with the demand for simpler and cheaper sheets rather than the demand for complex and expensive sarees. Christian missions promoted handloom factories of Malabar and pioneered the production of the cotton sheet in handlooms. In some towns of Tamil Nadu and southern Andhra, shifts toward stitched garments was accompanied by putting out on wages. The master weavers had 'taken care to maintain quality and are able to sell in competition with mills.' Ernest Havell described an Amritsar factory making cotton sheets, and Alfred Chatterton observed the connection between the factory and such undifferentiated goods as a checked cloth for men's shirts in Malabar.[40]

The artisan supplied a market for women's apparel that demanded traditional goods and yet was becoming fashion driven. It wanted bordered sarees but wanted variety in the borders. In designs, especially that of sarees, the consumer increasingly compared between numerous local decorative styles and a new type of decorative capability that could, simultaneously, simplify old designs, standardize them into fewer ones, and create new designs. The borders of high-quality sarees were one field on which such innovations concentrated. Geographically, this new capability tended to concentrate in the craft towns that were well connected and already were hubs of weaving, chiefly Benares, Surat, and Kanchipuram. That there was indeed such a choice in the handloom weaving industry and that preferences shifted from the former to the latter was noted by the Fact-Finding Committee.[41] Surat, for example, was not specialized in any distinct type of cloth. The weavers here used silk as a flexible raw material and shifted between garment types often. 'If there is a demand for a particular cloth, they convert themselves at once.' Kanchipuram acquired a similar ability to supply a wide variety of traditional designs in silk sarees (see the discussion on silk next).

Comparisons and cultural exchanges not only made the buyers aware of the existing differences but also made the producers aware of potential differences. Integrated trade at first caused the disappearance of many location names for silk saree borders in southern India. A few remained. But these few later began to innovate and branch out on the foundation of a core decorative style with which the town was identified. As these towns grew in scale and reputation (see also Chapter 6), trade information began to gravitate towards them. Thus, the most famous and the most capable of the silk towns were often the leaders in what some contemporary writers called 'decadence of taste.'

Artisans used the pattern-book creatively. The pattern-book expanded the artisans' horizon of what was possible. Imports encouraged import-substitution. '[I]n Southern India, while the shape of the saree, jacket and petticoat have remained unaltered, a radical change has taken place, in recent years in both design and colour owing to the wide-spread introduction of imported printed fabrics.'[42] Universally, the saree border absorbed design ideas from prints and pattern-books.

There was a reason why successful experiments tended to cluster in a few towns that acquired a brand name. Craftsmanship was a personalized resource. Innovations in designs and products were technically intellectual property that was not protected by property rights in these times. Therefore, a great deal of innovation occurred in an atmosphere of secrecy and stayed confined within communities living in a small area. If innovation were to happen at all, it would happen in the presence of a quasi-guild, and urban community, or led by somebody in authority. Only a few towns could create such conditions. The case of Madurai is described next, and more fully in Chapter 6.

Occasionally, we do hear of individuals breaking convention. Perhaps the most discussed example was a saree from Bengal that later became known as baluchari, after Baluchar, located on the river Bhagirathi in central Bengal ('baluchar' means sand-bank). The style of work was similar to the more well-known jamdani; that is, it involved raised floral patterns woven on a fine cotton cloth. There were also differences. Baluchari was made of silk. And the figures in baluchari were distinct. The borders and sides depicted, along with minute floral motifs, the performance of everyday tasks: women grooming themselves, men smoking hukka or riding horses, or a railway carriage complete with engine and European passengers. This form of incorporation of a modern concept on a traditional good was apparently the work of a talented weaver who had remained largely outside the community.[43]

More interregional competition led to attempts at branding products. The tendency was especially strong in handloom saree borders. Most of the established brands in the handloom saree market in the present times emerged around 1900. In the 1930s, Madras and United Provinces handlooms were making inroads into the Bengal market, and products of the factories of Bombay and Tamil Nadu towns threatened Hyderabad weavers. In Hyderabad, 'foreign' sarees, mainly the famous Ilkal, drove out locally made goods, causing alarm. The state representative on the Indian Tariff Board enquiry on silk attributed it to 'the standard quality and uniform size' of the former, whereas 'our workmen always try to deteriorate the quality by all questionable means.' This difference, it was believed, went with flexibility and innovativeness in Bombay and with advances in dyeing. The state's reaction confined to rhetoric, the local weavers must be 'awakened from their torpor . . . made to realize the seriousness, trained and taught.' Inside the industry, a more basic adjustment seems to have been underway. In at least three districts of Hyderabad, factories and contract workers made Ilkal sarees under the supervision of merchants from Ilkal.[44]

As the need for specialist handling of dyes was emphasized, master dyers diversified into weaving where the latter existed as a subsidiary to a dominant dyeing tradition. Thus, we find in Hyderabad 9 percent of the looms located in factories that the Rangrez and Nilgur people, dyers by caste, owned. Master weavers also invested in dyehouses, singled out as 'the direction in which developments can best be looked for'[45] The best example of weavers investing in dyehouses was Madurai where the Sourashtras owned much of the industry, concentrated in large 'colour factories.' Madurai was noted for the relative facility with which information on processes and dyestuffs was exchanged. The switch to mineral dyes was more successful in Madurai, famous for its accumulated skills in handling the chay-root red dye. The discoverer of the best reproduction of chay-root shade with alizarine was a Sourashtra trained in Japan. The 'spurious' red cloth of Madurai drove out competitors such as were being made in Kumbakonam, resulting in a decline and de-concentration of looms there.[46] In another, earlier, example of silks in United Provinces, the best-advertised methods of fast dyeing with aniline came from factories and dye houses of Agra.[47]

This importance of quality and innovation helps us understand why the craft writers around 1900 so persistently harped on the theme of instruction, particularly instruction in designs.[48] As designs themselves became saleable goods, designing showed signs of becoming a distinct profession. The art schools of the port cities realized this and adapted to the trend to some extent. Indeed, in many cases, the merchants and masters had begun employing professional artists and designers in the highly skilled crafts. Such a change characterized Madurai dyeing and that in the printing industry (such as Farrukhabad block-printing). But the supply of professional well-trained designers was far below the needs of the industry.

State policy in most provinces declared standardization as a useful goal. More direct action like reserving designs for handlooms was also contemplated, but this was unrealistic when the designs themselves were changing rapidly.[49] The Fact-finding Committee (1942) cited several cases in which cooperatives managed standardization. Banks and cooperatives, some suggested, should introduce patents and trademarks. Cooperatives should employ chemists and market researchers, they said. Caste guilds stepped in. A Koshti association in Nagpur 'affixed a stamp on the fabrics' guaranteeing fastness of dyes, a guarantee widely respected. Selectively, resources of the mills were used in finishing handloom cloth.

The expanding scale of consumption and integration of distant markets demanded standardization. In Tamil Nadu 'nowhere does the wholesale merchant place huge orders with small weavers, and the tiny weaving establishments cannot meet his demand. Unless the workers are organized in rural factories, their products cannot be standardized or marketed.' And where similar changes were already happening, 'sole agency, commission sale, sale on a consignment basis, mail-order house and canvassing agency are some methods of recent developments.'[50]

Richer weavers invested in handloom factories, sometimes to accommodate tools that needed more space than was available at home. In Dhaka and Santipur, richer weavers sometimes installed Jacquards and hired professional designers, but outside these towns, the weaving industry was not in good shape, thanks to the absence of any institution 'which could enable them to produce new types of fabrics to suit changing tastes.'[51] Rural weavers could not be easily trained, nor the average consumer made to appreciate new styles, as 'the great majority of the products are woven to suit the taste of the rural [M]uslims only.' Designs were 'clumsy and too showy' and changed little.[52]

In western India, especially Surat, Bhiwandi, and Ahmedabad, factories with a few looms operated with power, or powerlooms, as they were known, which were set up to weave art silk and spun silk sarees.[53] In Bombay-Deccan, powerlooms used mercerized and twofold to avoid processing.[54] Early powerlooms in western India were major users of silk and rayon. Being centres of import trade helped towns such as Bombay and Surat access silk and rayon cheaply. Between 1934 and 1939, the years of publication of successive Tariff Board reports on silk, there was a massive expansion in the number of silk mills, working both silk and rayon and a 'marked increase' in the number of handloom weavers who used rayon. A whole range of entrepreneurs, including these weavers and handloom merchants, seized the new opportunity to set up rayon factories in Bombay and Punjab.

Of the three main design technologies, printing/dyeing, embroidering, and loom-weaving, only the first rendered itself to larger-scale economies and was performed in a department inside a mechanized mill. Handlooms used all three; whereas the weaver made the designs on the loom, printing or embroidering existed as separate industries performed by specialists. I have discussed printing. What happened to embroidering?

How embroidering changed, and how that affected the weaver

Embroidering was a highly labour-intensive activity and therefore expensive. Rich people bought embroidery, like those involved in wall-hangings, shawls, some women's wear, and ceremonial dresses such as the kinkhabs.

In the embroidery process (as in printing), the decorative side of the industry was separated from weaving. The weaver supplying cloth to an embroiderer made a raw material and, for that reason, was often dependent on the merchant who gave shape to the final product and combined the processes. In draped garments like the bordered saree, the weaver created the design, retained control over craftsmanship, and, to that extent, was an entrepreneur himself. In most craft towns, weaving remained dispersed, whereas wire drawing (for embroidery involving gold or silver thread) was concentrated in factories. Merchants selling the most expensive material, like gotawalas of Benares, controlled the factories and the industry. Weaving was thus subject to outsider control. By contrast, saree manufacture allowed the weaver to become a capitalist and an innovator more readily.

From the end of the nineteenth century, the manufacture of fine cotton or muslin cloth containing gold and silver embroidery, notably the chikan work of Lucknow, saw a transformation in its market, together with changes in the pattern of goods produced. Designs became simpler and the consumers more distant than before. Something like a mass market emerged in the finest classes of such work.

An 1880 monograph on the urban manufacturers of Lucknow commented on the rapid decline of many types of skilled crafts in the city since the mutiny (1857–8), mentioning especially silk textiles. While the decline owed to the impoverished state of the aristocracy, Lucknow also at the same time lost some of its business to rivals such as Kanpur. The same report then mentioned the embroidery industry as an exception and a locus of growth and dynamism. The source of this dynamism was 'the exceptionally great skill of the Lucknow workmen.' Such skills developed through patronage under the pre-British rule but which successfully adapted to 'a new outlet in external markets in Bengal and the south of India.'[55] This observer said that the industry was dependent on domestic labour and local tastes.

> When one wonders through the mohullas of the City where reduced Muhammadan families reside and where there are poor Hindu families who need to add to the scant subsistence afforded by a small shop or by service, one can see women and even small children busy with needle and muslin. Thus the labour at the manufacturer's command is cheap and abundant.[56]

Domestic labour continued to sustain the industry. 'As a domestic pursuit, chikan was always favourite employment of the women of the same castes. . . . Hence there was a natural soil in which the similar industry should take root' (Ibid.). Lucknow chikan was fast acquiring a wider urban market. Almost the same process was described in a contemporary report from Punjab phulkari work, another form of embroidery.[57] But as markets for these goods became more national than local, the designs became simpler. In 1887, a monograph on Punjab phulkari reported that a distinct preference for simpler embroidery designs was driven by the 'desire of women for a lighter head-covering.'[58]

The top end of the quality scale in sarees was the bordered silk saree. Examples from silk weaving, therefore, illustrate well many of the processes of change discussed previously.

The market for silk

The pattern of silk consumption was changing in the early twentieth century in a manner that encouraged mechanized weaving. The pattern of change was rather similar to that happening in embroidered, printed, and handloom sarees – the emergence of a mass market and standardized tastes in design.

Silk, as far as one can gather, had been mainly commercial, mainly urban, and frequently traded over long distances in the precolonial period. A form of patronage was available so far as silk weavers were often settled directly by politically powerful classes. But silk was not necessarily consumed inside palaces. It was not a luxury in a narrow sense; rather it was a durable good consumed by 'the higher classes,' broadly defined. This demand, arising from 'the rajahs, courtiers, and zamindars,' probably declined from the mid-nineteenth century. An external trade in Bengal, nurtured by the East India Company, was also on the wane from somewhat earlier.

But there was still a large ritual usage of pure silk garments. Towards the end of the nineteenth century, the ceremonial function of silk was probably more important than a display of wealth. Gods, heroes of the epics, brides, grooms, priests, and devotees were more likely to wear silk. Both the rich and the middle-class people possessed some silk products. An 1880s description of the Punjab market for pure silk is a catalogue of festival attire, beginning with the Sawani, when young girls wore jewellery that used a large quantity of silk thread, on to the first of Bhadon, when 'every Hindu wears a wristlet of silk,' to weddings when a silk dress was mandatory, whether purchased or borrowed, and ending with child-naming ceremonies, when again silk dresses and jewellery were necessarily worn. Among the Pathans and Sayyads, women wore silk for a year after their marriages.[59] In Bombay in 1900, 'the ordinary use of silk is not common among members of the Hindu community . . . not even among the well-to-do.'[60] The same report found that in many better-off towns of Bombay 'women of the working classes' possessed silk garments because the ceremonial demand was strong.

And yet, the 1900 remark that 'it is upon the orthodoxy of the Hindus that the weaver must depend' would look out of place. Some earlier instances of decline, such as that of the industry in Berhampur, was attributed to a 'decline in the Hindu religion.'[61] Silk-weaving towns such as Pune and Yeola, which thrived on ceremonial dresses like the yellow pitambar, did not grow. On the other hand, there was almost continuous growth in Benares, Surat, and Kanchipuram thanks to their greater involvement in silk sarees, or 'the everyday attire of the well-to-do.' This is a function silk always performed among Parsis and mashrus (mixed silk-cotton cloth) among Muslims. As it did, silk substitutes, such as rayon or mixed cotton-silk cloth, became more popular because these served well the function of fabrics as a status marker. Silk and related goods were increasingly demanded for display value by the urban middle-class women.

Consistent with this tendency, the demand for clothes for ordinary use which utilized silk, such as silk-bordered fine cotton sarees, or silk-weft cloth like himroo and mushroo, also expanded. For example, in Punjab (Multan), 'there is less pure silk fabrics manufactured than formerly, but the increased demand for mixtures of silk and cotton cloth . . . has given ample employment.'[62] Correspondingly, there had been growth in a mass consumer demand for finer fabrics. As Hailey noted, raw silk imports into Punjab had been growing for some time even as the weaving of pure silk in some classes of clothing, such as turbans, was clearly in decline. Such declines were no cause of regret. 'It is better that fifty people should be moderately comfortable than that one should be magnificent.'[63]

East Asian imports of rayon yarn and Japanese sarees strengthened such uses of silk and silk substitutes. The imported clothes created a new use for silk as elevated daily wear from the 1920s. Imports consisted of flowered silks, satins, damasks, gauze, paj, and crepe. Much of it was meant to be used in stitched garments such as shirts or blouses, but some could be used as a radically redefined saree. The main markets for these goods were Bombay and Punjab. They touched Bengal marginally but Madras not at all. The import of pure silk fabrics dwindled from the mid-1930s under stiff protectionist tariffs. But by then it had created a market for simple, non-ritual, experiment-minded silk garments, and that effect lasted. From the 1920s, art silk (rayon or viscose) entered the production of cheap silk-like sarees and captured a part of the traditional demand for silk or fine cotton sarees. These new clothes did not involve distinct or intricate border designs. They could, therefore, be taken over by high-speed weaving systems. Rayon sarees circulated mainly in western India.

In southern India, silk sarees circulated more widely than before due to changing preferences. To see how trade affected producing regions, consider one example. Many sources from the first quarter of the twentieth century remarked on the decline of high-quality weaving in the Madras Deccan, whereas the region was overrun with silk cloth from beyond the district boundaries. Silk cloth came from two sides, the Tamil country in the south, and Bombay-Deccan, chiefly Pune in the west. In Bellary district, 'formerly the cloths of Kampli, Bellary, and Adoni were extensively used.' But the local 'better classes' preferred the southern product once they began to come in more easily after the railways. 'For about a year,' reported Edgar Thurston, 'the weavers have been trying to weave cloths like those manufactured in the south,' with partial success.[64] Similar examples come from coastal Andhra, and from Kurnool district, where one of the few silk carpet locations in India, Ayyampet, declined in the second half of the nineteenth century.

From the mid-twentieth century, the silk saree-weaving industry concentrated in a cluster of towns mainly in Tamil Nadu, most successfully in Kanchipuram, Madurai, Tanjore, and Kumbakonam. On a smaller scale, Arni and Kollegal also attracted new business. In Madurai, some weavers formerly engaged in fine cotton shifted to silk. Many of the products made in these locations were pure silk sarees with borders of jari, the type known as 'Kornad,' a garment whose demand has proven remarkably stable in the long run. Within Madras-Deccan or southern Andhra, survival was restricted to the small artisanal-trading town Dharmavaram. There were also a few successful silk factories, in coastal and southern Andhra, started by cloth merchants shortly before the First World War. Ventures in Uppada, Peddapuram and in Rayadurg in Bellary are examples.

Wool was the one large exception to the story I have told so far because the main handloom products in wool were not apparels. Silk, cotton, and rayon were similar in nature because of their attachment to the weaving of saree or fabrics for dresses. So far, therefore, the account of the handloom market could focus on a coherent range of products. But what about wool? Wool adds a different dimension to the discussion. Here, competition from mechanized production did play a bigger role than in the other forms of weaving, but the products were distinct. Only a short account is necessary.

The market for wool[65]

Wool weaving by hand was long tied to sheep herding. The modern history of wool production is a story of increasing concentration of commercial sheep herding from peninsular India (Deccan Plateau) and the plains (Indo-Gangetic Basin) towards the arid western zone (Rajasthan). The shift had owed to two main factors, changing land use patterns in the plains and the peninsula, and the growth of a railway network. The textile uses of wool were concentrated too. The range of use narrowed to three main fields, carpets, blankets, and winter-wear, including woven and knitwear. Industrial agglomerations emerged in the wool-trading towns of northern India.

The five main uses of wool in India were: blankets, carpets, shawls, felts, and garments. In the early twentieth century, semi-mechanized factories and knitwear factories started making woollen garments, so far confined to the cottage industry of handlooms. The increasing production of good-quality woollen garments was an effect of new middle-class choices as well as a new raw material, imported worsteds. Felts were a disappearing industry during our period. Shawls were manufactured mainly in Kashmir and remained at a distance from other branches of the woollen textile industry. Carpets were not woven products but knotted.

Until 1900, a considerable quantity of cotton cloth, usually woven with handspun cotton, was used as winter wear. This use was steadily replaced by woollen garments. Better storage of woollens and the growth of a middle-class urban market for garments contributed to this trend. This trend in the market touched wool weaving on handlooms marginally. In 1920, there were 100,000 handlooms engaged in woollens in British India and the princely states. For a comparison, cotton and silk handlooms numbered approximately two million. By contrast with cotton or silk, handloom weaving in wool was a minor tradition. The weavers adopted a rough process that dispensed with much of finishing and dyeing.

Interestingly, as in cotton or silk, artisanal weaving of wool withstood competition from factories quite well. In fact, the two traditions converged in the beginning when the factories wove wool with hand-powered looms.[66] Initially, the main business of the mills was to supply mass-produced but still hand-woven blankets and garments for the army and to spin yarn for the carpet industry. In the ten years after the First World War, dramatic changes took place. The war forced a rapid expansion in weaving capacity in the mills. Considerable excess demand remained, met by the resources of the cottage handlooms. Many small shops manufacturing tweeds and rugs mushroomed in northern India in response. There was also diversification in product lines. The mills began to make finer cloth using worsted yarn, for which the wool had to be imported.

The urban handlooms, especially in Muzaffarnagar and Bijnor in the middle-Gangetic plains, and Panipat and Ludhiana in Punjab, received great encouragement during World War I, when the Munitions Board began to contract orders in these cities for blankets and smaller articles. Many cotton weavers in these cities shifted to wool, and the existing woollen manufacturers expanded and diversified. The war orders were many times larger than the scale of the business before 1914 and were estimated to have used up practically the entire supply of blanket wool in India around 1917–18.

At the same time, imported better-quality woollen garments altered tastes and introduced new standards. Consumers increasingly did not want coarse rural blankets. They preferred the finer products made in new weaving establishments in the cities using traded wool. Competition from urban weaving and depletion of pastures adversely affected the practice of weaving by sheepherders themselves. In this fashion, the more commercialized part of the woollen textile industry came to concentrate in a few wool-trading towns of northern India, especially Ludhiana.[67]

Conclusion

There probably never was an age when the Indian artisan catered to a rigidly traditional, and therefore unmoving, market. And yet, unquestionably, the nineteenth and twentieth centuries altered the basic parameters of demand for consumer goods far more drastically than in times past. Competition from machine-made goods was one of the new drivers of change, but one of several, and its effects can be understood only when we notice these other drivers.

Large shifts in occupation, import of industrial goods, import of new design ideas, colonialism and nationalism, the European presence in India, migration of buyers and producers and their exposure to other cultural and technological practices, changed the demand for traditional products in ways that many contemporary observers saw as revolutionary. The accent of the change fell on costume styles, material, the association between clothing and occasions, and the design content of the goods. The design market cheapened designs and extended the master artisans' stock-in-trade. The readiness with which new ideas could be seized upon was itself a sign of the big role played by intellectual property, and a free market in such property, at work in the skilled Indian crafts.

These changes in consumption and the responses that these elicited made the industry different from before because any innovation carried risk and needed more capital. It would be wrong to follow the Indianist followers of the arts-and-crafts movement to claim that weavers were crazily experimenting. The point is, the value of knowledge as capital had risen. Not everyone could deploy that capital effectively. Who could, then? And what did they do?

Merchants and master-artisans controlled the industry more than before. The role of the merchant increased for several reasons. Marketing goods in distant markets required capital. Some merchants invested in dye houses or printing factories to control the most valuable process of manufacturing. And some highly skilled weavers and social leaders were also capitalists, as we will see in Chapter 4.

Notes

1 Clear evidence on this effect is available only from United Provinces, *Report on the Industrial Survey of the United Provinces*, Allahabad: Government Press, 1924, Etawah District, 17, Fyzabad District, 25, Hardoi District, 39. Fine weaving, on the other hand, was adversely affected by it, Bengal, *Report on the Survey of Handloom Weaving Industry in Bengal* (J.M. Ghose), Calcutta: Board of Economic Enquiry, 1937, 58.

2 According to the ethnographic reports produced around 1900, the caste groups that performed general labour in the countryside – Dheds of Gujarat, Katias and Mahars of Bombay-Deccan and Central Provinces, Gandas of Orissa, and Malas of coastal Andhra – did a lot of weaving on the side.

3 'In tracts situated at a distance of the iron road the village 'general shop' has not yet come into existence; the wants which it meets are not felt; the villager either tans his own leather and weaves his own clothing, or he journeys from time to time to some neighbouring fair or market,' A. Blennerhassett, *A Monograph on the Cotton Fabrics of the Central Provinces*, Nagpur: Government Press, 1898, 5.

4 Berar in Central Provinces, see Central Provinces and Berar, *Report of the Industrial Survey of the Central Provinces and Berar*, Nagpur: Government Press, 1908–09; on western United Provinces see United Provinces, *Industrial Survey*, Etawah District, 38, on Punjab see Imperial Gazetteer of India (Provincial Series), *Punjab*, Calcutta: Government Press, 1908, vol. 1, 81, on Bombay, Gazetters, Bombay Presidency, *Ahmedabad*, Bombay: Government Press, 1884–6, 135.

5 The Dheds were absorbed in public works, as both cultivators and mill weavers refused to associate with them. Handloom factories, however, employed Dhed labourers. Handloom factories of the east coast employed Malas. Gazetteer, Bombay Presidency, *Ahmedabad*, 80; India, *The Berar Gazetteer*, Nagpur: Government Press, 1870, 237; and India, *Report of the Textile Enquiry Committee*, New Delhi: Ministry of Commerce, 1954, 1250.

6 Gazetteers, Bombay Presidency, *Ahmedabad*, 136; Gazetteers (Bengal District), *Nadia*, Calcutta: Government Press, 1910, 92; Imperial Gazetteer of India (provincial series), *Bengal*, Oxford: Clarendon Press, 1908, 81; Gazetteers (Bengal District), *Sambalpur*, Calcutta: Government Press, 1909; A.C. Badenoch, *Punjab Industries, 1911–1917*, Lahore: Government Press, 1917, 1; T.N. Mukharji, *Art-Manufactures of India*, Calcutta: Government Press, 1888, 322; India, *Indian Industrial Commission*, Minutes of Evidence, vol. 3 of 5, Calcutta: Government Press, 1918, evidence of Theagaraya Chetty, 56; Gazetteers, *Mysore Gazetteer*, vol. 3 (Economic), Banglaore: Government Press, 1929, 239–40. The Mysore volume describes the weaving of handspun yarn in detail that suggests that some of it still carried on.

7 Sonia Ashmore, *Muslin*, London: V&A Publishing, 2012.

8 See Tirthankar Roy, *Artisans and Industrialization: Indian Weaving in the Twentieth Century*, New Delhi: Oxford University Press, 1993, for more discussion on this division.

9 A. Yusuf Ali, *A Monograph on Silk Fabrics Produced in the North Western Provinces and Oudh*, Allahabad: Government Press, 1900.

10 Seven of these were interviewed by the 1927 Indian Tariff Board enquiry on cotton textiles. The possibility of competition with handlooms was discussed. As a lobby these mills maintained a distinct identity and opposed tariffs on yarn.
11 Bombay, *Report of the Sholapur Handloom Weavers Enquiry Committee*, Bombay: Political and Services Department, 1948.
12 India, *Fact-Finding Committee: Handlooms and Mills*, Calcutta: Government Press, 1942.
13 C.G.H. Fawcett, *Monograph on Dyes and Dyeing in the Bombay Presidency*, Bombay: Government Press, 1896, 6.
14 John Forbes Watson, *The Textile Manufacturers of India*, vols. 5 and 6 (Garment Pieces for Women), London: India Office, 1866 (see also 'Selected biographies' at the end of the book).
15 G.S. Hardy, *Report on the Import Tariff on Cotton Piecegoods and on External Competition in the Cotton Piecegoods Trade*, Calcutta: Government Press, 1929, 5, 47.
16 The interview of Nalli Kuppuswami Chetti (2014), Chairman, Nalli Silk Saris, Creating Emerging Markets: Oral History Collection, Harvard Business School, available at www.hbs.edu/businesshistory/Documents/emerging-markets-transcripts/ChettiTranscriptWithCoverFinal.pdf (accessed 1 July 2019).
17 India, *Fact-Finding Committee*, 165; R.E. Enthoven, *The Cotton Fabrics of the Bombay Presidency*, Bombay: Government Press, 1895, 2; Bengal, *Report on the Survey of Handloom*, 86. In silk Tariff Board noted a long-term decline in sizes and weights of typical fabrics.
18 H. Maxwell-Lefroy and E.C. Ansorge, *Report on an Enquiry into the Silk Industry in India*, Calcutta: Government Press, 1916–18, 170; India, *Fact-Finding Committee*, 118–19, 122–5, 128–9: Bengal, *Report on the Survey of Handloom*, 86.
19 John Irwin and Margaret Hall, *Indian Painted and Printed Fabrics*, Ahmedabad: Calico Museum, 1971, 152.
20 The old trade name for cloths on which the pattern was drawn by hand was kalamkari. Ikat stands for a range of resist-dyeing techniques applied to the yarn (see also Glossary).
21 Essentially the following: kusum, kusumba, or safflower (*Carthamus tinctorius*) for red and yellow, madder root (*Rubia tinctorum*) for red, indigo (*Indigofera tentoria*) for blue, black and green. Alum or myrabolan (Indian gall nuts) were used as mordanting substances. Minor dyes included cochineal, lac, chay-root, all three for red.
22 For two descriptions on mordanting quality, George Birdwood, *The Industrial Arts of India*, Part 2, London: Chapman and Hall, 1887, 295; and Edgar Thurston, *Monograph on the Cotton Fabric Industry of the Madras Presidency*, Madras: Government Press, 1897, 7.
23 Out of the several scores of names occurring in the 1880s surveys, four major concentrations still appear in the mid-1930s sources: Lucknow and Farrukhabad in eastern United Provinces, Sanganer in Rajasthan, Ahmedabad in Gujarat. Dyeing, however, was far more widespread. Isolated instances of migration of printers were also reported. Mukharji, *Art-Manufactures of India*, 353n.
24 In the 1880s, E.A. Hobson, *Cotton in Berar*, Nagpur: Government Press, 1887, found block-printing 'a remunerative trade' in several Berar towns including Ellichpur. Ten years later R.V. Garrett, *Monograph on Cotton Fabrics of Berar*, Nagpur: Government Press, 1897, reported that printing was practically unknown in Berar. See also W.S. Hadaway, *Cotton Painting and Printing in the Madras Presidency*, Madras: Government Press, 1917.

25 Weavers being their own dyers was found to be common in the south about the mid-twenties, Madras, *Report of the Survey of Cottage Industries in the Madras presidency* (D. Narayana Rao), Madras: Government Press, 1925, 125. An earlier source on the north speak of it as a tendency, a 'retrograde step,' A.C. Chatterjee, *Notes on the Industries of the United Provinces*, Allahabad: Government Press, 1908, 66. In Bombay at the turn of the twentieth century, mineral dyes had 'thrown open the industry to almost all who choose to take it up,' Fawcett, *Monograph on Dyes and Dyeing in the Bombay Presidency*, 5. P.V. Kelkar wrote in 1929 that twenty years back in Sholapur dyeing was done by specialist dyers whereas now weavers do it, Maharashtra State Archives, File No 29 SH/1, evidence for the Banking Enquiry Committee, Bombay, 1929.

26 Irwin and Hall, *Indian Painted and Printed Fabrics*, describe many examples of hybrid styles, results of English designers copying Indian prints and the Indians, in turn, copying these imitations. Confusion was widespread. See p. 160, plates 93C, 8, colour plates VII and VIII for comparable instances of imitative and authentic work. Technical and art schools were also party to the process. See for example the debate between A.C. Burns, Principal of the J. J. School of Arts, a 'progressive' on synthetic styles, and E.B. Havell and Ananda Coomaraswamy, champions of authenticity. See also E.B. Havell, *The Basis for Artistic and Industrial Revival in India*, Madras: The Theosophical Society, 1912; and Mukharji, *Art-Manufactures*, 370. Switch to mineral dyes also loosened regional specificities in colour usage and printing styles, threatening the existence of any style at all. Prior to the shift every major location was known for its handling of a certain type of dye, Masulipatnam palampores for madder red, Kathiawar prints for deep brown and yellow, Umrer for cochineal red, Burhanpur for yellow and sparse use of indigo, Madurai for chay-root deep red, etc. These patterns were broken by the standardized mineral dyes.

27 S.M. Hadi, *Monograph on Dyes and Dyeing in NWFP and Oudh*, Lucknow: Government Press, 1896, 3; A. Latifi, *The Industrial Punjab*, Lahore: Government Press, 1911, 93. A whole literature exists on the apparent effects of the shift to chemical dyes. For a typical account, see B.H. Baden-Powell ('On Some of the Difficulties of Art Manufactures,' *Journal of Indian Art*, 1(5), 1886, 37–9): 'That a country in which the older work, . . . everything in which combined colour played a part, is so excellent; in which richness and depth, warmth and life, are combined with sobriety, delicacy and subdued harmony of tone, should delight in greens which are complimentary to no known colour, in violets which give one a disagreeable sensation at the bottom of one's throat, and in bluish crimsons which nature herself can hardly manage . . . is truly wonderful,' p. 32. Edgar Thurston wrote: 'And I have before me, as I write, a glazed label depicting a group composed of a native lady with turmeric complexion, clad in a pink saree, seated on a maroon cushion, and engaged in conversation with a naked little blue boy, while a chubby, pink child looks on round the corner of a violet purdah,' *Monograph on the Cotton Fabric Industry*, 6.

28 Imperial Gazetteer of India, *Economic*, Oxford: Clarendon Press, 1908, 185; Latifi, *Industrial Punjab*, 93.

29 Baden-Powell, 'On Some of the Difficulties of Art Manufactures,' 37–9; Thurston, *Monograph on the Cotton Fabric Industry*, 7.

30 United Provinces, *Industrial Survey*, Mirzapur District, 1; Imperial Gazetteer of India (Provincial Series), *Madras*, Calcutta: Government Press, 1908, 143; Latifi, *Industrial Punjab*, 97; evidence of P. Theagaraya Chetty in India, *Indian Industrial Commission*, Minutes of Evidence, vol. 3 of 5, 56; Irwin and Hall, *Indian Painted and Printed Fabrics*, various places; Gazetteer, *United Provinces*,

Benares, Allahabad: Government Press, 1909, 60; and Indian Tariff Board, *Sericultural Industry*, Report and Minutes of Evidence, Calcutta: Government Press, 1935, Written Evidence, 311.

31 India, *Indian Industrial Commission*, vol. 3, 153–7; Baden-Powell, 'On Some of the Difficulties of Art Manufactures,' 32.

32 Fawcett, *Monograph on Dyes and Dyeing in the Bombay Presidency*, 10.

33 S.M. Edwardes, *A Monograph upon the Silk Fabrics of the Bombay Presidency*, Bombay: Government Press, 1900, 50.

34 Thurston, *Monograph on the Cotton Fabric Industry*, 1899.

35 Agnes M.M. Lyons, 'The Textile Fabrics of India and Huddersfield Cloth Industry,' *Textile History*, 27(2), 1996, 172–94.

36 Deborah Swallow, 'The India Museum and the British Indian Textile Trade in the Late Nineteenth Century,' *Textile History*, 30(1), 1999, 29–45.

37 Kinkhab is a brocade sari. Brocade uses multiple threads, typically mixing silks with gold thread (see also Glossary).

38 Abigail McGowan, *Crafting the Nation in Colonial India*, New York: Palgrave, 2009.

39 Suchitra Choudhury, '"It Was an Imitashon to be Sure": The Imitation Indian Shawl in Design Reform and Imaginative Fiction,' *Textile History*, 46(2), 2015, 189–212.

40 E.B. Havell, *Handloom Weaving in India*, Calcutta: Luxmir Bhandar, 1905, 10; Chatterton, *Industrial Evolution in India*, 229.

41 India, *Fact-Finding Committee*, 127.

42 Thurston, *Monograph on the Cotton Fabric Industry*, 4.

43 For more on this artisan, Tirthankar Roy, 'Out of Tradition: Master Artisans and Economic Change in Colonial India,' *Journal of Asian Studies*, 66(4), 2007, 963–91. Dispensing with traditional floral motifs, in the 1850s, this weaver named Dubraj started to weave pictures on saree borders. It is interesting to speculate where he received his inspiration from. This is an uncharted field, but I do have a speculation to offer. In the late-eighteenth and early-nineteenth century, the southern districts in the Bengal delta witnessed a boom in temple construction. Bengal does not have enough stone but does have good clay. The temples were made of earth and had terracotta decorations on their outer wall. Traditionally, the decorations dealt with religious themes, as they should in a temple. But during the boom, many began to display the sentiments of the sponsor or the artisan. The sponsors were merchants and landlords who had come under the influence of a cosmopolitanism forged of long-distance trade with Europe. The temple decorations displayed everyday life, Europeans, warfare, commerce, and erotica (Shreela Basu and Abhra Basu, *Banglar Terracotta Mandir: Akhyan O Alankaran*, Bengali, Calcutta: Sygnet Press, 2017). There was a striking similarity between the pictures on saree borders and the pictures this expressionist movement of the temples produced. Only the medium was different. Were there other weavers like him who applied an inherited skill to make a new saree? Surely there were, but we do not know their story as much as we would like to.

44 Indian Tariff Board, *Written Evidence recorded during enquiry on the Grant of Protection to the Sericultural Industry*, Calcutta: Government Press, 1935, 300–1.

45 Evidence of Marsden, India, *Indian Industrial Commission*, vol. 3. In Hyderabad, 'almost all the dyers and printers are ignorant of the proper way of using and manipulating the synthetic dyes or of combining the same with mordants,' as a result 'majority of them *prefer* to work under master-dyer as labourers,' Indian Tariff Board, *Sericultural Industry*, 1935, Written Evidence, 309–10.

46 N.G. Ranga, *The Economics of Handlooms*, Bombay: Taraporevala, 1930; India, *Indian Industrial Commission*, vol. 3, 187; Thurston, *Monograph*, 8; Alfred Chatterton, *Industrial Evolution in India*, Madras: The Hindu Office, 1912, 134. There were a few cases of yarn merchants investing in dyehouses, from Howrah hat, Surat, Yeola and Nagpur, India, *Fact-Finding Committee*, 137; Indian Tariff Board, *Sericultural Industry*, Report and Minutes of Evidence, Calcutta: Government Press, 1940, Written Evidence, 412; F. Dewar, *Monograph on the Silk Fabrics of the Central Provinces*, Nagpur: Government Press, 1901, 30, Mukharji, *Art-Manufactures*, 339.
47 Yusuf Ali, *Monograph on Silk Fabrics*.
48 For example, Chatterjee, *Notes on Industries of the United Provinces*.
49 Indian Tariff Board, *Sericultural Industry*, 1940, Oral Evidence, 288. Proposal of Director of Industries, Bombay.
50 K.S. Venkatraman, 'The Handloom Industry in South India,' supplements to the *Journal of the Madras University*, 7(1) and 8(1), 1935–6, 95. Trade in non-standard items at the same time might have become increasingly speculative for information on these did not travel freely. This condition plagued raw silk and is likely to apply to fabrics as well.
51 Bengal, *Report on the Survey of Handloom Weaving Industry in Bengal* (J.M. Ghose), Calcutta: Board of Economic Enquiry, 1937, 86.
52 Ibid., 74.
53 Spun silk is silk made of waste and short silk fibres.
54 Mercerized is cotton chemically treated to improve lustre and dye absorption. Twofolds or two folds are yarns spun together to add strength.
55 William Hoey, *A Monograph on Trade and Manufactures in Northern India*, Lucknow: American Methodist Mission Press, 1880, 26–7.
56 Ibid., 28.
57 H.C. Cookson, *Monograph on Silk Industry in the Punjab*, Lahore: Government Press, 1885–86, 187, Appendix B by F.A. Steel, 7.
58 Ibid.
59 Cookson, *Monograph on Silk Industry in the Punjab*, Appendix B by F.A. Steel.
60 Edwardes, *A Monograph upon the Silk Fabrics of the Bombay Presidency*, 1900.
61 N.G. Mukerji, 'Silk Industries of Moorshedabad,' *Journal of Indian Art*, 5, 1894, 1–7.
62 William Malcolm Hailey, *Monograph on the Silk Industry of the Punjab*, Lahore: Government Press, 1899, 16, 21.
63 Ibid., 21.
64 Edgar Thurston, *Monograph on the Silk Fabric Industry in Madras Presidency*, Madras: Government Press, 1899, 7.
65 I draw on Tirthankar Roy, 'Changes in Wool Production and Usage in Colonial India,' *Modern Asian Studies*, 37(2), 2003, 257–86.
66 The first large-scale enterprises were established in 1876 by the British India Corporation, a north Indian managing agency firm at Dhariwal in Punjab and at Kanpur. Kanpur was an emerging textile mill centre, an important army base and a centre of army procurement activity. Both towns were conveniently close to trade-routes in country wool. The mills in Bombay and Bangalore that followed in the next decade, likewise, had easy access to traded wool from southern Rajputana and Mysore.
67 These towns, principally Ludhiana, expanded in knitwear manufacture after independence, thanks to the local manufacture of cheap machines and consolidation of the wool trade. See Manjit Singh, *The Political Economy of Unorganised Industry: A Study of the Labour Process*, New Delhi: Sage Publications, 1990.

The industry benefited greatly from trade reforms introduced in the 1990s. Easier access to technology, markets, and imported wool acted as a major boost. As small-scale production grew, the large factories stagnated. The British India Corporation had gone bankrupt in the 1970s and was taken over by the Government of India in 1981. It still possesses some of the best-known brands of wool in the Indian market, but the textile industry has developed stronger ties with the world wool market.

4

CAPITAL AND LABOUR

A series of craft monographs prepared at the turn of the twentieth century discovered differences within the industry and sometimes made a distinction between the 'rank and file' and the merchants, the social leaders, and the factory owners. By 1942, when a systematic enquiry on the industry was prepared, these differences were starker. The chapter shows how this differentiation came into being. The key processes were a concentration of skills and capital in fewer hands and in fewer places and increasing mobility of labour.

Along with growing inequality, there was also a change in the relationship between richer and poorer weavers. Many surveys of the industry in the twentieth century suggest that contracts of various kinds became more common in the industry, especially between weavers with access to capital and markets and those without. In turn, the marketing system for handloom cloth changed from local sales in periodic markets in which many producers could take part, to working to orders from a contractor. The Fact-finding Committee (1942) and a few other contemporary reports called this process a journey from independence to dependence or from free sale to tied sale.

Why did it happen? The insecurity of work was one reason commonly cited as to why weavers preferred some form of contract. There would have been other reasons. With the expansion of the railway network and a large fall in costs of trade, weavers could access distant and urban markets. If this was an opportunity for some, it was a risk for the others. Marketing over long distances needed more money and information. Neither money nor information was within easy access of most weavers. Also, migration increased and the migrants being without either looms or dwellings of their own worked under wage-based contracts.

In 1940, in this industry, the capitalists and the workers were quite distinct sets, with a large undefined middle space occupied by households and families who worked on contract. This chapter first describes the three classes, starting with the households, and then offers a few general remarks on changes in the relationship between these classes. I use 'class' loosely, referring to only one common benchmark, ownership of capital or lack of ownership, and not referring to feelings of class difference or solidarity. Such feelings, as we see, were often muted by caste ties and the fact that the employers were artisans themselves.

Households

Aware that relationships were changing, occasionally government surveys and independent observers tried to measure the degree of inequality in the industry. In 1909, a survey found one in five weavers in the Bombay Presidency to be without a steady address of his own. They went to weave at the house of the sowkars (the generic term for a capitalist) and 'invariably dies a serf.'[1] The 1921 census found a large group of cotton weavers who were neither factory workers nor 'home' workers and were probably wage-workers hired by households. Together with workers in registered handloom factories, they formed 17 percent of all handloom weavers in Bombay. The Fact-finding Committee (1942) carried out a systematic survey and found that the proportion of contractual weavers was high in almost all regions, but that the proportion of factories was variable (Table 4.1). Fifteen years later, the percentage of factory workers had increased from eight to 16 in Madras, was the same in Bombay, and was four in West Bengal.[2] The cooperatives were a minor new addition in this spectrum.

In cotton handloom weaving, the household was universal around 1900. Scattered evidence from the early twentieth century suggests that the weaving families were on average slightly larger than the average family, had a larger number of workers on average, and a higher ratio of female-to-male workers.[3] A 1947 survey again showed that the 'composite family,' a corporate of several distinct family units, was the typical form appearing among

Table 4.1 Status of weavers in 1940 (percentages)

	Independent	*On contract*	*Factory workers*	*In cooperatives*	*Total (no in '000)*
Bombay	21	24	54	1	100 (117.2)
Deccan States	15	70	7	4	100 (12.9)
Madras	28	60	8	2	100 (427.7)
Travancore	47	21	32	1	100 (19.0)
Hyderabad	26	32	40		100 (109.0)
Punjab	58	39	2		100 (355.9)
Bengal	36	64			100 (202.0)
Bihar	98	2			100 (102.7)
Orissa	20	79			100 (50.0)

Source: India, *Fact-finding Committee: Handlooms and Mills*, Calcutta: Government Press, 1942.

large households of Sholapur town.[4] Interestingly, the 1961 census reported that the proportion of males in weaver households of Madras was above the state average. The household changed between 1900 and 1960 in that it bought more services formerly performed by insider women from providers outside the household.

Women and girls performed warping of the yarn, winding the thread onto bobbins for use as a weft yarn, and shared with men the task of sizing, that is, applying the starch paste on the warp thread. Weavers, as a rule, were men, sometimes assisted by young adults, almost invariably boys. The children also did bobbin winding or the manipulation of the harness if it was a draw-loom. The adult male weaver had an additional job. 'When the cloth is ready, he takes it to the nearest bazaar every evening or shandies every week for sale. In some places, he hawks it in streets.'[5]

This sentence from a 1935 report described the type that many official reports meant by 'independent' weaver (see also Table 4.1), one who mainly employed family labour to weave cloth, hawked goods, was a retail seller, as well as a producer of cloth. 'Handloom weavers,' stated a 1929 report on Bombay, 'may be classified into three main divisions on the basis of organisation: (1) independent weavers who work at home on their own looms and have sufficient finance for purchase of yarn, (2) dependent weavers perpetually in debt either to a dealer in yarn or a *karkhanadar*, and relying on him for supplies, and (3) *karkhanadar* or entrepreneurs with a group of 8 to 10 or more weavers, working under their personal supervision. The dependent weavers form about 75 per cent. of the whole group, the independent weavers 20 per cent. and the *karkhanas* 5 per cent.'[6] The classification is too schematic. As I show next, many units combined these features, hiring in some workers but also relying on family labour, or purchasing yarn on one's own but selling cloth on contract. Contemporaries, however, used the classification often to suggest how institutional change was taking place: from independence towards dependence.

In most standard descriptions of the household, women would be seen as helpers. This is simplistic. Quite a few women in weaver families knew how to weave. They learnt it casually rather than from systematic apprenticeship such as the boys went through.[7] But because they knew the work, and some knew it very well, in interwar south India, in towns that were growing rapidly as weaving clusters, more women started weaving for wages. In Salem town around 1950, a significant percentage of women weavers could be found in small handloom factories.[8]

Warping-winding-sizing was not always done inside the weaver's home but was sometimes hired out to neighbourhood women. The significance of the 'composite family' (see previous description) should now be clear. Frequently it was done by teams of adult and young women in a commonly owned premise. Such pooling of labour of the community was standard in rural Bengal and Madras around 1900. Thurston described this system for a Tamil village: 'As you enter a weaver's grove, it appears at first as if those occupied in this industry were engaged in a pretty game. Rows of women walk up and down the shady aisles, each holding aloft in the left hand a spindle, and in the right a bamboo wand, through a hook at the end of which a thread is passed.'[9]

The formation of warp in silk was almost an identical process except for sizing. Thurston, again, is useful:

> Bamboo sticks, 120 in number, are fixed upright in the ground, generally in the shade of a tope or grove, at a distance of a cubit from one another, and ten women or children, carrying ratnams [hand-spindles] in their hands, walk up and down this line, one behind the other, intertwining the thread between the bamboos, until 1,920 threads of various colours, according to pattern desired, are thus arranged. For this work each gets half an anna – a small remuneration for walking four miles. To form a warp sufficient for eight women's cloths, 40 miles have thus to be traversed.[10]

Warping systems of this kind were communal, manual, and outdoor, usually done in common spaces within a weaver's village.

In both silk and designed cotton weaving, boys were groomed to become weavers and were taught the basics of dyeing.[11] A set of descriptions in the monographs (c. 1900) dealt with the apprenticeship. There is little discussion available on the training of girls. There was one major exception, however. The exception was embroidery, mainly in Muslim households.[12]

Among the silk-weaving Muslim weavers, or Momins, of Deccan, the household again ruled. 'Their women help largely in the weaving and embroidery of wearing apparel, and add as much as the husband to the monthly income of the family.'[13] Among the transhumant shepherd-weavers of Bombay, 'one of the weaver's family, generally a woman or a boy, [spins] the wool into yarn.' Similarly, Gareri women in south Bihar were spinners of wool, while their men reared sheep and wove coarse blankets.[14] The (wild silk) tasar-weaving industry of Chotanagpur 'gives employment to men, women, and children; the first weave, the second spin, and the third set the warp. Labourers are not employed . . . at all.'[15]

Households did not disappear quickly, but the majority worked under contracts with merchants in 1940 (Table 4.1).

The growth of contracts

Weavers selling retail became rarer in later sources. So did price-based contracts. Insecurity, as I said, was usually the reason why weavers preferred a contract.[16] Around 1936, K.S. Venkatraman, a careful scholar of the industry, said that the independent weaver, who came 'first in historical sequence, is fast disappearing . . . the fluctuations in prices . . . are too great for his slender means.' Workshops were 'a more humane system' than a price-contract. The rates were fixed and paid by the piece. Payments were never deferred, and no haggling took place.[17]

Around 1900–1910, in the towns of northern India, wage-based contracts were common.[18] But the rural weaver sold cloth on his own initiative. The weaver of Punjab was 'under the thumb of the moneylender.'[19] Still, the moneylenders or the shopkeepers who dealt in yarn and cloth did not control sales. The weavers received orders from local landholders, other residents, hawked about in the neighbouring villages, or sold at the weekly market. Twenty years later, the Punjab Banking Enquiry Committee, which had surveyed the craft towns of the province, found that contracts were common and that in many cases, 'the weavers . . . are virtually the wage earners.[20] Weavers selling cloth anywhere they wished, even if indebted to yarn sellers, or tied sales with a merchant or creditor seemed to be disappearing. Owners of small factories employed others on wages as well as gave out contracts. In Benares' large and hierarchical business system, the factory owners or karkhanadars were a growing class.[21]

In rural Bengal, the factory owner or karkhanadar was not so prominent; the wholesale merchant was. The mahajan, the generic term for the contractor, controlled the industry. Around 1900, contractual sales were not as widespread. The weavers were by and large free to choose customers, and several of them were wealthy enough to afford that freedom. In the 1930s, by contrast, merchants controlled the cloth and yarn trade, and free sale was rare. 'The small and cottage industries of the province . . . depend largely on the accommodation granted by indigenous bankers. The accommodation sometimes assumes the form of the loan of raw materials to the borrower on a definite understanding that the finished articles will be delivered at a favourable price to the moneylender who may happen to be a trader himself.' One of the later reports insisted that 'the weaver is not [the mahajan's] employee but attached to him.' Where producers could, they negotiated harder on the terms of the contract, and when they could, tried to bypass the local merchant and sell in the big city (Calcutta) directly.[22]

Whether in the towns or in the rural clusters like Bengal's, the contractor knew or had contacts in the final market. In Bengal's case, the big market was Calcutta. This was too expensive a city for weavers to settle in and yet was a lucrative market for them. The contractor-cum-mahajan was the bridge. The more expensive the cloth, and the more distant the market, the more valuable were these contacts. On the other hand, local sales carried risks and often dragged the weaver into debt. 'Freedom of operation also carries along with it considerable risks.' An independent weaver would more often fail to dispose of his whole produce, which brought him back to the yarn dealer who then tried to undervalue the cloth, and 'the weaver has to take the next supply of yarn from that dealer at whatever price the latter may exact.' A sample survey in Bengal (1932) found that 82 percent of the entire time weavers were in debt to the yarn merchant. The merchants watches the weavers in the market places and during the festive season and 'pounces upon the money as soon as it reaches the weaver's hands unless the yarn dealer himself purchases the fabrics in which case the matter becomes easier.'[23]

It would seem from these descriptions that market risks were high enough to make falling into debt more likely. Market risks were high either because markets were further away, or the 1930s were stressful years, or both. In that case, a contractual sale was a safer option. This was a benign type of change, one that did not affect the unity of the household as a production unit mainly using family labour. There were two other situations in which external pressures transformed the household itself.

Households displaced or transformed

Two forms of organization – factories and large household units that needed to hire workers – show us how the shift happened. Both employed labour more intensively (that is, the average hours worked per person rose) and reduced the scope of part-time work such as family labour would represent.

A speeding up of the warping and sizing processes encouraged factories. Between 1883 and 1910, weaving towns in Bombay-Deccan experienced 'a noticeable change in . . . the methods of production. That change was the gradual specialization of the preliminary processes of sizing and warping, by a different group of workers consisting of women and inefficient weavers.'[24] The specialization process led to an expansion of the processing shop. Around 1940, in all small towns, as a rule, the processing side of the business was done in a factory-like setup. The drum-warping system, installed in a factory, was more capital-intensive than its predecessor. Someone other than the household weaver would own the processing factory. It also popularized the use of the warp beam, thus enabling longer lengths of warp to be prepared at a time and allowed for sizing and warping to be performed as a joint operation.

In the weaving towns of Tamil Nadu and the Deccan, drum-warping was a well-known implement and had displaced stick-warping extensively in the mid-twentieth century. By 1918 Salem weavers owned all processing shops. Mechanization in other processes progressed slowly. Dresser sizers were a later introduction, and sizing was less sensitive to change. Sholapur had an equally impressive record, by 1940 over 90 percent of the warping here was done in factories.[25] Machine warping and sizing was not yet popular in Bengal or north India. That was partly because the warping mill was yet to find a satisfactory way of combining warping with hand-sizing, which gave handloom cloth distinctiveness. In places where it was adopted, weavers had to find ways of bypassing the problem. A few towns were vanguards in such processes.

In silk, the main processing jobs, twisting or re-reeling threads, were similarly being reorganized in factories in the interwar period. During the late-nineteenth century, the indigenous sericulture industry had suffered a series of shocks partly due to the pebrine disease of the worms and the withdrawal of foreign filatures from Bengal.[26] The immediate effects were deteriorating quality, falling prices, and loss of the European market to Italian and Levantine silks. Within the home market, a straight substitution was difficult because local and imported silks were of different quality. Some silk weavers switched to foreign silks because these took dye well; otherwise, local silk was acceptable as raw material. A stronger advantage of foreign silk was its ready-processed nature. The Canton steam filature silk came to the market reeled, twisted, and standardized, while the Bengal or Mysore varieties were neither uniform nor ready for the loom.

Threatened by a changeover, local silk merchants and master weavers set up twisting and re-reeling houses. In Mysore, the tendency received state patronage. Some of the largest plants, Peddapuram in coastal Andhra and Rayadurg in southern Andhra, were handloom weaving units with an integrated processing facility. In the two premier silk-weaving towns of Bombay Presidency, Surat and Yeola, yarn processing was partially mechanized. In Surat, proximity to the mill industry was turned to good account, reeling came to be performed by a machine adapted from the mill practice.[27]

While warping came into larger-scale semi-mechanized work sites, cotton handloom weaving too concentrated in factories. These factories, called 'karkhanas', were common in silk weaving also.[28] The karkhana literally means a factory. The word signified an urban workshop engaged in the production of high-quality craft goods in Mughal India. Whereas in the Mughal cities, these workshops were sometimes owned or regulated by consumers, the term later was attached to merchant-owned and artisan-owned craft workshops as well. In the handloom weaving towns of Bombay-Deccan, karkhana referred to any small factory and the karkhanadar to the owner of the factory.[29] In this region, in the early twentieth century, migrant handloom weavers set up workshops to produce textiles and gave employment to wage-workers, usually men from their own caste and places of origin. Karkhana, the word used to describe the workshops, had by then entered the vocabulary of the entire subcontinent.

The urban handloom factories employed migrants. The single male migrant dominated the working class. And yet, as the factory movement strengthened, many of these migrants brought their families into the textile towns, often braving a much harsher lifestyle in the process. For example, until the 1930s, many among the Sholapur weavers lived with their families in single-room tenements not larger than 8 feet by 10 feet.

Factories and wage-work were biased towards male employment. Although, at the turn of the century, factories still hired women if their menfolk worked in the same premises, this was becoming rarer in the early twentieth century. K.S. Venkatraman, based on his fieldwork in the mid-1930s, held that 'men have taken the place of women sizers who have gradually disappeared as a result of the introduction of long warps.'[30] The spread of handloom factories of the Malabar Coast run by the Basel Mission gave rise to 'the fear, that the organization of the factory will eliminate women labour or that women would not come to the factory for work.' This fear, however, appeared 'unfounded' at that time.[31]

Why would factories not normally employ women? For the reason that women must balance household duties with wage-work, combine 'the tiresome work of cooking, feeding, turning the winding wheel and preparing the warp,' and an employer interested in someone able to devote more hours per day was not happy about the mixed duties. N.G. Ranga, an observer of weaving in the 1920s, wrote these lines. Ranga saw a variety of systems in place in southern India, from household production to communal pooling of mainly female labour in processing, to a whole family working for wage: 'In most cases, a weaver and his wife go to work in the employer's house.' Factories were rarer in the Telangana region where he did most of his fieldwork, but not unknown.[32] Ranga wrote:

> The houses of employers in which these workers labour . . . have tiled roofs and are too long and too narrow and are crowded with half a dozen looms, many charkas [wheels, probably for winding], a dozen women and a score of men in addition to an unruly crowd of children, so that in them it is very hard to hear one another speaking.[33]

Such factories were halfway between a household and the handloom factories of Sholapur where few women worked on the loom.

From a long time past, in major weaving clusters, leading units of production would be a hybrid between a family unit and a factory, that is, a unit where some workers were from the family and the others were hired. In the towns of Deccan, around 1900 'few workrooms have only one loom.' Reports on Sholapur in 1872 reported more looms than there were weavers. Rich weaving families with five to six looms were common in Salem and Coimbatore at the time of the Industrial Commission (1916–18).

By 1940, when the Fact-finding Committee was published, in the Bombay Deccan region: 'The average weaver in the employ of an independent weaver who has more than one loom still retains some of his old social position especially if his employer is of the same caste, but those who work in the karkhanas are regular wage-workers and in that respect are at the bottom of the ladder.'[34] A few years earlier, a witness in a Tariff Board enquiry reported that in the western part of the United Provinces, town workshops hired workers, but they were all 'relatives' of the owner. The relatives did not live under the same roof as the owner. They were paid at rates lower than notional market wage rates. And yet, 'they would not serve anybody else for four annas.'[35]

Was such a paradox sustainable? We cannot say. There were already numerous worksites where wage-workers were migrants rather than the owners' relations.

Wage-workers

Around 1900, observers of the industry often described the individual weaver or weavers in small communities being in distress. Such reports were as frequent then as in the 1850s when Karl Marx wrote of 'the misery inflicted by the British on Hindustan' and singled out the weaver as the object of his concern. In the last quarter of the nineteenth century, weavers joined indentured workers going to the tropical colonies. Famines made their situation desperate because they lost the market for cloth quickly as buyers spent everything they had on food, and 'they did not like the field labour of the ordinary relief works.'[36] Town weavers joined food riots. Some of them nearer forest zones were called criminal tribes.

By the middle decades of the twentieth century, crises like famine were a distant memory. But weavers working for wages was common enough. They were poor and did not find it easy to sell cloth on their own. A Bengal report from around 1940 said that 'just as there were landless agricultural labourers there are also a large number of loomless weavers.'[37] In western India, the class of loomless weavers working in others' homes or factories was already many thousands strong.

Three examples of wage-contract, from Sholapur, southern Andhra and the Tamil Nadu towns, are of special interest. For, these examples show the different ways the wage system could work: the immigrant workforce of Sholapur where producers dominated the industry, the system in southern Andhra where large producers were subcontractors of merchants, and caste-based hiring in the deep south.

Sholapur, the premier textile town of the Bombay-Deccan, represented the most advanced form of mass production of handloom cloth in the twentieth century. The first factories in the town dated back to the 1880s. About a decade or so earlier Sholapur received many migrant weavers from eastern United Provinces, the Awadh area, and Telangana after the great Deccan famine of 1876. The dry and famine-prone Madras-Deccan saw large emigration of weavers towards the textile towns of the west, overseas, and to the plantations in the north-east of India. The major expansion in the town, therefore, was a relatively recent phenomenon. By the 1930s, the 8,000-loom-strong industry was the biggest hub of wage-based weaving. All types of contractual sales, as well as the karkhanas, existed side by side.[38] Both loom-owning and loomless weavers were available. Loom owners were usually locals, but hired workers formed a composite category consisting of locals and migrants (on migration flows, see Map 4.1).

The first group formed of inhabitants of the city, 'have homely surroundings of their classes and castes' and enjoyed greater freedom. '[T]hough . . . inferior in the position they freely mix with their masters.'[39] Workers in factories were 'wholly different and more miserable.' By and large, they were Telugu-speaking Padmasalis, immigrants from southern Telangana, where real wages were higher but employment insecure. On coming to Sholapur, they entered an agreement with a karkhanadar. The agreement provided for living quarters, really an 8 ft by 4 ft space 'by curtsey called rooms,' work for women and children, and triennial visits home. Against these privileges, piece rates were lower than wages, and the hours were longer. Consumption debts to the karkhanadar were both an instrument of bondage and an excuse for wage cuts. Sometimes the worker could go home only by leaving his family behind as a hostage.

In the 1950s, the frequency of homeward journeys came down, and more immigrant families settled in Sholapur. The Handloom Workers' Union had been formed and managed to enforce two relatively minor provisions of the Factories Act, regarding hours of work and weekly holidays.[40] There was no improvement, however, in living conditions, and wage bargaining was rare or ineffective, because reports of wage cuts continued, sometimes as fines for bad work. The contract weavers had also organized themselves meanwhile to confront the arbitrary impositions of discounts and commissions, sudden changes in orders, termination of the contract, and unscheduled price revisions.

The first workers' trade unions appeared in the Bombay-Deccan and the Malabar factories run by the missions. Widespread wage cuts in Bombay around the time of the Great Depression encouraged the formation of collectives. Somewhat later, threatened wage cuts in Sholapur led to a spate of strikes affecting 200 karkhanas. More often, however, demands centred on the implementation of specific clauses of the Factories Act. The weavers were partially successful in this endeavour. The ever-present option of putting out work made it difficult for them to bargain hard. Employers who did not register their units as a factory escaped labour laws. Caste sentiments cut across class lines. In Sholapur 'the weaver is unwilling to join hands with any force seeking to curb the power of the employers to whom he is sometimes related.'[41]

A late 1920s report said that most factory workers came from Telangana and the Madras-Deccan (Map 4.1).[42] What did weaving complexes look like in Madras-Deccan? This region is a very dry agricultural zone that had a few towns located on points of overland trade. These towns contained significant concentrations of artisans until the nineteenth century. The availability of local wool and cotton, and some silk, advantaged the urban handicrafts.

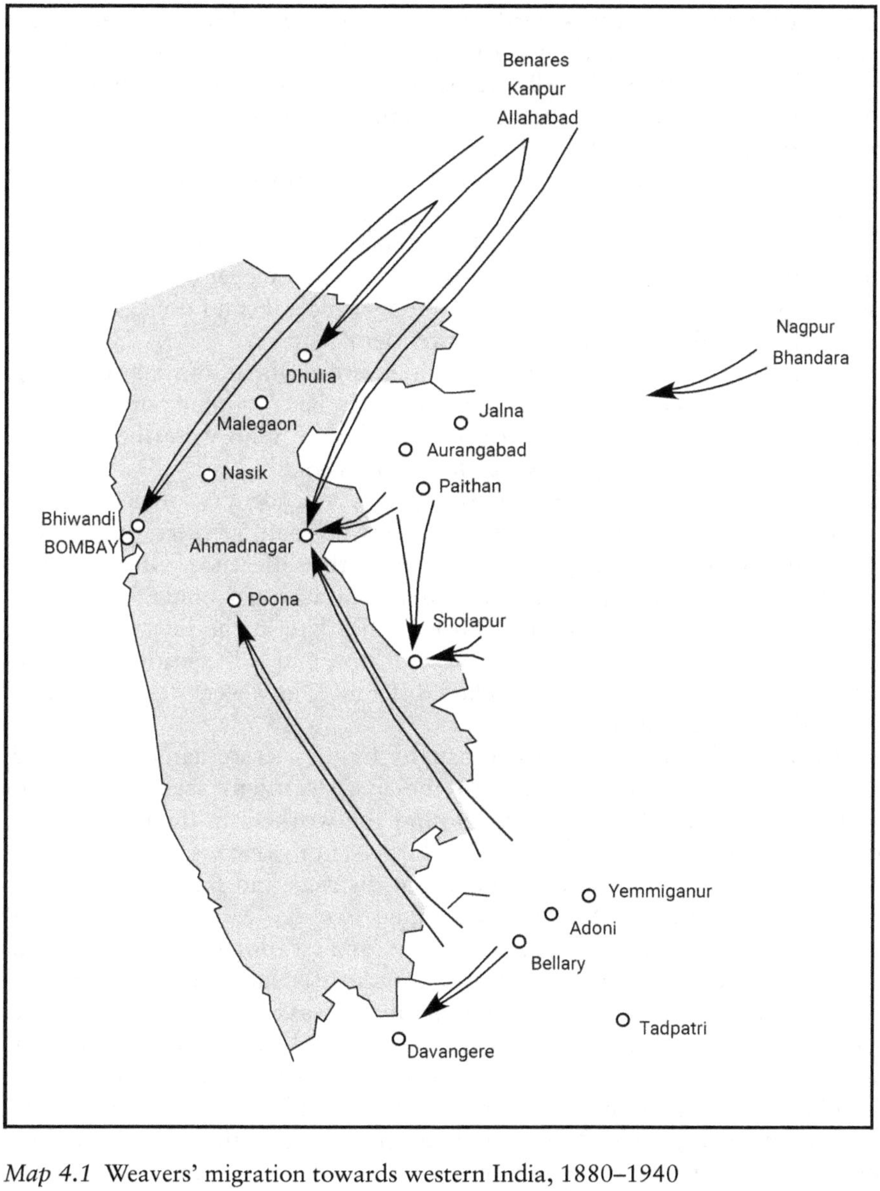

Map 4.1 Weavers' migration towards western India, 1880–1940
Source: Author

Descriptions of wage-employment suggest considerable uncertainty, for example, in the carpet and silk weaving business of Adoni, one of the bigger towns in the region. Yarn and dye merchants contracted with households. Some of the former set was north Indian traders settled in the recent past. In turn, the households hired workers. This three-tier vertical dependence was called mungani locally. All three tiers were secured together with never-ending debts, repaid over generations. Some local weavers still owned land but mortgaged it to master-weavers. Ranga's 1920 surveys found that the weavers were unhappy, restless, 'very mobile, impatient of any control, devoid of all sense of honour, very untrustworthy.'[43] Some of them left home to work in the Assam tea estates. Merchants sometimes reverted from mungani to piece work or offered fixed wages. But the bigger problem for the weavers was the region's aridity and poor agricultural conditions. The number of looms fell in the region in the twentieth century.

Factories of the size of Sholapur were rare elsewhere, but labour-hiring households were common throughout south India. A contemporary report on Tamil Nadu called them 'cottage workshops.' Who were the workers in the cottage workshops, also called coolies and 'assistants'? As in the Bombay-Deccan, they formed a working-class dependent on owners of handlooms for their livelihood. In return they were paid at piece rates lower than what the price-contract weaver received, the difference being a 'rental' on the loom. Grinding poverty and absence of a proper home drove them to migrate. The growth of nationalist politics late in the interwar period affected the weavers, whether on wages or not, and led to efforts to introduce collective bargaining.[44] The class difference, however, was never clear cut in the weaving towns.

Many people (we hear of them usually by their caste names) who had not done weaving before came to the factory towns seeking employment. In the 1930s, Venkatraman found the workers in the cotton handloom factories of south India to be largely non-weavers by caste, such as Panchamas and Muslims in the Tamil districts and Balijas and Malas in the Telugu country. Surveys conducted twenty years later show that the trend had continued. In Kanchipuram, immigration of workers (called coolies) was confined to the Vanniyas, Yadavas, Naidus and Nadars, all non-weavers.[45] Inter-caste wage employment was the trend in all textile towns. In the 1950s, the government survey, called the *Textile Enquiry Committee*, reported several instances. Labourers in Surat handloom and small powerloom factories were mostly 'Mahomedans, Harijans and other backward caste people.'[46] In contemporary Madras 'the majority of the nonhereditary weavers are first employed as Korvai [attached or bonded] assistants for low wages.'[47]

On the other hand, members of the weaver castes in south India, even if reduced to dependence, rarely joined wage labour. They did enter price-based contracts more readily. More than that, since they knew the work better than the others, they could take on the contract for complex work.

The merchant, the master-weaver, and the contractor, who was in the backdrop of all of these descriptions, should now take centre stage.

Capital

Weavers, we have seen, entered contracts frequently in the interwar period. At the other end of a contract was the contractor. Usually, to be able to give out a contract, one needed to own some form of capital, that is, be a capitalist. Accounts of the industry in the interwar period report many types of capitalists, factory owners, yarn merchants, cloth merchants, dye-house owners, gold-thread makers and merchants, bankers, buying agents, and others. A broad distinction existed between these categories. Yarn merchants were usually shopkeepers and not necessarily specialized in the textile business. Pure moneylenders too had little to do with weaving as such. Almost anyone in a small town with some money to spare tended to employ it in the credit business. Distinct from such mixed groups of people with some stake in textiles, there were other capitalists who had a big stake in weaving. They came in two sets: some weavers enlarged the scale of production, and merchants with access to market information and contacts tried to reach more distant markets, and, if successful, engaged more household weavers under contract. The former was more common in cotton weaving (such as in Sholapur), whereas the latter was more common in silk weaving (of south India).

Between 1880 and 1910, several reports on Bombay suggest that handloom weaving clusters contained large production units which had a stake in yarn trade and moneylending. 'Like other Khandesh moneyed classes,' one of these said, richer weavers did some credit business on the side. Sometimes they invested profits from trade and banking into production. The first Sholapur factory was set up in 1880. Around 1900, an enquiry done in Bombay described in rich detail a karkhana at Bhiwandi worked by immigrant weavers who shared the home of their employer.[48]

In the interwar period, factories and immigration were both more common. A 1937 survey of Bengal mentioned merchants who 'themselves take the risks for the losses or profits caused by the fluctuations in the market.'[49] In almost all the towns of western India, factories were a common organization. The factory owner of Sholapur was a weaver, a yarn processor and a wholesale cloth merchant, but not usually a yarn seller. The separation of yarn and cloth trades was systematic. The cloth traders included large producers, 'sowkars among weavers.' Yarn traders, by contrast, were the 'shopkeepers.' The Sholapur large producers were neither numerous nor powerful about the time of the Industrial Commission (1916–18), but 'since then the movement in this direction has been rapid.'[50] By the late-1930s 'the karkhanadar occupies the most important position in the structure of the industry.'

Once factories became an established institution in Sholapur, the growth of individual entrepreneurs depended as much on production as on trade. An example of such a trajectory is L.V. Tikekar.[51] Tikekar's early background in weaving is obscure. His factory started in 1899 and was unsettled for more than a decade as several experiments, with new looms and new products, failed. Finding skilled hands was difficult; his first recruits were persons who had no experience in weaving. But he was involved in weaving long enough to overcome these problems. In 1930, he was the owner of Tikekar Textile Mill, with 75 handlooms and 36 powerlooms, and of L.V. Tikekar & Co, making looms and accessories. Seen through his eyes, the preceding thirty years were an era of prosperity for Sholapur: the population of weavers increased, their proverbial vulnerability to famines were forgotten, new powerloom mills helped make new products, and a large labour force was available on hire. Tikekar himself was seen as a threat to other local weavers because of the better quality of cloth turned out in his factories.

Many examples of merchant capitalists came from silk and fine cotton weaving. In silk textiles, especially the traditional artisanal settlements like Kanchipuram in south India or Murshidabad in Bengal, descriptions available from around 1900 mention individuals who rose from the ranks to become shop owners in big city markets, wholesale suppliers of raw materials, campaigners of new tools and processes, community leaders, and 'master weavers' who put out work to neighbours.[52] In the 1880s, Joykrishna Mandal was one of the richer weavers of Mirzapur in central Bengal. He was the master-weaver for 40–50 local families. They executed his contracts under the supervision of Joykrishna himself, who was responsible for the quality of work done in his 'firm.' He took large orders from traders in Calcutta or Bombay and had 'great influence with . . . fellow caste-men' whom he hired. Mrityunjoy Sarkar was one of Joykrishna's men in 1887, who was, by 1900, the most important master-weaver of the same area. He died a wealthy man in 1903 and had been influential behind the adoption of many improvements in designed fabrics. Nalli Chinnasamy Chetti of Kanchipuram, a weaver of the Padmasali handloom weaving community, established in 1928 a saree shop in Madras, which became the nucleus for one of India's largest silk saree retailers today, Nalli Silks.[53]

Leading members of a social set sometimes campaigned for, successfully, the adoption of new tools and processes. Tulasi Ram of Madurai, a member of the Sourashtra weaving community of the town, was a dyeing technologist who revolutionized yarn-dyeing in Madurai and stimulated the handloom weaving enterprise of the entire Sourashtra community. P. Theagaraya Chetty, a weaver-capitalist, was instrumental in the spread of the fly-shuttle pit loom in Madras Presidency. In some of these cases, master-artisans became public figures by drawing upon the community and political resources. Tulasi Ram was known as a social reformer among the Sourashtra community. A member of the National Congress until the early 1910s, Theagaraya Chetty later played a role in the non-Brahmin movement and formation of the Justice Party. He was also the president of the Madras Corporation.

In the Tamil Nadu towns, there were many types of cloth merchants around 1900. The export merchants were mainly the Komati Chettis, village-to-village long-distance trade in cloth was associated with the Labbais of Karur, and Marwari moneylenders sold garments to the urban working class. None of these groups were weavers by caste. They kept an arm's length relationship with the weavers. For example, professional merchants were rarely willing to 'finance the weavers [to equip] their looms with improved sleys and harnesses.' Where the merchant or capitalist was also a weaver by profession, one would see more credit transactions occur. Thus, strong ties explain the 'peculiar' custom of Madurai silk weavers of borrowing only from their castemen and never from others.[54] The weaver-merchant also readily invested in technology and in the larger towns worked in close collaboration with the technicians and policymakers of Madras.[55]

Reports from the interwar period suggest that master-weavers exercised a great deal of control over trading. The Sourashtras of Madurai was 'a mercantile community,' the Devangas of Salem, their own sellers. 'The master-weaver,' Venkatraman wrote in 1937, 'is also a merchant.' The Fact-finding Committee mentioned weavers of Erode controlling 500 to 1000 looms each. The master-weaver was a full-time merchant but employed a head-weaver, someone he could trust, who in turn employed others on wages to work looms that might belong to him.

Unlike in south India, the Bengal silk industry took place in the villages of middle Bengal. Therefore, trade and landholding were both avenues of accumulation. It was not uncommon to 'rise from the ranks' to become a substantial weaver-merchant. A 1909 source called them 'guild mahajans,' weavers 'who have raised themselves to the head of the profession' and compared them to outsiders 'to whom usury is the sole motive.'[56] It appears, however, that in the interwar period, a reshuffle took place with the decline of Bengal sericulture industry and the increasing use of foreign silks. The changeover led to new entry in the cloth trading business. The 'local mahajans,' erstwhile master weavers, 'were thus eliminated' from trade.[57] In cotton cloth production in Bengal, the contractor was a powerful figure. Nadia weavers were said to be 'in the clutches of mahajans,' in Murshidabad 'practically enslaved' by them, in Dhaka the bani (advance) rates are 'the lowest possible', and so on. The other side of that process was, as in south India, elite merchant families setting up retail saree shops in Calcutta city, where the real action was marketwise.

Occasionally, cloth merchants set up factories and hired master-weavers as managers or supervisors. The weaver was a 'supervisor' in Amritsar carpets, in Benares silk, in Tanda printing, and Lucknow embroidery. Each product line was intensive in craftsmanship, and in some of them, the weaver's expertise in quality control was crucial to the success of the factory and mattered in his earnings. The workers were indebted to the head-weaver and practically bonded to him.

In the 1930s in Punjab, merchants set up rayon weaving factories. The cooperative promotion movement was prominent here, and often weavers tried to escape a contract with a merchant by joining the cooperative.[58] In Jullunder cheap cooperative credit was used by two small factory owners to move into the trade. In the weaving towns of western United Provinces, the north Indian Muslim Julaha weavers had headmen known as 'Chaudhuries.' They acted as creditors, traders, and social leaders (heads of the panchayat). In Budaun and Sitapur, in the early 1920s, attempts to set up a cooperative yarn store failed because 'this democratising system alarmed the Chaudhuries.'[59]

Conclusion

The chapter shows that there was considerable inequality within the handloom weaving industry. At one end there were businesspeople, social leaders, technology leaders, and campaigners, and at another end, migrant weavers without either a loom in their possession or a roof over their heads. In the huge space in between, we would find households working under a variety of contractual arrangements. Some of them hired workers and had some stake in the yarn or cloth trade. We cannot say if one form was slowly graduating to another. There is not enough material to tell how this world evolved.

But with hindsight, we can say something about the implications of inequality for the regions. Roughly, there was a negative correlation between the proportion of 'independent weavers' and concentration of looms across regions (Table 4.1), which should suggest to us how crucially survival depended on capitalist control over the business. The handloom weaving industry concentrated in two large regional clusters in the second half of the twentieth century – western India and Tamil Nadu – and several smaller hubs in other regions where highly skilled cloth was woven. In these vanguard areas, the capitalists were becoming more prominent in the industry as producers, merchants, and as public figures in the interwar period. Handloom weaving was becoming a business in these parts. Migrants and poor weavers came to these places because the places had that kind of energy.

A significant part of that energy went in trying out new tools and processes, as we see in Chapter 5. Innovation was never successful without the backing of a community leader of sorts, usually a figure combining wealth with social status and a progressive outlook. What did they do?

Notes

1 P.N. Mehta, *Report on the Handloom Industry of the Bombay Presidency*, Bombay: Government Press, 1909.

2 The mid-1950s estimates are from India, *Report of Textile Inquiry Committee*, New Delhi: Ministry of Commerce and Industry, 1954–8 The *Fact-Finding Committee* left out Bengal from their census. We have adjusted the Textile Enquiry Committee (1954) figures assuming factories to constitute a negligible proportion. Factory workers as a class do not appear at all in any of the surveys conducted in the 1930s.

3 Bengal, *Report on the Survey of Handloom Weaving Industry in Bengal* (J.M. Ghose), Calcutta: Government Press, 1937, 37.

4 R.G. Kakade, *A Socio-Economic Survey of Weaving Communities in Sholapur*, Poona: Gokhale Institute of Politics and Economics, 1947, 121.

5 K.S. Venkatraman, 'The Economic Condition of Handloom Weavers,' *Journal of the University of Bombay*, 5, 1936–7, 75–104, see p. 62.

6 Bombay, *Report of the Bombay Provincial Banking Enquiry Committee 1929–30*, vol. 1, Bombay: Government Press, 1929, 129–30.

7 About 1925, N.G. Ranga observed the general situation among 'caste weavers' in these words: 'About 10% of the women of Karnool are able to weave, but it is considered derogatory for a Padma Sale woman to weave,' *The Economics of Handlooms*, Bombay: Taraporevala, 1930, 69.

8 A study of women weavers in South India discusses this trend, Indira Parikh, Pulin K. Garg, and Indu Menon, *Women Weavers*, New Delhi: South Asia Books, 1992. From the 1990s, women were common not only in the handloom factories but also in the export-oriented garment units.

9 Edgar Thurston, *Monograph on the Silk Fabric Industry of the Madras Presidency*, Madras: Government Press, 1899, 9.

10 Edgar Thurston, *Monograph on the Cotton Fabric Industry of the Madras Presidency*, Madras: Government Press, 1899, 10.

11 For another description of apprenticeship of boys, see Ranga, *Economics of Handlooms*, 113. Boys of 10 were sent (near Dharmavaram) to other weavers, they were paid Re 1/month. They handled the dobby for the first year, prepared warp in the second, and were taught weaving from the third, when their wage increased to Rs. 2.5/month. At the age of 17 or 18, they tried to set up their own shops. In the Salem area, the period ranged from 12 to 20. They worked for 10 hours a day, and 'even the six to eight hours sleep that [they] get is disturbed by the tip tap noise of the blessed loom.'

12 S.M. Edwardes, *A Monograph upon the Silk Fabrics of the Bombay Presidency*, Bombay: Government Press, 1900, 51.

13 Ibid., 55.

14 N.N. Banerjei, *Monograph on the Woollen Fabrics of Bengal*, Calcutta: Government Press, 1899, 32.

15 N.G. Mukerji, *A Monograph on the Silk Fabrics of Bengal*, Calcutta: Government Press, 1903, 111, 115, 122.

16 See, for instance, Indian Tariff Board, *Sericultural Industry*, Report and Minutes of Evidence, Calcutta: Government Press, 1940, Report, 109, Oral Evidence,

249–56, and Indian Tariff Board, *Sericultural Industry*, Report and Minutes of Evidence, Calcutta: Government Press, 1935, Oral Evidence, 272.

17 K.S. Venkatraman, *Handloom Industry in the Madras Presidency*, Madras: The Diocesan Press, 1936, 62–4. Also Madras, *Report of the Court of Enquiry into Labour Conditions in the Handloom Industry* (B.V. Narayanaswami Naidu), Madras: Government Press, 1948.

18 Main sources on northern towns are: A. Latifi, *The Industrial Punjab*, Lahore: Government Press, 1911; Punjab, *The Punjab Provincial Banking Enquiry Committee, 1929–30: Evidence*, vol. 2, Lahore: Government Press, 1930; United Provinces, *Industrial Survey of the United Provinces*, Allahabad: Government Press, 1924, reports on districts; Indian Tariff Board, *Written Evidence Recorded during Enquiry on the Grant of Protection to the Sericultural Industry*, vol. 1 (Written Evidence), Calcutta: Government Press, 1935; Indian Tariff Board, *Oral Evidence Recorded during Enquiry on the Grant of Protection to the Sericultural Industry*, vols. 2 and 3, Calcutta: Government Press, 1935; Indian Tariff Board, *Sericultural Industry*, Report and Minutes of Evidence, Calcutta: Government Press, 1940.

19 Latifi, *The Industrial Punjab*.

20 Evidence of R.C. Rawlley, Director of industries, Punjab, Punjab, *The Punjab Provincial Banking Enquiry Committee, 1929–30: Evidence*, vol. 1, Lahore: Government Press, 1930, 42.

21 On the karkhana in north India, Latifi, *Industrial Punjab*, 53–4; United Provinces, *Industrial Survey*, Lucknow District, 24–5, Fyzabad District, 27, and Benares District; Census of India, Punjab, Calcutta: Government Press, 1901, vol. 1 (Report), 369; A.C. Badenoch, *Punjab Industries, 1911–1917*, Lahore: Government Press, 1917, 52; Indian Tariff Board, *Sericultural Industry*, 1940, Written Evidence, 717.

22 The basic sources are Bengal, *Report on the Survey of Cottage Industries of Bengal*, Calcutta: Department of Industries, 1929; Bengal, *The Report on the Survey of Handloom Weaving Industry*; Bengal, *Handloom Cotton Weaving Industry in Bengal*, Calcutta: Department of Industries, 1940; and Indian Tariff Board, *Sericultural Industry*, 1940, Oral Evidence. The quotes here are from memorandum of the Bengal National Chamber of Commerce and Industry to India, Banking Enquiry Commission, Bengal, 1929, 386.

23 Bengal, *Report on the Survey of Handloom Weaving Industry*.

24 N.M. Joshi, *Urban Handicrafts of the Bombay-Deccan*, Poona: Gokhale Institute of Politics and Economics, 1936, 72.

25 Gazetteer (Madras District), *Salem*, Madras: Government Press, 1917, 268; Madras, *Report on the Survey of the Handloom Industry in Madras State*, Madras: Directorate of Statistics, 1954, 26; Joshi, *Urban Handicrafts*, 104; Kakade, *A Socio-Economic Survey*, 26.

26 See on this tendency Indian Tariff Board, *Sericultural Industry*, 1940, Written Evidence, 414 and Oral Evidence, 669, 689, 693, 700–2 and memorandum of Bengal National Chamber, op cit. Also, Brenda M. King, *Silk and Empire*, Manchester: Manchester University Press, 2005, 66–83.

27 Indian Tariff Board, *Sericultural Industry*, 1935 and 1940, Evidence.

28 Joshi, *Urban Handicrafts*, 120.

29 Tirthankar Roy, 'Karkhana,' in Kate Fleet et al., eds., *The Encyclopaedia of Islam Three*, Leiden: Brill, 2018, 143–6.

30 Venkatraman, *Handloom Industry*, 54.

31 Venkatraman, 'Economic Condition,' 72.

32 Ranga, *Economics of Handloom*, 76.

33 Ranga, *Economics*, 66.

34 Bombay, *Report of the Sholapur Handloom Weavers Enquiry Committee*, Bombay: Political and Services Department, 1948, 37.
35 Indian Tariff Board, *Report on Woollen Textiles*, Evidence, New Delhi: Government Press, 1936, 264–5.
36 Gazetteer (Bombay Presidency), *Belgaum*, Bombay: Government Press, 1884–6, 347. Also, Kakade, *A Socio-Economic Survey*, 10.
37 Bengal, *Handloom Cotton Weaving Industry in Bengal*, 1940.
38 The basic sources on Sholapur used here are Joshi, *Urban Handicrafts*; Kakade, *A Socio-Economic Survey*; Bombay, *Report of Sholapur*; and Maharashtra State Archives File No 29/SH/2 1929–30 of Bombay Provincial Banking Enquiry Committee records. This is on Sholapur and includes written and oral testimony of L.V. Tikekar, an entrepreneur, more on him below, of V. Kelkar, Inspector of Weavers' Cooperative Societies, and of Tukaram Kanna, representative of weavers.
39 Joshi, *Urban Handicrafts*, 110.
40 India, *Fact-Finding Committee*, 86.
41 Bombay, *Report of the Sholapur Handloom Weavers Enquiry Committee*, 37.
42 Ranga, *Economics of Handloom.*
43 Ibid.
44 For a study of mobilization and unionization in South India, see Karuna Dietrich Wielenga, 'Repertoires of Resistance: The Handloom Weavers of South India, c.1800–1960,' *International Review of Social History*, 61(4), 2016, 423–58.
45 Venkatraman, *Handloom Industry*, 181; and Census of India, *Silk Weaving of Kanchipuram*, 1961, vol. 9, Part 7-A, Handicraft Survey Monograph No. 1, Madras: Government Press, 29–30.
46 A.B. Trivedi, *Post-War Gujarat*, Bombay: Publisher n.a., 1949, 450.
47 Census of India, *Handlooms in Madras State*, 1961, vol. 9, Part 11-A, Madras: Government Press, 110.
48 R.E. Enthoven, *The Cotton Fabrics of the Bombay Presidency*, Bombay: Government Press, 1895.
49 Bengal, *Report on the Survey of Handloom Weaving Industry in Bengal* (J.M. Ghose), Calcutta: Board of Economic Enquiry, 1937.
50 India, *Fact-Finding Committee*, 78.
51 Tikekar's testimony in Maharashtra State Archives File No 29/SH/2 1929–30 of Bombay Provincial Banking Enquiry Committee records.
52 I draw on Tirthankar Roy, 'Out of Tradition: Master Artisans and Economic Change in Colonial India,' *Journal of Asian Studies*, 66(4), 2007, 963–91.
53 Interview of Nalli Kuppuswami Chetti (2014), Chairman, Nalli Silk Saris, Creating Emerging Markets: Oral History Collection, Harvard Business School, available at www.hbs.edu/businesshistory/Documents/emerging-markets-transcripts/ChettiTranscriptWithCoverFinal.pdf (accessed 1 July 2019).
54 S. Srinivasa Raghavaiyangar, *Memorandum on the Progress of the Madras Presidency during the Last Forty Years of British Administration*, Madras: Government Press, 1892.
55 India, Indian Industrial Commission, Evidence, vol. 3, Calcutta: Government Press, 1918, 185. 'The small workshop system . . . is a feature of that branch of the industry where strict supervision of the work is required,' Venkatraman, *Handloom Industry*, 66–8.
56 G.N. Gupta, *Resources of Eastern Bengal and Assam*, Shillong: Government Press, 1909.
57 Indian Tariff Board, *Sericultural Industry*, Written Evidence, 414, Oral Evidence, 693.

58 See, for a typical description, Banking Enquiry Committee, *Punjab*, vol. 2 (Evidence), 856–7. Reference to Gurdaspur. The decline was attributed to legislation restricting usury. This came in 1930, but cases of large-scale bankruptcy occur in immediately preceding years as well. This might reflect anticipation of the new laws.

59 United Provinces, *Report on the Industrial Survey of the United Provinces*, Budaun District, Allahabad: Government Press, 1924, 29.

5

TOOLS AND TECHNIQUES

Productivity in handlooms registered extraordinary growth in the first half of the twentieth century. To some extent, the growth derived from redistribution within the industry, away from part-time and low-valued work and towards full-time, specialized, and higher-valued work. But technological change contributed to this process too. Where did the tools and the techniques come from? Why were they adopted? Who adopted them? The chapter answers these questions.

What does technological change mean in this context? There was little inventive activity in India. The key issues were adapting European tools and processes to local conditions, mainly to augment craftsmanship. I will use the word 'innovation' to mean that kind of change. Individually, the changes were small, but as Table 5.1 shows, collectively they could have a significant effect.

By the end of the nineteenth century, not only had many weavers survived competition from British cloth, but they were also investing in new tools and processes. The fly-shuttle was practically unknown before 1900. In 1940, there were 700,000 of them in an estimated loom-size of two million. There were about 20,000 'frame looms' with more than double the productivity of a fly-shuttle, and 15,000 'powerlooms' or mechanized looms located in small factories usually owned by handloom weavers. From the last quarter of the nineteenth century, basic raw materials such as dyes, gold thread, and silk yarn were mainly imported to India. Some were cheaper than local substitutes and some (like dyes and silk) delivered variety. As Chapter 4 shows, systems of warping changed in many places from the old ones that were slow, extremely labour-intensive, and not compatible with mass production in weaving, to drum-warping, which was superior on all three counts.

This whole movement is puzzling because by and large weavers were poor and susceptible to a fluctuating market due to frequent harvest fluctuations. Often only a succession of good years persuaded the weavers to adopt a new tool.[1] Officers, as we have seen in Chapter 3, shared the anxiety that the weavers needed to improve quality to compete, and yet most seemed to resist the idea. Any deterioration in the quality of work tended to be blamed on whatever

Table 5.1 Productivity in handloom weaving, 1901–1939

	Looms (million)	*Workers in handloom industry (million)*	*Cotton Cloth Output (in million lbs of yarn equivalent)*	*Output per Loom (Index)*	*Output per Worker (Index)*
1901	2.2	3.3	207	100	100
1921	2.0	2.4	235	125	156
1932	2.0	2.1	379	202	288
1939	2.0	n.a.	426	227	n.a.

Note: Output is the average of two adjacent years. Looms and workers exclude Burma. For 1901 there is available a total figure of 2.7 million looms including Burma, which probably accounted for about half a million looms. A handloom census in 1921 found 1.5 million looms excluding Burma, but the census had poor coverage. The correct figure should be around two million. Looms and workers include cotton as well as non-cotton fibres. Cotton accounts for over 70 percent of the looms. The percentage was higher for the earlier years. For calculation, see Tirthankar Roy, 'Acceptance of Innovations in Early Twentieth Century Indian Weaving,' *Economic History Review*, 55(4), 2002, 507–532.

was new so that a temporary depression in the industry caused a reversion to the old tools.[2] Weavers, in short, displayed risk aversion and conservatism.

Indeed, technological dynamism was not universal at all but characterized the urban and design-sensitive consumer markets. The weavers who could target these markets adopted new ideas more readily than did the others. What were these weavers trying to do? They aimed at doing two very different things. When installing a new warping machine, the fly-shuttle, or a powerloom, they were trying to speed up the operation. But when they installed the frame loom, or Jacquard, dobby, or a drop-box, they were trying to deliver more variety in design by making warp- or weft-manipulation easier to effect. These decisions could become interconnected because fitting attachments was easier in a frame loom than in a pit loom. Neither of the two tendencies can be explained as a simple response to competition from machines. They were instead responses to changes in consumption patterns, the demand for affordable variety within traditional designs.

Historians, however, do not usually see the significance of technological change in quite this way. How have they seen it so far?

How technological change is seen

Why did technological change happen and why was its reach limited? While addressing this question, scholarship has focused on specific regions where conditions varied a great deal from one to another. Thus, Peter Harnetty's study of central India generates a picture of slow change and resistance to change, whereas the work of Douglas Haynes on western India suggests a readiness to accept new tools. On the other hand, Haynes concentrates on certain institutional forms more prevalent in western India. These studies suggest that the common factor between regions was the interaction between technology, market, and organization, but that the nature of these interactions was variable.

Following that line of thinking, I suggest that technological diffusion accelerated during a period of good profitability. But investment needed not only capital or good returns but also some form of a public good. It required a large transregional market, agglomeration that enabled utilization of economies of scale and reduction in transaction costs, and a cooperative community with influential and progressive leaders.

General interpretations of technological change in handloom weaving claim that the change was a response to competition from machines. As Chapter 2 has shown, from the 1880s, handloom cloth production was stable and then rose steadily in the interwar period. This was precisely the period when mechanized weaving in Bombay, Ahmedabad, and other Indian textile towns expanded from less than 400 million yards of cotton cloth to about three billion. Many officials dealing with the industry believed that the weavers on average worked harder for less in the interwar period than they had in the early nineteenth century.[3] It was sometimes the case that when faced with competition, the weaver accepted lower wages and standards of living. But this was not a sustainable option in the long term or on a large scale. What then did they do to survive the competition?

The economic historian Amiya Kumar Bagchi attributes the survival to the new improved tools that were made available to the weavers by government agencies from around 1900.[4] Other historians have followed Bagchi in saying the same thing.[5] How credible is this view that the state imparted knowledge and knowledge saved the industry? I have discussed elsewhere (Chapter 1) that the state played a very limited role in improving the industry. Even when it did campaign for new tools, without the agency of leading members of the weaving communities, the capitalists-cum-social-leaders, nothing would likely be adopted. The question remains: Could knowledge at all bridge the gap between the machines and the artisans?

Comparisons of the average cost per yard show that technological change in handloom weaving cannot be explained by the need to compete with the power-driven loom. We can compare three loom types, the fly-shuttle, the frame loom, and the powerloom. Given capital cost, physical output per loom, yarn price, interest rates, labour requirement per loom, and the life of looms, cost per yard can be calculated. The reference cloth is cotton that does not involve material or techniques affecting physical productivity to any great extent, such as fine or coarse yarn, or borders made of other material. Such standard cloth can use yarn of counts from 20s to 40s, and its ends and picks a range between 40 and 60. Within this range, physical productivity should not differ greatly between cloths for a specific loom type.[6] The cost per yard is calculated once by assuming the wage rate to be identical between the loom types, and next by investigating relative wage rates to see which ratio achieves equality in costs.

These calculations suggest two points. First, the difference in physical productivity between the 'improved loom' and the powerloom remained wide. And second, while the mill weavers did earn higher wages than the handloom weavers, the wage gap did not meet the productivity gap. The ratio of relative wages between a pit flyshuttle loom, a frame loom, and a powerloom that would enable all three to achieve the same average cost is approximately 1:2:8. The ratio has to be wider if (a) the labour required for a powerloom is smaller than the ratio taken (two looms per person), (b) the cost of capital is higher for the small firms, which it was, and (c) the cost of yarn is higher for the handloom, which was often the case. In reality, the wage differential was much narrower.[7] The reference cloth is precisely the kind the handlooms were abandoning. The extent of diversification can be estimated reliably for the 1930s, when the share of 'non-cotton fabrics,' nearly all of which included higher-valued and skill-intensive goods, rose from 27 to 43 percent of the value of handloom output (Chapter 3).

In short, competition with machinery cannot explain the technological change, because the better looms fell far behind the powerlooms, even with a wage gap. Why install equipment, then? The answer is, most types of new tools allowed the weaver to make a traditional saree differently and thus access wider and more diverse demand. Weavers installed new tools to augment their skills to make a different quality good. As Chapter 1 showed, the general tendency was to offer a greater variety of simpler designs within the basic framework of a traditional garment like the saree.[8]

Before discussing how this happened and where, a description of the technological system is needed.

The technological system

Production of cloth in the handloom consisted of three major steps: processing of yarn before weaving, the weaving process itself, and processing of cloth after weaving. The first task, again, consisted of several steps: winding weft yarn on shuttle pirns, winding warp yarn on cones or bobbins, preparation of the warp, sizing, and winding the warp on a beam. More rarely, in a few towns with a reputation for coloured clothes, dyeing yarn was an important preparatory task. By contrast with the mills, the handloom production system integrated the post-weaving processes to only a small degree. Dyeing and printing of cloth was an industry in which the weavers took a decreasing part. The connection seems to have been closer in the eighteenth century. But in the twentieth century, the application of colours to handloom cloth was a distinct industry and much smaller than its counterpart in the mills. The reasons for this were that there were considerable economies of scale in dyeing and printing, and printing required standardized fabrics, which the weavers could not supply. Besides, as Chapter 3 shows, the quality of dyeing posed a challenge to the industry. The designs for which the handlooms were known, therefore, were mainly woven on the loom. In a traditional handloom system, some of the pre-weaving tasks, such as winding, were performed by family labour at home. Others, notably warping, needed either the pooling of domestic labour or machines when communal labour was not an option, as in a town.

The average Indian weaver in 1900 produced a complex cloth using equipment that was astonishingly crude in appearance (Figure 5.1). This apparent

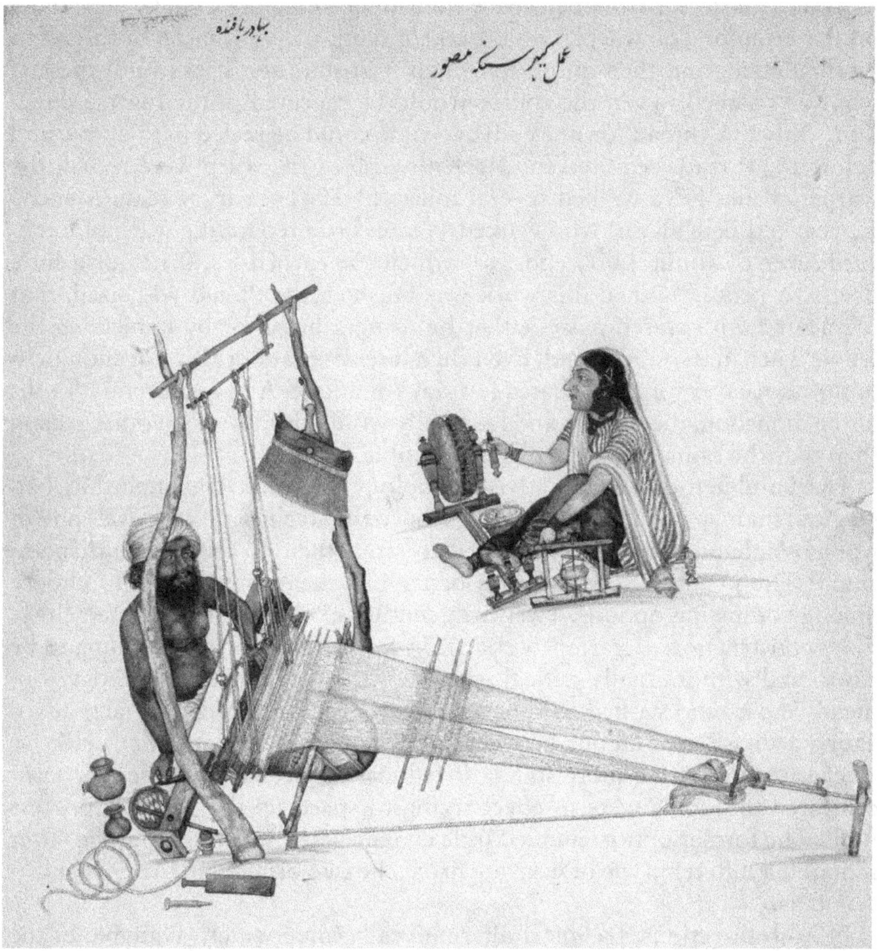

Figure 5.1 Weaver and spinner, 1860

Source: The Cleveland Museum of Art, www.clevelandart.org/art/1987.162

incongruity had struck European observers from a long time past.[9] The weaver sat in a pit dug in his living room, in front of a wooden frame which held the few pieces of roughly carved sticks that functioned as reeds and heddles or healds, laboriously passed the shuttle from one end to another, and then manipulated the warp threads by hand or with the help of a child to weave the most complex designs. The pit retained moisture, which made the threads break less often. The house was constructed to allow light to fall on the loom. That is, the windows in a weaver's house tended to be placed low. The warp threads stretched a few feet in front, and were tied to, or hung from, another horizontal stick.

The preparation of the warp was just as remarkable. At the centre of the weavers' quarters, in an open space shaded by trees, a few sticks were fixed on the ground. The warper would take a hank of yarn, fasten a thread to the first stick, and then go on unreeling it around the sticks until the last one was reached, when the course would be repeated in the reverse direction. Only one thread (or one end) at a time could be reeled in this way, and before the threads required for a given width of the warp were reeled, the warper would have walked several miles. In 1941 a survey team found a 12-year-old Bengali girl who walked 17 miles to prepare the warp of a ten-yard saree of about 3,000 ends, for which she earned Rs. 0.125 or a little over two pence.[10] When this work was finished, the thread was sized, that is smeared with starch paste, either by using a brush or by immersing the whole warp in the compound. Even such intensive labour was not enough to occupy a weaver for more than a few days at a time. And for several months of the monsoon, the weaver and his family would be idle for no other reason than that the rains made warping impossible.

The combination of primitive technology and fine craftsmanship had inspired many provincial officials to believe that technological development was possible and that it was needed to strengthen or preserve craftsmanship.[11] The problem was to find a better but cheap option and to choose among competing options. Twentieth-century experiments addressed either loom construction or yarn processing. In India, the two spheres came to be associated with mutually critical schools of thought on handloom development. Those who wished to concentrate on processing were, in fact, advocating a division of labour between processing and weaving, and selective mechanization of the more standardized task, processing. Those who concentrated on looms were in effect trying to speed up the weaving process itself. The former option entailed little change in the weaving firm; the latter required a different type of weaving firm. The two differed in their organization bias.

In both directions, technical alternatives became widely available in the twentieth century, partly due to the efforts of provincial governments in popularizing them. It would not be wrong to say that this was the only significant example of direct government intervention in the promotion of small-scale industry. By 1900, three key innovations had been introduced in demonstrations in India and selectively introduced to weavers. From the traditional pit loom and stick warping, there was a change towards the fly-shuttle loom, a set of 'frame looms' and 'semi-automatic' looms, mounted on wooden or cast-iron frames, and drum warping.

The frame loom took up much less space, could weave longer lengths of yarn, could be used to attach warp beams and 'take-up motion,' and thus became popular with the handloom factories. The drum-warping system was more capital intensive than its predecessors, but it popularized the use of a warp beam and allowed for sizing and warping to be done as a joint operation. The Salvation Army in central and western India, the Basel Mission in Malabar, and the British machinery manufacturer Hattersley had been pushing semi-automatic looms with some local success, whereas the government of Madras began to promote warping and sizing mills. Individual weavers modified the loom to meet specific needs. A locally famous example of the 'naksha' or design loom was created by the weaver Dubraj, said to be a carpenter before he became a weaver (Figure 5.2).

Figure 5.2 'Naksha' loom for design weaving in Murshidabad area, c. 1900

Source: N.G. Mukerji, *A Monograph on the Silk Fabrics of Bengal*, Calcutta: Government Press, 1903.

Among looms, the fly-shuttle was easily affordable, whereas frame looms and the warping mill required a great deal more capital. There were several advantages of a fly-shuttle or frame loom over the traditional loom. The shuttle moved faster. Weaving broader widths in a throwshuttle required two persons. In the fly-shuttle, the picking motion was considerably easier, and one person could do the work. With the adoption of a yarn roller beam, it was possible to weave longer lengths of warp to save time on frequent dressing, drawing in or twisting in of warps, and to replace the slow and laborious country warping systems with a warp which was sized and wound on a wooden roller. With an attachment such as the 'spring tension,' the risk of broken threads was reduced. When improved looms were installed in many firms near a concentration of processing firms, the processing firms reaped economies of scale, and the weavers enjoyed lower transaction costs in buying raw material or selling cloth.

From the frame loom, the idea of a power-driven loom was a small step. In the interwar period, power-driven looms were being discarded at scrap rates by the mills. Buying such a loom and reconditioning it to fit the weaver's factory shed was not expensive. Relatively well-off weavers started to replace handlooms by power-driven looms in products where such a switch was possible. The first such looms in India appeared in handloom towns around 1900 and were run on fuel oil. At the same time, and probably unaware of this small beginning, A.C. Chatterton, the Director of Industries, Madras, predicted that 'small power loom factories might be worked with great success in this country.'[12] From the 1930s, the powerlooms spread much faster when electricity became available in many interior towns with handloom industries. The ground was prepared for what was to become India's largest industry at the end of the century and the most fertile 'training ground for the development of indigenous manufacturing genius,' to quote the prescient Chatterton again (see also Chapter 4).

The cloth-processing side remained an activity separate from weaving. However, woven designs were a potential field of change. There were two possible ways of implementing these: one intensive in the handling of warp threads and the other intensive in the handling of weft threads. The Jacquard punch-card was a method of manipulating warp threads, whereas effecting designs that required manipulating the weft needed a frequent change of shuttles with the help of an extra hand. The distinction, of course, was not rigid because most borders on a garment such as the bordered saree needed both techniques, but the emphasis could differ. The advantages of a Jacquard over a draw-boy or dobby were greater standardization and smaller labour costs. Jacquards were not unknown in the towns that made designed apparel using a significant quantity of silk and gold thread, but the method was not used extensively during the colonial period.

Three circumstances can explain the slow diffusion. First, it was less useful in designs that involved several shuttles and in products that required each piece to be unique, such as bordered sarees. Jacquards continue to be rare in such types of hand-woven products. On the other hand, in more standardized goods such as the furnishing fabrics of Sholapur, or certain types of 'jamdani' sarees made in Benares, Jacquards began to be used at the end of the colonial period. Second, it used metal parts that were not easily replaceable. And third, the diffusion was dependent on the development of the use of punch-cards as a separate skill. In most places, this task was and continues to be performed by a specialized set of firms, thereby making the Jacquard feasible only in a well-developed textile town offering diverse services.

The new tools were an improvement over the throw-shuttle in lines of work in which the weaver enjoyed a market niche. The fly-shuttle was not easily accepted in the complex figured weaving because the weavers felt it would lead to excessive breakage of thread or would interfere with the quality of the design. But it was more popular in clothes that combined a special preference for handlooms with a simplicity of design. Thus, in plain cotton weaving with the 80s or 120s yarn, for which central Bengal was known, the fly-shuttle was popular. It was also much used in the Madras handkerchiefs of the eastern coast. The frame-loom was relatively more common in silk-weaving factories.

The new tools did not spread either rapidly or uniformly. By 1940, in the three major weaving provinces, Madras, Bengal, and Bombay, about two-thirds of the looms used fly-shuttles. But the proportion dropped sharply as one moved to the interior, the 'up-country,' and into rural weaving. Not for another two decades would there be a mass conversion of looms. The warping mill was even rarer. In the weaving towns of Tamil Nadu and the Deccan, it was a well-known implement and had displaced stickwarping almost completely, but it was not popular in Bengal or anywhere in the north. That was partly because the mill had yet to find a satisfactory way of combining warping with hand sizing, which gave handloom cloth a certain distinctiveness. However, in places where it was adopted, weavers had found ways of bypassing the problem.

The slow diffusion must, in part, be attributed to the absence or inadequacy of information systems. The history of public effort towards technological improvement in handlooms started in the nineteenth century with a weaving institute at Srirampur or Serampore, a town in Bengal that was once an important centre of Danish and British trade in Indian cloth. However, the idea of state aid for handlooms came on its own between 1900, when provincial governments carried out surveys of handicrafts with a half-hearted intention of reviving them, and 1918 when the Indian Industrial Commission endorsed the philosophy of state aid for technological improvements. During this period, the first Departments of Industry were started in the British provinces, closed by imperial order, and restarted around 1914. In this phase, the efforts of the Madras government under the leadership of Chatterton were especially noteworthy.[13] In the brief first phase of the Industry Department, Madras held a few exhibitions and competitions to popularize the new looms and was quick to establish a school on the Serampore model in the weaving town of Salem. The school was closed in 1909 on government orders, ostensibly induced by financial stringency, but the idea of technical schools for weavers survived. In the interwar period, the provinces set up some weaving schools in major towns. For the more remotely located weavers, there were travelling demonstrations.

The industrial schools did have some effect in showing the more complex tools at work, but the peripatetic demonstrations responsible for spreading this knowledge deep into the interior were not effective. A party of three or four, one superintendent and a few *maistries* [foremen], visited a village, where the revenue officials announced their arrival by beating tom-toms and stayed there for anywhere between a day and a few weeks, depending on how quickly the local weavers received their message. Each province had one weaving superintendent. It is impossible to believe that the party could visit more than a few hundred weavers in a whole year, and a province such as Madras had more than 400,000 of them. There was never a chance of a party returning to a village once visited. Besides, the men involved were not always equipped for the task. The secretary of the Madurai dyers' association remarked that one superintendent he knew had 'never woven a yard of ordinary cloth.'[14] Often, the foreman, on the strength of his formal education, looked down on the assistants, who knew the craft better. Government failure, however, should not be exaggerated. There are few reported instances in the interwar period of the non-adoption of a device because the weaver did not know about it. Haynes shows that numerous actual cases of adoption occurred without help from the government.[15] There were also countless cases of rejection of a known alternative.

In short, the government, while it did supply a service, was not the crucial link between the weavers and technological decisions. The slow and uneven diffusion of new tools must be explained partly by product specialization of different groups of weavers, and partly – as will be shown next – by risks, returns, markets, resistance, and organizational compatibility.

Another major field of challenge and opportunities was yarn dyeing. Traditional 'vegetable' dyes could provide striking and fast colours but could not create a great variety either in shades or in designs. Coloured cloth survived in handlooms where dyed yarns were used in making woven designs, as in bordered sarees. Traditional printing, on the other hand, had suffered because of foreign competition. Until the 1870s, the printing industry was depressed because of the popularity of Lancashire-printed textiles, the class where imports held their own against Indian mills for a long time.

As we have seen, a crisis occurred within yarn dyeing after the discovery of coal-tar dyes in Europe and their wide usage from about the 1870s. Colours now came in little packets that anybody could buy in a shop.

Universally, the new colours threw the process of dyeing yarn open to anyone who wished to take it up. This meant a loss of livelihood for hereditary dyers, whose worth depended on their knowledge of the plants, roots, and insects from which the natural dyes were extracted.[16] The colours being thus dependent on the local flora, different regions and peoples had specialized in different shades, a position that was now about to change. Increasingly, weavers started to dye yarn, or remnants of dyeing castes took up the new processes in weaving towns.

While the synthetic dyes made a whole knowledge system redundant, they required a lot of expertise of their own, which the new practitioners of dyeing did not possess. This had the curious result of Indian cloth losing just that distinctiveness for which it was once world-famous: fast colours. In mineral dyes, fastness and shades depended on strict adherence to the permissible recipes by which the basic colours could be mixed. The dye-maker's agents disseminated these prescribed formulae through demonstrations, but they rarely reached the small-scale user, who in any case did not seem interested. As a result, by 1900 colour on cotton cloth woven in handlooms was known to be as a rule 'ephemeral,' and the shades themselves had been reduced to a 'common character.'[17] Good, expert handling of the synthetic dyes was rare; no more than a handful of such references can be found in the sources.

How did weavers respond to bad work? In cotton weaving, there was always the option of buying ready-dyed yarn from the mills. Thus, the Madurai Mill yarn eventually eliminated much local dyeing of cotton over a large area of the south. Second, there was the option of switching to plain weaving, which usually implied a switch to coarser and thicker weaving, that is of cloth where the texture mattered more than the colour. This happened in many small towns of Bombay distant from the mills, where coloured yarn sold at a premium. Third, the weavers could return to the vegetable dyes despite the increased cost. This option was important especially for silks where quality mattered much more than the cost of the cloth. The option was not overly cost-ineffective, either, for such dyes as indigo, where the price difference between local and imported dyes was narrower than in the other major shades. Fourth, the dyer or weaver handling the mineral dyes had the desperate choice of cheapening his labour as the quality of the cloth degraded.[18] Finally, there was always the option of exit, and in numerous instances weaving simply declined because of degeneration in colour use.

None of these options made the craftsman better off, and some were impossible to sustain. Even where mill-dyed yarn was bought – the least painful of the alternatives – the weavers were paying the mills an implicit dyeing charge that they could easily appropriate if they knew the right recipes. The need to learn, therefore, was obvious. This realization manifested itself in demand for dyeing schools from urban weavers. But the Industry Department's demonstrations in dyeing, as much as those of the dye suppliers, were confined to the big cities where both coloured yarn and information were cheaper to obtain.

Thus, by and large, learning was as badly needed as it was rare. I have before quoted Marsden, a textile expert in the employ of the Madras government, who noted that the informal knowledge of the Indian dyer was not enough. Trained chemists would do a better job (see Chapter 3). Marsden was probably right about the general rule. There were exceptions to the rule, where capitalists and cooperation worked to reorganize knowledge (discussed next).

The state, I have argued, was a weak agent in technological change. The profit-motive was a more powerful agent. But the profit-motive needed to join the leadership of powerful people. Any technological adaptation could anger and upset some members of the community. The leadership was crucial to contain such sentiments.

Market, institutions, and technological change

Access to long-distance markets had a bearing on technological change in two ways, by expanding marketing opportunities and by providing avenues of accumulation. At the tum of the century, a common argument heard from weavers against the fly-shuttle was that it would raise production, glut the market, and reduce prices.[19] Forty years later, such arguments became rare, and the more usual objection to new tools was simply the higher cost of some of them. Some contemporaries saw the argument as a sign of the proverbial conservatism of the weaver. The solution was education.[20] In fact, the fear was a justifiable one in a rural and traditional setting, where the market was small and local, and too dependent on the harvest. That is, the argument made sense when the prospect of marketing the additional output was not obvious. This problem was less serious in points of trade or in cloth with a developed long-distance trade. For an example of a product, the fly-shuttle 'conferred a boon where kiles, Madras Handkerchiefs, Sarees and Dhotis of finer yarn and clothes with borders are manufactured.'[21] These were commercialized cloths with rising markets.

In explaining limited diffusion, officials routinely alleged 'conservatism.' There are indeed instances of resistance, rejection, and even violent collective reaction to experiments. In one case, local weavers burnt a loom-inventor's house along with all traces of the loom. Workers in the Madras School of Arts factory went on strike for being asked to learn the use of spring tension. Their fellows boycotted fly-shuttle users in Bihar.[22] It is difficult to assess these cases because almost always it is the action that is recorded, not its antecedents. They might stem from a fear of competition. But equally, the entrepreneurial activity might have been seen as a breach of collective unity.

In some cases at least, resistance stemmed from the extent to which merchants with a background outside weaving dominated contracts. Learning was potentially a means of shaking off such domination, so 'the banias don't like it' if the weavers did 'earn a little more to be able to purchase flyshuttle looms.'[23] In other instances, from Madras, from southern and coastal Andhra, and Bengal, merchants resisted change or forced progressive weavers to backslide.

Most new tools and processes in weaving created a problem for the existing institutional setup. Around 1900, the standard organization of production in the rural areas and much urban weaving was the family. Its division of labour based on age and sex was peculiarly suited to textile production. But the family was not compatible with many of the new tools and processes. For example, a warping mill could not be set up in a house. Poorer weavers' houses were not always adapted to broad-width weaving, whereas experiments showed that the wider the cloth, the greater were the gains from the fly-shuttle. The new changes also sometimes saved on labour, which was attractive only when labour was hired. For example, a new sizing machine designed in Madras made seven out of ten workers redundant for the same quantum of work. 'So our people are unwilling to see their women thus deprived of their domestic employment.'[24]

Again, the fly-shuttle was not a problem when installed on a small scale. However, mass installation of fly-shuttles raised the prospect that the pace of weaving would get ahead of the processing capacity of local family labour. Processing machines such as the warping and sizing mill not only displaced family helpers. A collection of such factories could encourage weaving factories to start with frame looms and hired labour. And once that shift was made, it was only a small step from the weaving factory to a powerloom workshop. This sequence – fly-shuttle to warping mills to handloom factories to powerlooms – is a rough characterization of how large weaving towns progressed.

In explaining their rejection of processing machinery, weavers did argue that new machines would render family labour unemployed and should not be accepted.[25] We cannot say precisely what alternatives the women and children of rural weaving families considered. Weavers did not often work as farm labourers, especially in south India. Wages, as far as one can see, were low, lower than those of field labour. Processing wages were low because in the summer months when weavers were busy, the demand for farm labour was usually low. If these conditions made it attractive for most workers to work from home, the low wage was an attraction for the employer to induce them to go to a factory.

In many industrial and trading towns of relatively recent origin, these conditions weakened. A 1950s report summed up the Tamil Nadu experience, 'in the race of improving techniques and producing new lines, owners of factories generally led, and the master-weavers avidly followed.'[26] These towns offered concentrated and diverse markets, opportunities of accumulation, a labour market in both weaving and processing, and a fluid class structure. Technological dynamism flourished on this ground. The largest of the weaving towns fulfilled these conditions. They grew as markets with the opening of the railways arid new trade routes. They were destinations for some of the recent mass migrations of weavers, who came to the towns as sellers of labour. Jointly induced by capital and wage labour, these towns saw the growth of a new institution, the handloom factory, which pioneered the use of new looms and warping mills. The wider product range of a large textile-trading town presented the weavers with the opportunity to specialize. Some of the products taken up in the factories were new ones capable of large-scale production but were not standardized enough to be taken up by the mills.[27] This process is seen in the experience of Sholapur in western India and Salem in the south. In 1950, these were two of the four largest weaving towns in India, with about 10,000 handlooms working in Sholapur, and more than 20,000 in Salem. In the major towns (see also Chapter 6), new technologies accompanied accumulation by weavers and the development of new divisions of labour.

The first Sholapur factories were established in the 1890s. Migrant workers, usually single males, increasingly populated these factories.[28] In the interwar period, this work happened in a shop attached to the factory. Stick-warping (discussed previously) was never common in Sholapur. Peg-warping, where the function of the sticks was performed by pegs attached to a wall, was more common. By the early 1930s, this was giving way to beams prepared in the factories, and fly-shuttle pit looms were becoming popular, clearly at a faster rate than in the other weaving towns of the region. The rapidity of these changes can be seen by comparing two reports on Sholapur, N.M. Joshi's in 1932 and R.G. Kakade's eight years later. Within this time, warp mills had completely taken over. Winding of hank yarn onto bobbins for the weft thread, the last operation to be mechanized, was done in multi-spindle winders. Two-thirds of the looms were fitted with overhead attachments for designed weaving. And even dyeing, which previously had no significant presence in Sholapur, was beginning to emerge as a separate branch of the industry.

Salem had, in 1905, the good fortune to be selected as the site for one of Chatterton's major projects, a model handloom factory that would demonstrate the use of the warping mill. The factory did not survive beyond 1909. Even during its lifetime, the factory faced problems with its workers, who were neither good enough nor steady, being the 'waifs and strays' of the community. But the factory achieved its aim. According to the Madras District Gazetteer for Salem, published in 1918, street warping had been 'almost completely superseded by the hand warping mill, . . . an ingenious adaptation of the old-fashioned horizontal warping mill used in Europe.'[29] Thereafter, many factories were set up in Salem. A 1950s source defined a factory as a unit that received warps ready for use from a warping mill. All units hired labour. But the workers preferred factory work, as there they could use a ready-made warp and did not have to perform a variety of tasks. In appearance, however, these various units were not markedly different. The astute master-weavers, in a ploy to avoid the labour inspector and the trade unionist, did not allow the factory 'to present an imposing facade of prosperity.'[30] The factory worker was said to earn a better wage than the puttingout weaver. But, in times of crises, the Sholapur factories did impose wage cuts, which led to the first major strikes in a handloom town.[31]

The successful diffusion of tools in these towns involved the agency of castes and individuals. The community that saw themselves as specialist 'caste weavers,' prided themselves on their skills and wanting to retain and develop these skills was more likely to share information about new tools within it. The significant contrast here was with a large number of rural weavers. Although mobile and urbanizing, these groups were not associated with the new forms of urban enterprise in weaving.

'Community' could become an important resource in several senses. First, in these towns, the handloom trade was dominated by persons with a background in weaving who saw themselves as the weaver elite. Capital accumulated in the hands of people who understood the production process closely and retained direct ties with production. Second, social organization and associations among weavers made it possible for some of the profits to be channelled into the common good, which ranged from schools to temples to the work of charities during famine relief. A sentiment about 'caste' thus bridged inequality to some extent. Third, 'community' could play a guild-like role, in that it could disseminate technical information more easily within a group while restricting its access by outsiders. Finally, a community in some cases played a role in the learning and diffusion of new tools. The problem with training was that while formal systems of training had poor reach, systems of informal learning were not always efficient in handling new principles as the history of dyeing illustrated. The solution, where one was obtained, was found within the tradition.

The term 'community' is used here in the sense of a group that communicates internally with relative ease. It is not necessary to assume that a communicating group was also a group made of equals. Some of the weaving communities widely regarded as innovative were far from egalitarian.[32] And yet, a shared sense of skilled artisan status did cut across the hierarchy. Thus, inequality was often built into caste identity. Almost without exception, 'leaders' who combined trade with education and training bridged inequality and played a role in the propagation of ideas. One of the striking examples of this appears from Madurai (see Chapters 4 and 6).

'Community' has had a range of applications in Indian business history but usually in the context of mercantile-financial groups who set up large-scale industrial or trading firms.[33] The literature on small firms has recently discovered 'community,' mainly in its social role. Haynes, for example, shows how charitable expenditure was a means to diffuse the tensions arising from increasing economic differentiation in a formerly relatively homogeneous weaver group.[34] It is clear from these works that caste associations and collective bodies were often revived, recreated, and invented in the interwar period, especially among migrant groups or groups that were changing rather rapidly in economic terms. Such institutions were prominent in Sholapur and Salem, but their technological role is almost always hidden from view and can at best be inferred.

With the Sourashtras of Madurai, where some of the most successful adaptation to the mineral dyes occurred, this role was more obvious and a subject of considerable discussion among contemporaries. The Sourashtras, like the Padmasalis of Sholapur, were producers-cum-merchants and had a strong hold on the local industry. They were educationally advanced relative to the average weaver in south India. They were a relatively small group and spatially concentrated, accounting for a remarkable level of cohesion revealed in various community-bound activities. The main products for which Madurai was known were coloured silk garments, especially sarees. Madurai silk derived its distinctness from the red dye with which the yarn was coloured.[35] The dye came from a local plant, chay-root.

In 1895, Tulasi Ram, a weaver trained in Japan, realized by chance the possibility of reproducing the chay-root brownish-red shade with alizarine, thus making it a fast colour. The technical success of his experiments, and the commercial success of a factory he later set up, derived from a suitable mix of local mordanting materials and techniques with German dyes. Once the technique was found usable, it spread quickly among the community, and 'red factories' mushroomed. Most of these factories were small-scale extensions of weaving establishments. Some contemporaries attributed the quick spread of the new knowledge and yet its restriction to one town and one group, to the role of 'caste' as a craft guild. What mattered was not only that the owners of the dyeing factories knew the specific formulae, but that they could secure cooperation from the workers not to work for or divulge these to outsiders. There was an unstated pact not to employ any outside labourers in processes 'wherever an element of brainwork is wanted.'[36] Dyeing was not the only example of innovation in Madurai, which was generally a site of active experimentation. As Chatterton wrote, 'nearly all the so-called improvements have been tried in Madurai, and the fact that they have rejected most of them may be taken . . . as evidence of their unsuitability to Indian conditions.'[37]

While in general weavers' handling of the new dyes led to bad work, the Madurai experience suggests that only a weaver could creatively adapt to the crisis. A hereditary dyer knew the uses of plants and roots, but a weaver knew the cloth. Where the cloth was as delicate and as expensive as silk sarees, it was natural that the weaver would have a say in dyeing. A cooperative community made the weaver better equipped in sharing and restricting access to the results of experiments. It is this combination of the characteristics of the product and that of its makers which ensured that one of the most striking examples of learning occurred in Madurai.[38] A final lesson of this episode is that some types of knowledge allowed a greater role for the community. Certain dyeing formulae never became widely diffused in the way the fly-shuttle or the warping mill did, because chemical processes were embodied in the persons who practiced the craft and therefore were relatively excludable. An employer would need to hire a skilled Sourashtra weaver to obtain that knowledge. Relationships mattered more here.

Conclusion

The main message of the chapter is that technological change in handlooms was a response to changes within the handloom-weaving industry. That is, the process was driven, not by government campaigning, but by the profit-motive of the artisan-capitalists who served markets that did not directly compete with the machine-made cloth. Those weavers who did not face such market prospects and did not have many leaders among them stayed conservative for a good reason.

Profitability or leadership alone does not explain innovation. Institutional change was another precondition. The traditional mode of organization was incompatible with many of the technological alternatives. The family firm in rural areas had limited means to employ new tools or labour, limited means to experiment with new tools, and supplied markets too dependent on seasonally variable rural demand. The diffusion of new tools needed different circumstances, that is, new firms, collectives, different markets, and products. This requirement explains why diffusion was limited.

The factories were the best sites to install some of the new tools like bigger looms or more overhead attachments or warping systems. The towns that became the main settlements of skilled weavers saw significant changes. Technological change, therefore, had an urban bias and a scale bias. Economic constraints were weaker in the towns. Social capital played a positive role; leading members of the weaving groups were sometimes politically connected as well. The fact that capitalists and producers regarded themselves as part of the same community enabled cooperation, maintenance of trust, easier contract-enforcement and dispute-settlement, greater commitment to production, and the spread of new techniques within the community while keeping these techniques a secret from others. These functions were not equally important everywhere, but they were critical in an informal industry that lived without too much reliance on public authority or formal law.

A great deal of the more successful adaptations was taking place in clusters or hubs, rather than in the isolated village. Why did the settlement pattern change?

Notes

1 Madras, *Preliminary Report on the Survey of Cottage Industries in Cuddapah District*, Madras: Government Press, 1927, 11; D.M. Amalsad, *The Development of the Madras Handkerchief and Lungy and Kaily Industry in the Madras Presidency*, Madras: Government Press, 1926, 6.

2 Amalsad, *Development*, 4; N.M. Joshi, *Urban Handicrafts in The Bombay-Deccan*, Poona: Gokhale Institute of Politics and Economics, 1936, 105; Peter Harnetty, 'Deindustrialization Revisited: The Handloom Weavers of the Central Provinces of India,' *Modern Asian Studies*, 25(4), 1991, 455–510, cited text appears in p. 494.

3 India, *Fact-Finding Committee: Handlooms and Mills*, Calcutta: Government Press, 1942, 22.

4 A.K. Bagchi, *Private Investment in India, 1900–1939*, Cambridge: Cambridge University Press, 1970, Section 7.2.

5 See the section 'Deindustrialization' in Irfan Habib, 'Studying a Colonial Economy: Without Perceiving Colonialism,' *Modern Asian Studies*, 19(4), 1985, 355–81.

6 See Tirthankar Roy, 'Acceptance of Innovations in Early Twentieth Century Indian Weaving,' *Economic History Review*, 55(4), 2002, 507–32. In more detail: (1) four samples were taken from the list of cloths where mills and handlooms competed keenly (source: India, *Fact-Finding Committee*, XXIX). The samples were all from Madras, and the plain cotton apparel called 'dhoti.' (2) Yarn cost was estimated from yarn prices, on the assumption that each lb of yarn makes 5 yards of cloth (source of yarn prices: *Fact-Finding Committee*, 93). (3) Capital cost was estimated on the assumption that the average life of a loom is ten years, and rate of interest 6% p.a. Capital cost includes the cost of looms, reeds and heddles, shuttles, and of loom construction. Loom cost was approximately one-third of the total capital cost of setting up a fly-shuttle factory in the mid-1930s. It is assumed that the same proportion applies to the other loom types as well. (4) Handloom wages were estimated as piece rates (weaver's net receipt per yard). The average wage is an average of three samples from costs of production data in *FactFinding Committee*, XXVIIl. These wages were converted into time rates. In the case of a family, the 'wage' is the weaving charges received by the family. (5) The number of workers required per loom was taken as two for a fly-shuttle loom and frame-loom, and one for a powerloom. The average costs that result tally closely with the reported final sale price of these products, the cost being about 80 per cent of the price.

7 A mill weaver (tending one loom) earned about double the wage of a fly-shuttle weaver in the 1930s, K.S. Venkatraman, 'The Economic Condition of Handloom Weavers,' *Journal of the University of Bombay*, 5, 1936–7, 75–104.

8 Market segmentation is explored in Chapter 3. See also Haruka Yanagisawa, 'The Handloom Industry and Its Market Structure: The Case of The Madras Presidency in the First Half of the Twentieth Century,' *Indian Economic and Social History Review*, 30(1), 1993, 1–27.

9 'The . . . tools . . . are so coarse, and apparently so inadequate to their purpose, that it creates surprise how he can ever effect his undertaking,' H.T. Colebrook, *Remarks on the Husbandry and Commerce of Bengal*, Calcutta, 1804, 31.

10 India, *Fact-Finding Committee*, 295.

11 A comprehensive statement of the technological problem in handloom can be found in three essays presented at the first industrial conference at Benares, 1905, and published in the proceedings of the conference. The essays are by Raoji Patel, Director of Agriculture, Baroda state ('Handloom weaving in India'), E.B. Havell, Superintendent of the Calcutta School of Art ('Powerloom mills

and handlooms'), and Alfred Chatterton, then Superintendent of the Madras School of Art ('Industrial work in India'). Havell played a significant role in popularizing the fly-shuttle slay in Bengal, and Chatterton is associated with the warping mill. *Report of the First Indian Industrial Conference (Benares, 1905)*, Allahabad, 1906. See also 'Selected biographies' at the end of the book.

12 Cited by A.C. Chatterjee, *Notes on the Industries of the United Provinces*, Allahabad: Government Press, 1908, 24.

13 Chatterton served at different times as a professor at the Madras Engineering College, superintendent of the Madras School of Arts, and director of industry at Madras and at Mysore.

14 See discussions in India, *Indian Industrial Commission*, vol. 3 of 5, Calcutta: Government Press, 1918, 186, 483.

15 D. Haynes, 'Logic of the Artisan Firm in a Capitalist Economy: Handloom Weavers and Technological Change in Western India, 1880–1947,' in B. Stein and S. Subrahmanyam, eds., *Institutions and Economic Change in South Asia*, New Delhi: Government Press, 1996, 173–205.

16 Dyeing is a good example of the way in which castes disappear as occupations do. Nineteenth-century sources represent dyers as distinct communities. For nearly 60 years after the first occupational census, 1881, dyer castes appear in one census only to be merged with other occupations, excluded, or forgotten in the next.

17 S.M. Edwardes, *A Monograph upon the Silk Fabrics of the Bombay Presidency*, Bombay: Government Press, 1900, 13.

18 For examples of each, see N.G. Ranga, *Economics of Handlooms*, Bombay: Taraporevala, 1930, 6; S.V. Telang, *Report on Handloom Weaving Industry in the Bombay Presidency*, Bombay: Government Press, 1932, 9; Madras, *Preliminary Report on the Survey of Cottage Industries in Bellary District*, Madras: Government Press, 1927, 6; India, *Indian Industrial Commission*, vol. 3, 155.

19 'The use of improved looms would vitally affect their interests by cheapening production,' Chatterton, cited by Chatterjee, *Notes on Industries*, 23. Harnetty describes an outburst of resentment towards the fly-shuttle in central India during market crises in the years of the depression, 'Deindustrialization revisited,' 494.

20 Chatterjee, *Notes on Industries*, 23. Also, evidence of a weaving assistant of the Madras government at the *Indian Industrial Commission*, III: 'the preliminary step should be to educate the weavers before they could receive any improved ideas,' 185.

21 Ranga, *Economics of Handlooms*, 269.

22 Edgar Thurston, *Tribes and Castes of Southern India*, Madras: Government Press, 1909, 4, 270; India, *Indian Industrial Commission*, vol. 3, 125.

23 India, *Indian Industrial Commission*, m, 185; *Census*, 196.

24 Ranga, *Economics of Handlooms*, 268.

25 See previous n.; Harnetty, 'Deindustrialization Revisited,' discusses another example.

26 All India Handloom Board, *Survey*, 29.

27 In Malabar, the Basel Mission's factories switched to shirting, a wholly non-traditional product. In Sholapur, and several regions of the north, weavers took up furnishing fabrics. In Punjab, narrowwidth cloths were associated with the first factories and the use of the fly-shuttle.

28 Joshi, *Urban Handicrafts*, 72.

29 *Salem Gazetteer*, 268.

30 All India Handloom Board, *Survey*, 32, 135.

31 Venkatraman, 'Economic Condition,' 99; All India Handloom Board, *Survey*, 32; Bombay, *Report of the Sholapur Handloom Weavers Enquiry Committee*, Bombay: Government Press, 1947.

32 The Madurai Sourashtras, for example, were not generally well off, even though on average better off than other weaver groups. 'Many writers have mistaken the skill, energy and organising capacity displayed by a few big successes among [the Sourashtras] for general prosperity,' Ranga, *Economics of Handlooms*, 156.

33 For a discussion of related works, see Tirthankar Roy, 'Capitalism and Community: A Study of the Madurai Sourashtras,' *Indian Economic and Social History Review*, 34(4), 1997, 437–65.

34 D. Haynes, 'Artisan Cloth-Producers and the Emergence of Powerloom Manufacture in Western India, 1920–1950,' *Past and Present*, 172, 2001, 170–98.

35 The following paragraph draws on Roy, 'Capitalism and community.'

36 K.R.R. Sastry, *South Indian Gilds*, Madras: Indian Publishing House, 1925, 26.

37 Cited by Thurston, *Tribes and Castes*, vol. 4.

38 From elsewhere in the country, a few examples of a successful switch to mineral dyes can be found. Both Salem and Sholapur expanded this branch of the industry, and did so successfully. On Sholapur, see R.G. Kakade, *A Socio-Economic Survey of Weaving Communities in Sholapur*, Poona: Gokhale Institute of Politics and Economics, 1947, 21. But in general, cotton weavers were not keen on experiments with colour, since coloured mill yarn was available.

6

TOWNS AND REGIONS

'Handloom weaving,' the Fact-finding Committee report said in 1942, 'has now become largely an urban industry.' This was true. In parallel with the concentration of capital, the industry concentrated regionally. The main hubs were a few towns in Maharashtra and clustered settlements in Tamil Nadu. These towns and regions enabled a substantial increase in the capacity to trade over long distances, attracted migrants, led to improvements in technology, and to the emergence of politically connected and influential groups and individuals from within the weaving community. The chapter studies these emerging urban systems.

The first part of the chapter will look at the statistics available to show which regions and which towns were leading this change. The second part will study the history of a cluster of towns in western and southern India to illustrate the point that urbanization of looms was much more than just urbanization of looms, it was part of the many-sided process that Douglas Haynes calls the emergence of small-town capitalism.

An estimate of urbanization, 1899–1940

An estimate of urbanization in the Madras Presidency can be made by comparing two surveys forty years apart, looms in major centres in 1899 from Edgar Thurston's monograph on silk (the looms were both cotton and silk), and the Fact-finding Committee's appendix supplying similar data for 1940–2, but only on cotton looms. Neither of these two sources claimed to be a proper census or was based on a definition of what made a handloom town. Still, it is unlikely that any major centre that would qualify for inclusion had been left out.

Table 6.1 shows that the concentration of looms in towns more than doubled in these 40 years. In 1940, weaving, if it was not mainly an urban occupation, was not a rural industry either. However, these data come from south India. The regions did differ a lot. The comparable figure for Bombay, in 1940, is 35 percent and for Central Provinces 19 percent. In Eastern India, too, the industry was semi-rural. For other provinces in British India estimates are not available as the statistics are not detailed enough. This gap, however, suggests the absence of large agglomerations and a smaller urban percentage in northern and eastern India. For a visual description compare Maps 6.1 and 6.2.

The 45 percent in Madras Presidency (Table 6.1) could be a low estimate. First, 1940 data are only on cotton looms, whereas silks had always concentrated in the towns. In 1961, 74 percent of the silk looms in Tamil Nadu

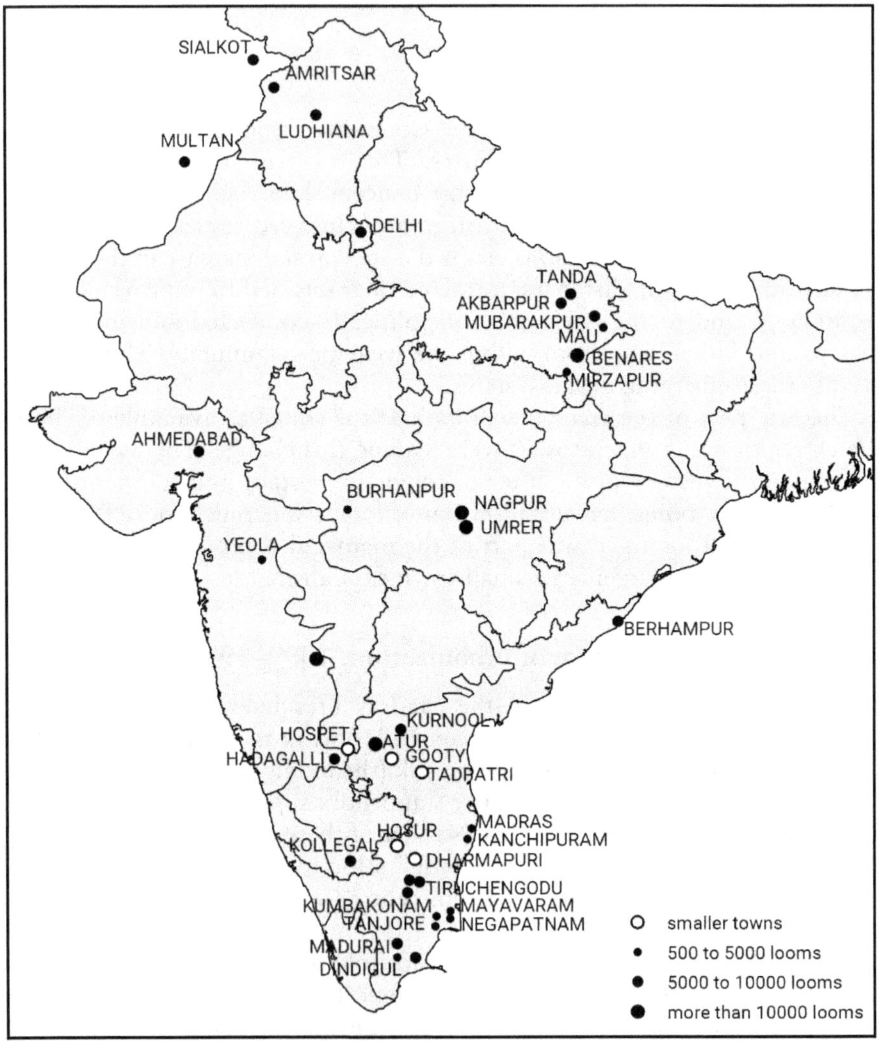

Map 6.1 Weaving towns around 1900

Source: Author, based on data discussed in the text

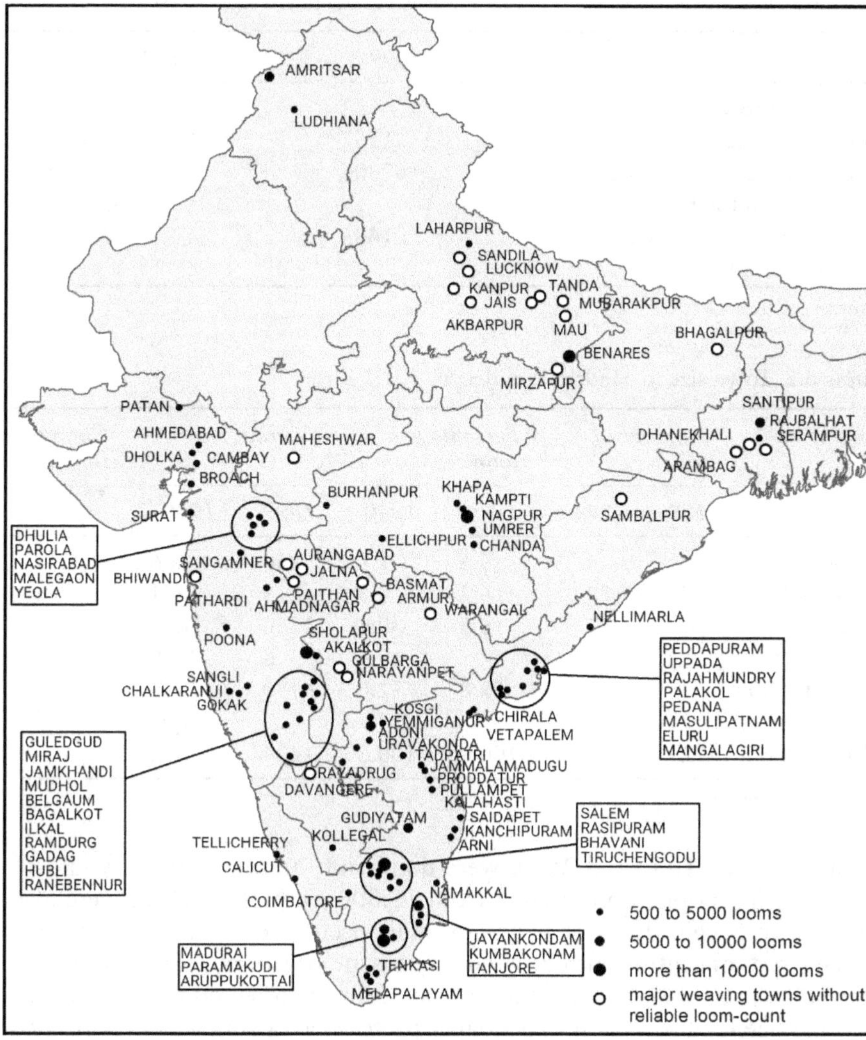

Map 6.2 Weaving towns around 1940–1950

Source: Author, based on data discussed in the text

were based in nine towns, the smallest of which had 300 looms and the largest, Kanchipuram, 6500. Second, Fact-finding Committee's list excludes centres with less than 300 looms. Even the coverage of large centres was not quite complete; data related only to 'centres visited' by the committee's members.

A break-up by town-size shows where the growth occurred (Table 6.2). In number, share in looms, and average size, the medium-sized towns with

Table 6.1 Urbanization of weaving in Madras Presidency, 1899–1940

	1899	*1940*
Number of towns	22	51
Looms in these towns	31557	121028 (cotton)
Looms in Madras Presidency	167806	269306 (cotton)
Percentage in towns	19	45
The average size of towns measured in looms	1434	2373

Source: See text.

Table 6.2 Town size in Madras Presidency

Looms	*Number of towns*		*Percentage of looms*		*Average size*		*Common to both years*
	1899	*1940*	*1899*	*1940*	*1899*	*1940*	
< 500	8	6	6.6	1.8	256	366	3
501–1000	7	10	16.2	6.3	716	761	1
1001–2500	4	22	16.5	30.4	1350	1674	1
2501–5000		7		19.5		3379	
5001–10000	3	5	59.8	32.0	6190	7749	2
> 10000		1		9.9		12000	
Total	22	51	100.0	100.0	1434	2373	7

Source: See text.

looms between 1000 and 2500, were dominant. Normally these would be towns with a population ranging from 15,000 to 50,000. These were also places where typically weaving was the main occupation. On the other hand, in the large concentrations like Madurai, Salem, or Coimbatore, handlooms existed as part of a diversified industrial structure oriented to textiles. The average size figures suggest that smaller places were giving way to mid-sized towns. The column 'common to both years' suggests that most mid-sized towns had emerged between these years. In turn, that ties up with the high frequency of weavers' migration.

Madras Presidency was an enormous tract of land, diverse both geographically as well as in terms of the weaving industries within it. Table 6.3 on regional distribution shows where the growth happened and the location of some of the new agglomerations. There are four sub-regions in Table 6.3. As the Maps 6.1 and 6.2 suggest, handloom towns clustered in four areas, Tamil Nadu, Malabar, coastal Andhra Pradesh, and southern Andhra Pradesh, straddling the British Indian districts of the Madras-Deccan and some districts of the Hyderabad state in Telangana.

Table 6.3 Weaving towns by major region

	Coastal Andhra		*Southern Andhra*		*Tamil Nadu*		*Malabar*	
	1899	*1940*	*1899*	*1940*	*1899*	*1940*	*1899*	*1940*
No of towns	1	15	6	10	15	25		1
Average size	256	1054	1660	2049	1423	3368		546
Looms ('000)	0.3	15.8	10.0	20.5	21.3	84.2		0.5
% of the Presidency	0.8	13.7	31.6	16.9	67.6	69.6		0.5
Common instances	None		2		5		None	

Source: See text.

The regions produced different things, and each region had a somewhat different history. The industry along the coasts came under greater outside influence. The coastal Andhra weaving clusters correspond to the region that European traders called Coromandel. Their records suggest that the handloom weaving industry in this part of the eastern coast was spread in groups of villages making mainly exportable textiles. Some of these textiles survived into the twentieth century. In the southwestern coast or Malabar, there was not much export trade. But the Christian missions in this area made efforts to advance handloom weaving. In the interior of the Deccan Plateau, in Bellary, Anantapur, and Warangal, towns did manufacture some traded goods such as carpets and blankets made of local wool, but the area mainly produced plain cotton cloth using a vast supply of local cotton. Before the railways, the expensive method of bullock caravans served trade in this area. The railways revolutionized trade. But trade also invited merchants from outside the region to come into the towns and settle here. Some of them had influence in the handloom weaving industry in the interwar period. The Tamil Nadu cluster had some similarity with southern Andhra until 1900, but the two diverged later. Later in the chapter, descriptions of Salem will discuss more fully the distinctness of Tamil Nadu.

Settlement patterns also differed. For example, Map 6.2 shows that some large towns enabled the emergence of satellites around them. This neighbourhood effect will be discussed later. Leaving out the eastern and the western coastal regions, the data of the tables and the two maps show that the new towns and additional looms were concentrated in Tamil Nadu. The southern Andhra towns were larger in 1899, but the ranking reversed in 1940. In other words, the region which suffered a relative de-urbanization was southern Andhra.[1] Repeated famines in the Deccan region between 1876 and 1899 caused considerable dislocation to the weaving industry in this area. Adoni, the premier town of southern

Andhra, did not expand at all in 40 years. In the 1920s, N.G. Ranga's description of urban weaving in this area appears (in 1928–9) quite dark in tone. Here ordinary weavers were bound in an exploitative three-tier hierarchy involving yarn traders, master-weavers, and wage-workers. Perpetual indebtedness secured a form of bondage extending over generations. Reports of physical oppression were not uncommon. Weavers were migrating towards the Maharashtra region.

Masulipatnam, a trading port of the seventeenth and eighteenth century, was often mentioned in the nineteenth century but mainly in connection with dyeing and printing. In the 1920s, Ranga toured this area and confirmed the rural character of it, except for the manufacturer of a highly successful export fabric called Madras handkerchief.[2] This was manufactured in a few towns in the Krishna and Godavari deltas. The trade was controlled by wholesale merchants based in Madras city. The two deltas experienced economic growth based on commercial agriculture and trade from the late-nineteenth century. The rising urbanization here reflected the effects of agricultural commercialization.[3]

By contrast with all other regions, the growth of looms in the two main Tamil Nadu towns, Salem and Madurai, was quite extraordinary (Table 6.4). Both towns grew by attracting trade, capital, and skills away from some of the smaller centres. Around 1900, Edgar Thurston compared Madurai and Kumbakonam, both silk-weaving centres and both known for their use of the red dye, but one rising and the other stagnant. He attributed the difference to the greater success of Madurai dyers in adapting to the new colours. The same reason was cited elsewhere for the stagnation of looms in another silk-weaving town, Tanjore.[4]

A closer look inside the towns that grew so much so fast will reveal what made them such business hubs.

Table 6.4 Looms in some southern towns

	1899	*1908*	*1918*	*1929*	*1940*	*1955*
Adoni	7000				7280	
Kumbakonam	6300	2000			1766	3000
Kanchipuram	5270				4700	6500
Madurai	2000		7820	9500	6580	
Salem	neg				8000	22300

Notes: Based on Edgar Thurston, *Monograph on the Cotton Fabric Industry of the Madras Presidency*, Madras: Government Press, 1897; India, *The Imperial Gazetteers of India*, London: HMSO, 1908–9, articles on the places cited in the table; H. Maxwell-Lefroy and E. C. Ansorge, *Report on an Enquiry into the Silk Industry in India*, Calcutta: Government Press, 1916–18; Provincial Banking Enquiry Committee reports and evidences; India, *Fact-finding Committee: Handlooms and Mills*, Calcutta: Government Press, 1942; India, *Textile Enquiry Committee*, Delhi: Government Press, 1954; and the Census of India, 1961, various state reports.

Salem and Madurai

In the mid-nineteenth century, Salem was not a large textile town. It had a branch of the East India Company, which effectively ended in the 1820s. It is the railways (opened in 1862), together with the cotton export trade and the growth of cotton spinning, that made it a hub of handloom weaving later in the century. The railways connected the cloth, yarn, and cotton trade, and connected Salem with nearby villages where peasant families invested in looms. As trade grew, so did the prominence of capitalists. Many rose from the ranks of the artisans to join trading in cotton, yarn, dyes, cloth, and gold-thread.

In Salem, the dominant capitalists were handloom weavers by their caste occupation. The weaving caste group Devanga, who formed about half the weaver population, spoke Kannada and Telugu, the former linguistic group tracing its entry into the Tamil region to the Anglo-Mysore wars, and the latter to the fall of the medieval empire Vijayanagara in the sixteenth century. The other castes in Salem were Tamil-speaking people. In the twentieth century, there was another kind of influx to Salem. Many people without prior experience in weaving and many women took up weaving in Salem.[5]

Ownership of capital had a positive association with weaving. The weaving caste groups known as Kaikolars and Salis owned the processing houses. At the end of the twentieth century, random lists of social leaders in Salem would include families that had been artisanal a hundred years before. Some of them invested money in factories, like spinning mills or dyeing workshops.

Around 1940, some master-weavers owned handloom-weaving factories and engaged household weavers on contract in Salem. The common unit was not a factory but a substantial household that operated four to five looms each and employed hired labour. The hired labourers or loomless weavers, called by the generic epithet for labourers, coolies, were of recent origin in Salem.[6]

The emergence of artisan-capitalists in these two towns derived from the weavers' control over the yarn and cloth trades. With the start of spinning mills locally, weavers could build direct transactions with spinning mills and bypass one set of traders. By contrast, in regions that depended on long-distance trade in yarn, the power of traders of non-weaving background was greater. Another factor was the weavers' ability to sell via 'commission agents.' Commission agents sold cloth over a much wider area than a weaver would be able to access and shared the risk with the producer. In Salem, the former system expanded between 1900 and 1925, and, according to a senior merchant, made ordinary weavers better off.[7]

Map 6.2 shows that Salem was one of a set of substantial weaving towns in the region. Over 60 or 70 years, this region emerged as India's premier textile industry complex. Salem, Erode, Tirupur, and Coimbatore are located on a straight line on the highway and railways that connected Madras with the western coast. As the twentieth century ended, these four towns and roughly 20 kilometres north and south of them defined India's most concentrated textile production belt. Coimbatore was a centre of production of spinning and textile machinery; all towns had numerous spinning mills. And several hundred-thousand powerloom factories were working in this area that included two large weaving clusters, Pallipalayam and Komarapalayam. The trajectory of growth started about a century earlier, when Salem – and handloom weaving – were the driving forces.

The growth of Salem as a weaving hub was much noticed and written on. In the Salem Manual of 1883, weaving receives passing mention.[8] Salem does not appear in the Imperial Gazetteers of 1909. The district as a whole of the same name had 13 percent of looms in Tamil Nadu in 1921. From 11,000 looms in the district in 1921, the number increased to 186,000 in 1961, and the percentage increased from 13 to 32. This growth did not all occur inside one town, though the other centres were much smaller and spread out over a large area.

As mentioned before, a government weaving factory was established in Salem in 1906, which through demonstrations, influenced the system of local processing. A.C. Chatterton, the industrial adviser to the provincial government, played a role in its establishment and the campaigns in which the factory was involved.[9] Chatterton's writing suggests that a partnership developed between substantial weavers and the factory in the matter of experimentation with new tools and processes. Although the government factory shut down in 1921, Salem had developed several large warping mills. In 1936, K.S. Venkatraman's compilation of village records in Salem district showed that weavers migrated locally to work in the processing factories or in the large weaving units.[10]

About 40 miles southwest of Salem is one of India's largest textile markets and hubs of the clothing industry, Erode. In the early 1900s, Erode and Salem were both parts of a growing cluster of small towns and big villages that were expanding in population and their engagement with handweaving. The whole cluster moved into powerloom weaving and spinning mills after 1950, rapidly in the 1970s and the 1980s. The most important local resource here was the handloom weavers belonging in the caste groups Kaikolars and Devangas. The farming group known as Gounders joined them later. The traders dealing in handloom cloth came from the weaver castes. Erode emerged as the main point of trade. Merchants based here contracted with weavers spread out over an area 15–20 miles from the town.

The peasant-weavers in this area were an unusual set, not found anywhere else on such a scale. Farmhouses belonging to individuals who owned some land, cattle, and poultry took up weaving on the side. The type was present in the Tiruppur, Palladam, Avanashi, and Pallipalayam areas; all emerged as diversified textile towns later in the twentieth century. Was this an example of 'protoindustrialization,' a strategy of peasant-families to employ their surplus labour? If it was, then why here, why not elsewhere? After all, peasants existed everywhere. Geography suggests one answer to the question. In much of this area, the water table is 300–500 feet below the surface. Investment in looms was a way to diversify and secure incomes; it was a strategy to deploy surplus capital rather than surplus labour. At the same time, the scarcity of water made farming both labour- and capital-intensive. It did not release much surplus family labour. In fact, the weaving workshops in this region hired labour.

If in the Salem story, the capitalists among handloom weavers dominated the industry through their access to trade and processing, in Madurai they did via access to skills and community-based knowledge-exchange. Madurai rose as a centre of political power from the seventeenth century, after the fall of the Vijayanagar Empire empowered some of the former vassals or Nayakas. From the time it became a centre of Nayaka rule and power, Madurai was famous for its textiles, and as a pilgrim centre, being home to the seventeenth-century Meenakshi temple. In the nineteenth century, commercial agriculture was well developed in this region, and, thanks to commodity trade and administration, the district was relatively more urbanized, literate, industrial, and middle class. In the early 1900s, handloom textiles had a singularly dominant presence in the town's retail trade and industry. The population of the town grew from 51,000 in 1871 to 139,000 in 1921, and 425,000 in 1961. The number of handlooms increased from 2,000 in 1897 to 10,000 in 1929 to 20,000–30,000 in 1960.[11] Traditional cloth production grew at the same pace as general urban growth.

The weaving community called Sourashtra dominated the industry, services, and town population. Sourashtra's number increased from 23,000 in 1891, or about a quarter of the town population, to about a hundred thousand or 30–33 percent of the population in the mid-twentieth century. As Edgar Thurston observed in 1909, Madurai owed its growth and position as the second city of Tamil Nadu 'mainly to the Saurashtra merchants and silk weavers, who have now grown into nearly half her population, and who have also come to a foremost place among the ranks of her citizens.'[12] This combined expansion of population, looms, and Sourashtra presence happened because handloom weaving was a source of employment and a field of investment. Handloom weaving was the foundation for the combined growth.

At the end of the twentieth century, when the town was still a major weaving hub, the Sourashtra specialties were silk saree with gold-thread border, and a fine cotton saree tie-dyed on cloth and bordered with gold-thread, called 'Chungadi.' A century earlier, the town manufactured similar products, but used more gold thread than coloured cotton. In any case, in the twentieth century, Madurai developed a huge brand-equity in handloom silk and fine cotton sarees. With that reputation as the basis, the industry also made a wide variety of other types of clothes in the twentieth century.

Around 1900, two factors had come together to contribute to the reputation Madurai had developed in handloom sarees: the skill involved in handling unithread silk yarn and the quality of hand-dyeing. Both skills were Sourashtra 'secrets.' The former skill seemingly disappeared later, but high-quality dyeing remained for a long time a Sourashtra enterprise.

The three permanent sites involved in the making of a saree were: the weaver's home, the dye-work, and the shops that dealt in both the retail and wholesale business. Merchants who owned the shops linked these sites to outstation agents and sometimes owned the dye-work. Another connecting agent was the master-weavers who mediated between the weavers and the merchants. All of these actors were Sourashtras in the early-twentieth century if we consider the arrangement inside the town. They were not only 'skillful and industrious workmen,' but also 'themselves retail the cloths which they weave without the intervention of [non-Sourashtra] middlemen.'[13] However, in the 1920s and the 1930s, marketing of Madurai cloth found outlets in distant cities, and the agents and shops in Bombay, Madras, and Calcutta were not Sourashtra enterprises.

The growth of the cloth and yarn trade was a major source of the weavers' accumulation of capital. In the 1920s, much of Madurai output still went to south Indian towns such as Madras, Salem, Tanjore, and Kumbakonam. But a lot went beyond the Presidency via Madras. Some of the distant markets for Madurai cloth were new ones: Southeast Asia, Ceylon, Bombay, Calcutta, and Delhi.[14] The main raw materials, silk and cotton yarn, dyes and gold-thread were once locally made or made within India. By 1900, all of these were mainly imported. China silk replaced the coarser and badly graded Bengal silk, French jari replaced costlier native south Indian around the 1890s, and German dyes replaced, though partially, the vegetable dyestuff from the 1870s.

Manmade dyes, as Chapters 3 and 5 showed, had a traumatic impact on the quality of dyeing almost everywhere. But not in Madurai. That story need not be repeated. One corollary of that story was that the successful use of the dye was associated with cooperation, leadership, and entrepreneurship. Madurai had all three. Around 1930, Sourashtras controlled the textile trade in a city that accounted for about half of Tamil Nadu's silk cloth production.[15] Innovations were not restricted to dyeing. Around 1900, a Sourashtra weaver took a patent for a loom which had a shedding apparatus better-suited to weave borders. Others quickly adopted it, though in disregard of royalty rights, leading to a long lawsuit. The switch from stick-warping to pegs and beams happened en masse in Madurai under the initiative of K.L.M. Balaraman. Another leading figure, Varada Iyer, redesigned the Jacquard for handlooms in the 1940s.

Handloom weaving was the foundation for industrialization here. The history of the five richest business families of the town around 1996 showed that in 1900 their assets were in the silk cloth trade, China silk trade, jari trade, and dyehouse ownership. A generation later, they had invested in agricultural land, rice and oil mills, powerloom weaving, spinning mills, and the making of gold jewellery. In the second half of the twentieth century, Sourashtra capital moved into basic metals, engineering, spinning mills, grain mills, powerloom weaving, and chemicals; whereas many ordinary weavers became masons, brick-layers, tile-makers, carpenters, blacksmiths, drivers, and jewel-smiths. All of these families, over several generations, made donations to various community-bound charities and social programmes. Education drove the community out of textiles and into the services. In 1900, the middle class would consist of brokers and commission agents. In 1960 or 1970, the Sourashtra middle-class included doctors, pleaders, engineers, photographers, priests, goldsmiths, astrologers, and teachers.[16] At the end of the twentieth century, most members of the community worked outside the town.

With trade and production so secure, and their population growing, Sourashtras experienced a sort of cultural rebirth. The period between 1880 and 1920 witnessed the most significant attempts to recreate a Sourashtra identity. The institutions and cultural movements which involved Sourashtras as a collective and defined their community-ness – linguistic and literary movements, Brahmanic claims, the Sourashtra Sabha, education, guilds, and cooperative societies – had their origins in these decades. This was the period of Sourashtra renaissance in the double sense of revitalization of language and reinterpretation of tradition. The three key elements in this movement were language, religion, and social support. The idea of a community took shape through these efforts. It was a product of Sourashtra enterprise as much as it shaped it. To some extent, and perhaps increasingly, collective institutions like temples, charities, and schools were being used as the means to reduce and overcome economic inequality within the group. This story has been told in more detail elsewhere.[17]

The Salem or the Madurai model reappears all over India, more rarely in the north or the east, and somewhat more frequently in the west. Consider some of these examples.

The rest of India

The Indo-Gangetic Basin had emerged as a major concentration of urban artisanal activity from the time of the rule by the Mughal Empire. Following the collapse of the empire, this region de-urbanized. With the railways connecting it with the port cities and their middle-class consumers from the late-nineteenth century, some of these towns revived again.

Table 6.5 shows that the larger weaving towns in the Indo-Gangetic Basin – Benares, Ludhiana, and Tanda in the table – saw significant growth. The somewhat later growth of Kanpur is striking because Kanpur was not an old weaving centre. It was a garrison town that industrialized rapidly thanks to European investment, easy access to raw materials like cotton and leather, and railway access to Calcutta and Delhi. As it did, the growth of population in the town created a large in-house market for locally produced

Table 6.5 Looms in some northern towns

	1862	*1904–10*	*1923*	*1940*	*1955*
Benares		18000			29000
Tanda	1122	1150	2600		
Kopaganj		500	600		
Mubarakpur		1700	800		
Kanpur			nil		3000
Amritsar		2700		6000	
Ludhiana		350		3000	

Notes: Based on various District Gazetteers; A. Latifi, *Punjab Industries*, Lahore: Government Press, 1917; United Provinces, *Report on the Industrial Survey of the United Provinces*, Allahabad: Government Press, 1924; India, *Fact-finding Committee: Handlooms and Mills*, Calcutta: Government Press, 1942; India, *Report of the Textile Enquiry Committee*, New Delhi: Ministry of Commerce, 1954.

Table 6.6 Towns in western and central India

	1884	*1903–05*	*1927*	*1936*	*1940*	*1948*	*1955*
Sholapur	6425			7500	7000	13000	20205
Yeola		3600			2000		
Nagpur		5000			5156		17000[1]
Umrer		10000			1800		2100
Burhanpur	4500				1300		
Ahmedabad		1000	750	200	100		
Surat					700		5000[2]

Notes: 1. Nanekar's estimate is 10,000 (K.R. Nanekar, *Handloom Industry in Madhya Pradesh*, Nagpur: Nagpur University, 1968); 2. The figure may include 3,000 lace weaving looms. Other sources: George Birdwood, *The Industrial Arts of India*, Part 2, London: Chapman and Hall, 1887; N.M. Joshi, *Urban Handicrafts of the Bombay-Deccan*, Poona: Gokhale Institute of Politics and Economics, 1936; India, *Fact-finding Committee*; Bombay, *Report of the Sholapur Handloom Weavers Enquiry Committee*, Bombay: Political and Services Department, 1948; A.B. Trivedi, *Post-war Gujarat*, Bombay: Bhagirathi Press, 1949; India, *Textile Enquiry Committee*, Delhi: Government Press, 1954.

textiles, both handmade and machine-made. Benares is the only north Indian town comparable to Salem and Madurai. It was distinctive too. Handloom weaving in Benares combined three features, huge regular inflow of Hindu pilgrims who would also shop for sarees (as in Madurai), convenient position in a trading zone secured later by the railways (as in Salem), and transactions with imperial cities in the Indo-Gangetic Basin.

Table 6.6 shows that central and western India display mixed tendencies. Of the three most famous places, Sholapur, Nagpur, and Burhanpur, in the first two looms remained stationary and rose only after 1940, whereas in Burhanpur there was a decline. Also in decline were the silk towns Yeola, Umrer, and Ahmedabad.[18]

Stagnant looms in some of the bigger towns until 1940 need not surprise us. Descriptions, mainly from the Gazetteers produced at the turn of the twentieth century, suggest that urbanization in Bombay-Deccan was a process connected with the railways and cotton trade. The impetus derived from these factors was not equally strong everywhere and was weak in the twentieth century.

Sholapur, however, took off. Sholapur is in a cotton-growing region in the western part of the Deccan Plateau. It became a major mill town and a cotton trading point soon after the railways connected it with Bombay. From the 1890s, Sholapur received many migrant weavers from the Telangana region 200–300 miles east (Map 6.3). Some of them came to work in the mills. But the majority settled down as handloom weavers. In the interwar period, the town had 7,000–8,000 looms located in small factories owned mainly by the Telugu-speaking Padmasali weavers. These weavers dominated both capital and labour.[19] By 1930, there was a mixture of small family firms with 3–8 looms and large factories with 20–40 looms. The second type relied on migrants who lived in dormitories or as paying guests of weaver families. For a long time after that, the Sholapur cluster maintained a combination of full-fledged wage-labour and community-based hiring with shades of personalized relationship. Initially, the migrants were adult males who had been trained inside their own families before migration. Even when younger persons and trainees were employed, the handloom factories recruited mainly from within the Padmasali caste. If they did share the cost of training, the caste-based hiring ensured that changing jobs would not be easy for anyone without the consent of the employer.

In Surat in western India, migrant handloom weavers and the local Khatri weavers performed the industry in the early twentieth century. This was a silk-weaving town mainly, which switched to Japanese and Chinese silks and rayon yarn in these years. From then on, merchants in these goods also began to control production. In the 1950s, Surat exported a lot of handmade cloth and soon after switched over almost wholly to production in powerloom weaving factories. Many of these factories the leading textile merchants had set up.

A common feature of several prominent crafts centres was their strategic location in long-distance trade and transport systems. Benares, Amritsar, and Kanpur were thus advantaged both before and after the railways. Benares' position as a premier pilgrim town combined with its location on the riverborne east-west trade and later, on the main railway route. Amritsar was the point where four trade routes converged: Kashmir and central Asia from where raw silks and clothes were imported till the mid-1930s; the hill-trade on the east and northeast to which Punjab supplied coarse handspun yarn and cloth made out of it; Ahmedabad on the southwest from where mill-made yarns were received; and the plains and deep south which had a market for Punjab silk and later, rayon goods. The scale of transfrontier trade eventually declined, but those of the others expanded.

The main railways bypassed and therefore damaged the trade of Burhanpur, which was a significant craft town in central India during Mughal times and later. The opening of the railways in the 1870s destroyed its position as a clearing centre on the Deccan-Malwa trade route. This reinforced the effects of the decline of court patronage to the cloth printing and painting industry for which Burhanpur was once famous and that of the rise of machine printing in Bombay.

Ahmedabad had an unusual history.[20] This city is one of the few places where from the 1870s mills and handlooms existed together. Therefore, competition from the mills cannot explain the later eclipse of handlooms. Being a mill town, in Ahmedabad, installing powerlooms as an alternative to expansion within handloom weaving was more feasible for the weavers than it was elsewhere. This was so because of the plentiful supply of cheap local machines and electric power. Indeed, one of the first instances of converting a handloom factory into a powerloom shed came from here.[21]

In varying degrees of practicability, this option presented itself in the towns of Bombay-Deccan and the neighbouring regions (about 1960 in Tamil Nadu) and no doubt was one of the reasons why growth in handloom generally appears slow in these towns. In Sholapur in the 1940s and 1950s, and in Ahmadnagar, Malegaon and Sangamner, weavers switched to powerlooms when they could. Ahmedabad was similar. And in Burhanpur 'the powerloom industry rose out of the ashes of handlooms.'[22] In Surat, powerloom growth far outstripped that in handlooms.

The limited data on eastern India prevents us from constructing another table like the others. The limited data is symptomatic of the fact that large urban concentrations were few in Bengal, Bihar, Orissa, or Assam, though in all four regions, handloom weaving was performed on a large scale. It was done mainly by households based in the countryside or a village within easy reach from a city. In 1940, Santipur in Bengal was 'the only municipal area' with many handlooms, about 10,000. And yet Bengal weaving does not appear as thinly spread as in the United Provinces countryside, or Assam and Orissa.

The typical spatial organization, at least with handlooms serving long-distance trade, was clusters of villages all well-connected with Calcutta, the main market for handloom sarees. Four of these clusters were very large: western and central Hooghly (Arambag-Dhanekhali), Hooghly along the west bank of the river (Serampur-Farasdanga-Rajbalhat), within an eight-mile radius of Dhaka town or the oft-quoted 'Manchester of Bengal', and the Malda-Murshidabad silk complex. We do not have good estimates of looms in these. In 1940 the Dhaka concentration alone had about 25,000 looms, and another 850 in the Nawapara-Rupsa-Tarabo complex close by, together about 25 percent of looms in Bengal. By this standard, anywhere between 60 and 75 percent of the looms could be found in just these four areas.

Trade in Bengal was urban and dominated by Calcutta merchants. Only three markets were between themselves the 'clearing centres' of the bulk of the handloom output in Bengal: Howrah hat near Calcutta, Baburhat in Dhaka, and Kumarkhali in Nadia. None had much weaving. The main actors in each of these hats were traders and moneylenders, with a few weavers among them.

The urbanization process

So far urbanization has meant a quantitative process, increasing the percentage share of towns. In fact, what I call towns were not just places with lots of looms but places with a distinct type of trading. This point needs elaboration. Consider Table 6.7, which gives a snapshot picture from around 1950, using survey data on 43 centres in Madras. The table makes a simple point – the bigger the weaving industry in one town, the more likely it is that the weavers would sell to contractors who came from outside the town. The visit by outsiders is what I called market-integration. And loom size stood for the presence of bigger merchants and factory owners, and more innovations. These things were related.

The 1900 monographs usually described marketing with reference to smaller centres and villages. Within these, the cloth was made and sold, either on orders from consumers, or by hawking, or in the local hat, or to the village shopkeeper, or in weekly fairs at slightly distant locations. An extension of this arrangement was the itinerant traders covering many villages and towns. The few exceptions were the export production areas engaged in carpets, hangings, or Madras handkerchiefs of the east coast. The weekly fair, or hat (Bengal), or a shandy (south India), were places where the weavers did not lose touch with the consumers, but the shopkeepers often mediated the transaction. In large periodic fairs, such as the one described in Surat Gazetteer (1877), tailors, dyers, printers and weavers figured along with merchants from outside the area. While the typical shandy was to be found all over India, visits from outside merchants became more frequent in Bengal where bigger hats coexisted with smaller hats; the latter being one in which the weaver sold to outsider merchants and the bigger hat the one where transactions occurred between different kinds of merchants.

The other component of the rural system was mobile trade. In Deccan many weavers themselves, presumably large households of the bigger

Table 6.7 Disposal of fabrics made (percentages of row), c. 1950

Loom size-class	*Home consumption*	*Sold locally*	*Sold to outsiders*	*Exports*
< 100 (8)	0.6	52.0	47.4	
101–500 (24)	0.2	36.0	61.2	2.6
501–1500 (7)	1.0	34.9	50.0	14.1
> 1500 (4)		17.8	66.0	16.2

Notes: Number of observations in brackets

Source: India, *Textile Enquiry Committee*, Appendices.

villages, were travelling salespeople. The practice had to do with seasonal cycles in weaving. In Khandesh, peddlers included craftsmen who wove in the rainy months and 'in the fair season move from village to village.' Carrier trade had also to do with the seasonality of demand. The Labbais of Karur, a trading group, hawked clothes on long credit, making rounds twice in a year, selling clothes in monsoon and returning at harvest to collect their dues. Another element that influenced mobile trade was a facility for barter. In Mysore at the end of the nineteenth century, where trade in the rural tracts was carried on by 'small journeymen' carrying their goods in the country carts, on pack animals or by headload 'as is being done even now [about 1925], the prevailing medium of exchange was grain.' In Sholapur 'the traffic is conducted for cash payments though barter is not unknown.'[23]

Such village-to-village exchanges became weaker in the early-1900s. Carrier trade was in decline in the 1920s because merchants could visit the production sites more easily. With 'the advent of metalled roads and railways' came merchants from the towns and long-distance trade between villages came to be managed by the town trader. In Khandesh the craftsmen-cum-itinerant traders, since the 1870s, 'had to fight against two very dangerous rivals. Vanis from Marvad and Bhatias from Bombay . . . masters of the new system of trade by rail and wire'.[24] Perhaps only in the Tamil Nadu towns the 'masters of the new system' were members of the prominent weaver castes themselves.

All over India, the general effect of the opening of the railways was for towns on railway routes to grow faster than the countryside around them. Trade and manufacturers of the 'small country towns . . . left on one side of the railways, is at once diverted to places more conveniently situated.'[25] Handloom towns, both old and new, the recent growth of which could be directly attributed to railways included Salem in Madras, Gulbarga in Hyderabad, Amritsar, Batala, Kanpur in the north and a cluster of towns in Bombay which owed their growth to cotton and oilseeds trade. There is some data from Khandesh about this time which suggest that with the completion of the railways transprovincial trade in handloom cloth increased faster than trade in English cloth.[26]

There were limits to how far integration of markets and trades could go. The obvious barrier to spatial concentration was the dispersed nature of the consumption of handloom cloth itself. The medium-sized towns combined the economies of scale in weaving and trade with that of not being too distant from rural consumers. Within the large town with a reputation in designed weaving, only a few products dominated the trade. Therefore, nonhereditary weavers, women weavers, and coarse or 'utility' weaving were more common in smaller towns of relatively recent origin.[27] Now we see why some new mid-sized towns could do better than either the very small town or the very large. They were closer to local consumers and at the same time had some of the advantages of concentrated production.

Urbanization, the concentration of trade in large towns and consequent dependence of the country on the towns showed up in migration from village to towns and from old and decaying towns to new ones. The evidence is fragmentary, but whatever is available suggests that most immigrants came from the United Provinces, Hyderabad, and interior Madras. This refers to long-distance inter-urban shifts and not large towns drawing labour from their immediate neighbourhood. Reports on Salem and Amritsar refer to the latter type of movements.

About long movements, many places in Bombay-Deccan received weavers from the Indo-Gangetic plains in the north, Hyderabad in the east, and Madras in the southeast. The exact origin of immigrant labourers who came here to work remains obscure. Isolated instances suggest United Provinces often meant Kanpur, Allahabad, and Benares, Hyderabad meant Paithan and Aurangabad, and Madras meant the southern Andhra districts, Bellary in particular.

Momin weavers in the northern towns, in Khandesh, were migrants from United Provinces about the time of the 1876 famine. Ahmadnagar was the southernmost town to receive a large number of Momins though Muslim weavers were present in the southern towns also. Sholapur, on the other hand, received its labour force from areas closeby, mainly Hyderabad and Madras. This shift too had owed to the 1876 and 1898 famines, although there are previous instances (about 1800) of migration from the same region to Sholapur.[28]

While some mid-sized towns grew fast, weaving came to be concentrated in western and southern India mainly. A comparison of similar institutional data from the 1942 Fact-finding Committee and the 1953 Textile Enquiry Committee reveals some of these regional differences better (Tables 6.8 and 6.9). Table 6.8 shows that growth in Madras was associated with more active looms and more product-diversity. On all of these benchmarks,

Table 6.8 Regional differences in some key benchmarks

	Increase or decrease in looms, 1920–1940	*Proportion of idle looms in 1920 (%)*	*Proportion of idle looms in 1940 (%)*	*Noncotton looms*	*Finer yarn*	*Yards produced per lb of yarn*
Bengal	−34	15	25	18	40	4.6
Orissa	−17	19	19	5	2	–
Bihar	2	27	40	4	29	–
South India	100.	13	13	18	40	5.8
Bombay	17	12	12	24	52	4.8
Hyderabad	0	5	21	35	21	–
Punjab	6	20	19	7	6	3.6
UP		21	25	21	7	4.8

Notes: 'Finer yarn' refers to above 30s count. 'Yards/lb' is an average for the region. South India consists of Tamil Nadu, Andhra, and Malabar regions. Eastern India includes Bengal and Orissa. Proportional figures are percentages of provincial totals. Tables 6.8 and 6.9 are based on India, *Fact-finding Committee*, and India, *Textile Enquiry Committee*, appendices.

Table 6.9 More regional differences, 1940

	Factory workers proportion	*Looms per production unit*	*Powerlooms*	*Looms per town*	*Looms in the largest town*
Bengal	–	1.4	16	93	658 (Rajbalhat)
Bihar	0	–	104	–	–
Orissa	0	–	–	–	–
Tamil Nadu	8	3.0	270	622	22,200 (Salem)
Andhra	–	2.0	–	478	3,470 (Proddatur)
Malabar	–	12.3	–	446	1,513 (Pudukode)
Bombay	54	2.2	6,400	214	17,000 (Nagpur)
Hyderabad	40	–	240	240	–
Punjab	2	3.1	1,170	116	218 (Batala)
UP	–	1.9	–	131	3,000 (Kanpur)

Notes: The first two columns in percentages. Looms per centre calculated excluding the largest centre.

Bombay and Madras were ahead of the other regions. As we have seen, these were also the regions where weaving was more urbanized.[29]

Conclusion

The chapter shows that the axis of production, trade, and innovation shifted towards the towns of western and southern India. Handloom weavers took closer control of both the industry and the business in the larger centres in these regions.

Capital and labour involved in the industry became increasingly mobile. There was migration from rural regions towards new points of trade and towards the towns connected by the railways and containing spinning mills. One of the more visible and consequential flows occurred between textile towns in western India such as Sholapur, Malegaon, Bhiwandi, Burhanpur and Surat, and handloom weavers from the famine-hit Hyderabad region or southern Andhra Pradesh, and overpopulated regions like eastern United Provinces.[30] By 1950, in nearly every major town of western India, the older quarters housed settlements of handloom weaver communities.

Another twenty years, and many of these business people and workers, while continuing in textiles, had given up handlooms for powerloom weaving.

Notes

1 The 1901 census reported an absolute decline in population of weavers in southern Andhra districts while the number increased generally in Tamil Nadu. See also Madras, *Report of the Survey of Cottage Industries in the Madras Presidency* (D. Narayana Rao), Madras: Government Press, 1925, 71–2 and 86.

2 See also Tirthankar Roy, 'Madras Handkerchiefs in the Interwar Period,' *Indian Economic and Social History Review*, 39(2–3), 2002, 285–300.
3 Evidence of P. Theagaraya Chetty, India, *Indian Industrial Commission*, vol. 3 of 5, Calcutta: Government Press, 1918.
4 Thurston, *Monograph*, 5, Imperial Gazetteer of India, Provincial series, *Madras*, Calcutta: Government Press, 1908
5 About 16 percent of Salem's weavers were not of the weaver castes. All India Handloom Board, *Survey of Handloom Industry in Madras State, 1955–56*, Bombay: Government Press, 1959, 32–5.
6 Ibid., 29.
7 N.G. Ranga, *The Economics of Handlooms*, Bombay: Taraporevala, 1930, 134.
8 Henry Le Fanu, *A Manual of the Salem District in the Presidency of Madras*, Madras: Government Press, 1883.
9 Alfred Chatterton, *Industrial Evolution in India*, Madras: The Hindu Office, 1912, 223–44, on the Salem factory and introduction of faster frame looms in handloom weaving. A comparable example to Salem is Madurai where the large dyers themselves mooted the idea of a dyeing school and advised the government on the nature of its activities.
10 K.S. Venkatraman, *Handloom Industry in the Madras Presidency*, Madras: The Diocesan Press, 1936, 269–77.
11 F. Nicholson and E. Thurston, eds., *Gazetteer of South India*, Madras: Government Press, c. 1900, 'Madurai District'; J.H. Nelson, *The Madurai Country: A Manual*, Madras: Government Press, 1868; A.J. Saunders, 'The Sourashtra Community in Madurai, South India,' mimeo prepared at American College, Madurai, c. 1920–22; K. Bharathan, 'Handloom Industry in Tamil Nadu: A Study of Organisational Structure,' PhD dissertation of Madras Institute of Development Studies, Madras, 1988.
12 Edgar Thurston, *Tribes and Castes of Southern India*, Madras: Government Press, 1909.
13 Nelson, *The Madurai Country*, 87.
14 Saunders, 'Sourashtra Community,' 67–9.
15 Venkatraman, *Handloom Industry*, 180–1.
16 I.R. Dave, *The Saurashtrians of South India*, Rajkot: Saurashtra University, 1976.
17 Tirthankar Roy, 'Capitalism and Community: A Study of the Madurai Sourashtras,' *Indian Economic and Social History Review*, 34(4), 1997, 437–65.
18 George C. Birdwood, *The Industrial Arts of India*, Part 2, London: Chapman and Hall, 1887, 250 and John Irwin and Margaret Hall, *Indian Painted and Printed Fabrics*, Ahmedabad: Calico Museum, 1970, 24–5.
19 On Padmasali migration into Sholapur and the history of handloom factories in this town, see Douglas Haynes and Tirthankar Roy, 'Conceiving Mobility: Weavers' Migration in Precolonial and Colonial India,' *Indian Economic and Social History Review*, 33(1), 1999, 35–67; and D. Haynes, 'The Logic of the Artisan Firm in a Capitalist Economy: Handloom Weavers and Technological Change in Western India, 1880–1947,' in B. Stein and S. Subrahmanyam, eds., *Institutions and Economic Change in South Asia*, New Delhi: Government Press, 1996, 173–205.
20 Ahmedabad guilds were quite unique among Indian craft towns.
21 The Ahmedabad Fine Weaving Mill, for instance. See A.B. Trivedi, *Post-War Gujarat*, Bombay: Bhagirathi Press, 1949, 89.
22 India, *Report of the Powerloom Enquiry Committee*, New Delhi: Ministry of Commerce and Industry, 1964.
23 On similar systems of exchange, see Gazetteers, Bombay Presidency, *Khandesh District*, Bombay: Government Press, 1884–6, 194, 218; Gazetteers, Bombay Presidency, *Sholapur District*, Bombay: Government Press, 1884–6, 264. Also

Gazetteers, Madras District, *Salem District*, Madras: Government Press, 1918, and Gazetteers, *Mysore Gazetteer*, vol. 3 (Economic), Bangalore: Government Press, 1929, 300–1.

24 Gazetteers, Bombay Presidency, *Khandesh*, 194.

25 Census of India, *Punjab, Its Feudatories, and the North-West Frontier Provinces*, Part 1 (Report), Simla: Government Press, 1902, 18.

26 Census of India, *Madras*, Part 1 (Report), Madras: Government Press, 1901, 14; Census of India, *Punjab, Its Feudatories, and the North-West Frontier Provinces*, 21; Census of India, *Bombay*, Part 1 (Report), Bombay: Government Press, 1901, 12; Imperial Gazetteer of India, Provincial Series, *Bombay*, Bombay: Government Press, 1908, 397, 480; Imperial Gazetteer of India, Provincial Series, *Hyderabad State*, Calcutta: Government Press, 1909, 252; Khandesh railway returns quoted in Gazetteer, Bombay District, *Khandesh*, 216.

27 On Madras, see Census of India, *District Census Handbook* (Salem District), Madras: Government Press, 1961.

28 R.E. Enthoven, *The Cotton Fabrics of the Bombay Presidency*, Bombay: Government Press, 1895, 4; Gazetteers, Bombay Presidency, *Sholapur*, 244; Gazetteers, Madras District, Madurai District, Madras: Government Press, 1906, 108–9; A. Blennerhassett, *A Monograph on the Cotton Fabrics of the Central Provinces*, Nagpur: Government Press, 1898, 6; F. Dewar, *Monograph on the Silk Fabrics of the Central Provinces*, Nagpur: Government Press, 190, 4; Gazetteers, Bombay Presidency, *Khandesh District*, Bombay: Government Press, 1884–86,194.

29 The raw data were collected through a nonstratified sample of all handloom centres in India. The range was extremely wide, from the smallest village with ten looms in the remote corners of Assam to towns such as Salem with more than 20,000 looms. Numerically the small places dominate, but economies of scale were immense and inadequately captured. This produces a general bias in the data for the village. The bias gets magnified in the case of Bombay for which none of the important towns except Khasbag, a suburb of Belgaum, was included.

30 See on weavers' migration, Haynes and Roy, 'Conceiving Mobility: Migration of Handloom Weavers in Precolonial and Colonial India.'

7

HANDLOOMS AND POWERLOOMS, 1920–1990

Chapter 3 mentions that the border between hand- and power-weaving was never fixed. None knew this better than the weavers themselves. Their strategy to cope with this instability was to cross the border and invest in powerloom weaving if the decision was consistent with their skill set and market access. The chapter shows the beginning of this process in the interwar period, when the availability of East Asian silks and rayon made crossing the border an attractive option, continuing the story into about 50 years after independence when the powerlooms emerged as the dominant cloth producer in the Indian market. They did thanks partly to their own intrinsic advantages and partly to the policies of a state that could not make up its mind whether the powerloom was politically correct or not (see also Chapter 8).

For most of the mid-twentieth century, powerlooms were a common and numerous industry in India. These were weaving factories with power-operated looms. Unlike the big cotton mills of Bombay and Ahmedabad, which integrated operations, these factories purchased yarn from spinning mills and had the cloth processed by local firms. Therefore, they usually operated as one part of a diversified urban industrial system.

Official data on the industry is almost never reliable. In official definition, any weaving done outside the integrated mills would be called a powerloom. However, this residual definition could accommodate a wide range of cloth producers, from those operating six to eight looms each to make cotton cloth, to the producers of polyester fibre cloths, who built giant factories in the 1980s. In debates and discussions, however, powerlooms referred to the bottom-end of the scale.

The shift of capital began in the interwar period and speeded up in the 1960s and 1970s. In all major urban clusters of hand-weaving – Sholapur, Salem, Bhiwandi, and Surat – handloom weavers or cloth merchants who did business in handmade cloth invested in power-weaving factories. It would be wrong to suggest that these units were a higher stage in the evolution of the handloom industry. The handloom industry was too differentiated to evolve into a single type of entity. Besides, powerloom factories received investment from a wide variety of local capitalists, not just handloom weavers. But the overlap between the two industries was close enough in the handloom weaving towns to deserve a chapter in this book. The chapter, in other words, restricts to that part of the power-weaving industry which had close ties to handloom weaving.

The chapter draws on extensive but scattered scholarship on the origin of powerlooms. It ends in 1997–98, when I did a series of fieldworks and interviews in south India, and jointly with Douglas Haynes, visited Ichalkaranji and Bhiwandi.[1]

A short history: 1920–1990

The first powerlooms appeared in major textile towns of western India at the turn of the century. Their number grew steadily in the interwar period, but not before 1940 did they attract attention in contemporary reports. The pioneer powerloom entrepreneurs were of mixed occupational background. However, the first phase of investment owed to those groups with experience in handloom cloth production and marketing. The earlier chapters advanced two propositions that help us understand why handloom weavers invested in powerlooms. First, there was already capital accumulation in handlooms. Moneyed people who understood the technology and the business side of selling sarees would find it sensible to move to a faster loom if possible. And second, the boundary of specialization in hand-woven and machine-woven cloths was constantly shifting. The rise of rayon cloth and simplification of saree design made the boundary even more unstable, encouraging weavers and merchants engaged in sarees to cross the technological dividing line.

Like the handlooms, the first powerlooms wove sarees. The powerloom sarees fell into two classes, one did not compete with handlooms and the other one did. The former consisted of rayon sarees, which may have provided some competition to silk weaving. Rayon sarees were first imported from Japan in the 1920s. After a tariff was imposed, weaving factories started to weave the new material. The designs were simple, like stripes, which could be standard and mass-produced with a dobby. The mills too were doing this in cotton sarees. The sarees that did compete with the handlooms usually had woven borders.

Not all handloom weavers were able or willing to switch. Weavers were arranged in a hierarchy. At one end were the agricultural workers who occasionally did coarse weaving on the side, but rarely took an active part in trade. At the other end were the silk saree weavers in south Indian towns. Over this progression from the basic skills to complex skills, and the less to the more organized, the ability to invest in new and better looms increased. But the willingness to invest fell because the opportunity cost of leaving handlooms increased too. Thus, in advanced pockets of silk handloom weaving, powerlooms made only hesitant inroads. The weaver or the merchant who did start powerlooms tended to fall somewhere in the middle of this range.

From the 1950s, and accelerated in the 1960s, several other drives joined this endogenous transformation. Some of these factors were organic, and some were added externally by state intervention. The organic factor was the way industrial cities were changing. The original homes of cotton mills in India, Bombay, Ahmedabad, Kanpur, or Madras, saw a rising cost of living and a rise in wages and rents. For a new cloth-producing factory, it made sense to relocate in a smaller town where costs were lower. In choosing where to go, the preferred option was a town with a sufficiently well-developed textile business already in existence. Further, the Green Revolution in the 1970s led to the growth of local markets and local merchants who invested money in the small-scale industry. These other drivers did not necessarily favour the families traditionally engaged in handloom weaving. Many other types of capitalist, even rich peasants, and professionals entered the business. Still, usually the investment happened in towns that had some association with textiles and therefore with handlooms.

State intervention attracted such entry. Independent India's development strategy placed a heavy accent on building the capability to produce machines, metals, and chemicals at home. These industries required a great deal of capital to build; the technology needed to do so was not available domestically, so they needed a great deal of foreign exchange too. The state decided to license investments to conserve capital, invest taxpayer's money in these fields, license foreign exchange to conserve its use, and offered high levels of protection to machines, metals, and chemicals to make them domestically competitive against imports. The implication of all this was that cotton textiles, in which India had for millennia built and nurtured a capability that was competitive at home and abroad, now lost priority. Cotton textile producers had no chance to get either foreign exchange or an investment license to modernize and expand operations. The cotton mills, under this onslaught, started to decline rapidly from the 1970s.

Besides these macroeconomic measures, a special package was created to help the handloom weavers withstand competition from mechanized mills in the domestic market.[2] Between 1950, when a Textile Policy came into existence, and 1985, when a new Textile Policy eased some of the restrictions earlier imposed on them, the government prohibited the cotton mills from expanding capacity and reserved products exclusively for the handlooms to make.

The powerloom factory had a rather ambiguous position in the policy. The philosophy that produced this policy took shape at the time of independence. Two influential government enquiry reports prepared in the 1950s are its best expression.[3] While both had recommended that mill-weaving capacity should be frozen, there was ambiguity about powerlooms. One of them correctly judged the powerloom as a sign of upward-mobility of handloom weavers and recommended easier conversion. The other either did not understand or did not give importance to the handloom root. It also had a more militant Gandhian agenda and recommended a blanket restriction on powerlooms (see Chapter 8 on the Gandhian programme). In the end, powerlooms became technically illegal. The federal (central) government prohibited their operation beyond a capacity size.

Enforcement of this strategy, however, was left to the states, who did not believe in the philosophy underlying it. Locally, state officials and politicians almost openly helped them grow, or at least did not carry out the federal policy to stop them from growing. At the same time, the distressed cotton mills scrapped looms and sold these at a huge discount. The individuals who bought these and administrators of the towns where these machines were brought for reuse, agreed that there was good business to be had from making the looms work.

The handloom lobby, especially the voice of the master-weavers, was always heard in the regional politics in Tamil Nadu. After 1950, in the wake of the Textile Policy statements from Delhi, which were pro-handloom, regional politics in most states needed to take an informal stand on powerlooms. States in which powerlooms mattered took an unofficial view that adopted Delhi's ideology but only piecemeal. Gujarat was pro-powerloom in noncotton. In Tamil Nadu, leaders of handloom communities themselves switched to powerlooms such that the state could stay committed to handlooms and yet leave powerlooms free.

Most powerloom factories started between 1950 and 1990 came up in three states: Maharashtra, Gujarat, and Tamil Nadu. These states were generally friendly towards small businesses and not too keen to insist on those regulatory measures, such as the Trade Union Act and the Factory Act, that made the small entrepreneur reluctant to expand operations. The factory workers increasingly came from outside the state, which reduced their lobbying power. And these states already had advanced forms of handloom weaving.

The death blow to the cotton mills came during the 1982–83 Bombay Textile Strike, and a spate of bankruptcy in Ahmedabad, Kanpur, and Madras, leading to the widespread closure of these mills. These events gave an enormous boost to powerlooms. They grew in number and capacity by making clothes that the mills made formerly, such as grey or bleached sheets. They also used rayon and polyester fibres to produce printed sarees that captured a big part of the handloom market in sarees. One of the best-known saree brands of the 1980s, Garden, came from a weaving factory in Surat which made sarees for home and export markets. In south India, they made a wide range of household textiles that the government had reserved for the handlooms alone. These goods sold in the market as handloom goods but were not produced by the handmade process.

From the mid-1980s, another driver encouraged the emergence of a powerloom weaving factory. In 1985, the old Textile Policy was reformed, and the worst excesses of the investment-cum-exchange regime were over. Import of machines was permitted just when textiles and clothing began to experience an export surge following the exchange rate and tariff reform, or India's economic liberalization. Not all powerlooms could either import machines or export cloth. Doing business in the home market meant making poor-quality cloth as cheaply as possible and did not demand timely delivery, market-research, up-to-date technology, and access to information. These aspects of doing business the average powerloom firm or the industry associations did not worry about. Now they were falling behind. The export market insisted on quality and standardization not ordinarily attainable with plain non-automatic looms. The export market entailed a new economy of scale. A powerloom firm which wanted to export fabrics by itself was constrained by minimum export units, such as 'container quality', or 60,000–70,000 metres of cloth in one single yarn type. All this needed high levels of standardization. A new set of factories with a large number of automatic and shuttleless looms came up to meet the demand. Families with ties in handloom weaving did own and start some of these factories, perhaps more in Tamil Nadu than anywhere else, but overall, the ownership pattern was diverse and had moved further away from the handloom root.

A big shift in the consumption pattern helped the modern segment of the industry change faster. The Indian consumer – men and women – started wearing more readymade garments, as opposed to buying sheets and having these tailored by the neighbourhood tailor. Any weaving factory that tried to sell grey and bleached sheets to the city markets had its days numbered, even though it did not disappear, nor decline quickly. Even now (2019), bleached sheets of cloth are available for sale in the small-town cloth shops to meet a variety of uses. But most fabrics now went to the clothing industry. With the improvement in the average quality of the fabric, consumers in the domestic market became more demanding too. Thus, with globalization and the emergence of a modern and competitive segment within the powerloom weaving factories, the generic small factories fell behind and from time to time fell into crises.

The garment and cloth export boom of the 1980s and the 1990s encouraged investment in complementary activities. Thus, there was phenomenal growth of small cotton-spinning factories in Tamil Nadu, usually clustered around powerloom hubs. Looms in Tamil Nadu expanded from about 100,000 in 1990 to 450,000 in 1996. Cloth trade, machinery, and processing expanded. Coimbatore became what Bombay and Ahmedabad had been in an earlier time, that is, concentrated the production of yarn, machinery, spares, and trading services and made these goods and services cheaper to buy. In the 2000s, the impetus of growth in labour-intensive manufacturing weakened somewhat, partly because the government did not follow up tariff reforms with reforms in labour law.

In the mid-1990s, the main textile regions of India were in Maharashtra, Gujarat, and Tamil Nadu. These regions were not similar. The west processed more manmade fibres. The standard output of a western Indian loom was polyester shirting or sarees. The south processed mainly cotton. The west developed powerlooms in the interwar period. The south entered late, from the 1950s, but grew rapidly. The main growth phase in the west was in the late-1970s to the late-1980s when Indian consumers began to substitute cotton for polyester. The main growth-phase in the south began from the mid-1980s when garment and yarn exports re-established the importance of cotton.

The small spinning mill was a distinctive feature of the south Indian textile hub. After the economic reforms began, India emerged as a major producer and exporter of cotton yarn. Indian yarn came in a wider range than most of its competitors. The quality of cotton yarn was not always good, but it was improving. India, like Pakistan, sold yarn to other Asian textile and clothing exporters such as China. Because of this link, the East Asian economic crisis of 1997 hurt India, which then had few other connections with the rest of Asia. Tamil Nadu benefited from the yarn export upsurge more than other states. The state accounted for 4 percent of cotton produced in the country but over half of the cotton yarn produced.

As weaving factories or powerlooms developed, a contrast emerged between western India and south India on their industrial organization. In western India, powerlooms concentrated in towns. Trade, processing, and production all operated in the same town. In the south, a small set of towns specialized in trade and processing, whereas production was semi-rural. One factor underlay the difference, the countryside had better infrastructure and a higher standard of living in Tamil Nadu than the countryside in Maharashtra. Whereas migrant wage-workers from poorer states of India populated these towns in increasing numbers, in Tamil Nadu, the industry developed by using mainly local resources, both capital and labour.

The Tamil Nadu countryside was remarkable in another way. Acute scarcity of water limited processing options. The dyed or printed cloth was relatively rarer here. Grey cotton and woven designs in coloured yarn were more common. There were few large process-houses in south India, except in the few water-abundant pockets (along the Kaveri and Vaigai rivers) and as adjuncts of spinning mills. In the mid-1990s, no more than 30–40 percent of fabrics were processed locally. The rest were sold as grey or designed by means of the drop-box, dobby, or Jacquard.

Powerlooms never touched eastern and northern India in a big way. Eastern and northern India lacked powerlooms not because of higher costs. Labour was cheaper in the east than in the west. But urban handlooms and weaver-capitalists were rare in the region. The handloom root to the powerloom was weaker in the towns of eastern and northern India. Upwardly mobile urban handloom weavers being rare in these regions, the industry was poorer, less skilled, and more rural. Agglomeration and prior accumulation in handlooms were the critical factors behind the origin of powerlooms.

These conditions existed in western India in the 1920s and did not materialize to a comparable extent in eastern India.

Not all this story deserves to be retold in this book. I will only discuss the handloom-powerloom connection over the next two sections, concentrating on just two areas where the connection was the strongest, Maharashtra-Gujarat and Tamil Nadu.

Western India

In 1948, all the districts of Bombay province where there were 100 or more powerlooms had at least 1000 handlooms. Malegaon, Bhiwandi, and Surat, then the main powerloom towns, had each at least 2000 handlooms.[4] The region emerged as the most important destination for migrant weavers from both northern and southern India. In Bhiwandi, Malegaon, Dhulia, and Burhanpur, migrant Momin weavers from Uttar Pradesh led the progression to powerlooms. In Sholapur, Padmasalis from Telangana played a similar role (see Figure 7.1).

In Surat, the handloom root was of a different nature. The local Khatri weavers did take part in the transition to powerlooms. But the pioneering families were mainly cloth traders. Their business was with silk, rayon, and gold thread. Surat powerlooms retained this orientation towards cloth trade

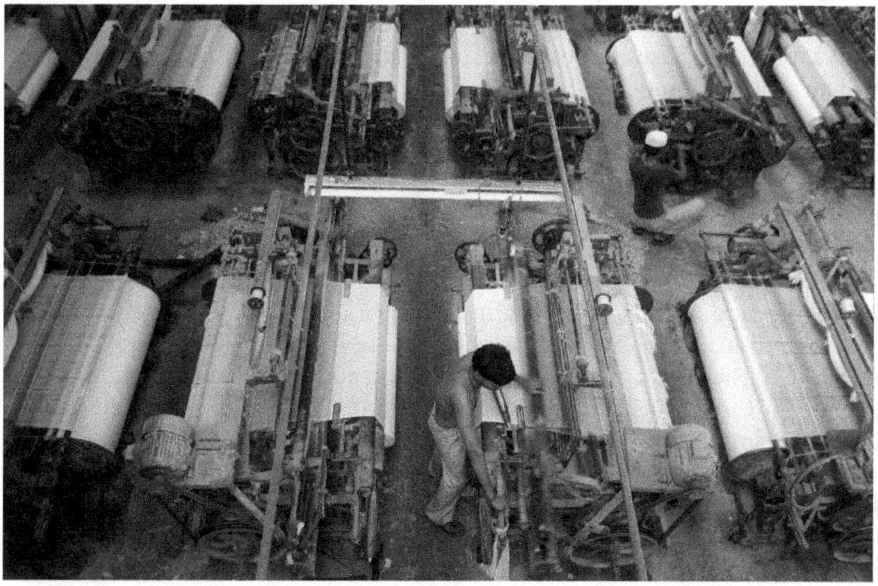

Figure 7.1 Interior of a powerloom factory in Malegaon, 2009
Source: Dinodia Photos/Alamy Stock Photo

and noncotton fibres. Beginning with Chinese silk in the 1920s, Surat shifted to Japanese rayon until the war stopped supplies. From 1950 it began to develop a virtual monopoly in printed rayon and nylon filament yarn sarees, and in the 1970s, diversified into polyester men's wear. In another significant cluster, Ichalkaranji, the handloom root was weaker. Initially, Koshti weavers-cum-merchants set up powerlooms. But from around the 1940s, a development-minded princely ruler encouraged investment in the industry, which diversified the participants in the powerloom industry. The story was somewhat similar to that in Mysore, where again the state encouraged investment in textiles.

About 30 years after independence, these towns had moved on and changed in several ways. In each case, the handloom root was diluted further, even disappeared. A survey conducted in Ichalkaranji in the 1980s showed that owners of small factories had been mill workers, accountants, and foremen in the first powerloom factories. Some were families who sold or mortgaged land to buy looms.[5] In all towns, the textile processing business had developed greatly. Originally done in and around Bombay, increasingly processing came to be done in the weaving town. The processing required a lot of capital. Some owners of these shops were rich factory owners; others were merchants. In Ichalkaranji, development of the sugar industry under the cooperatives led to a considerable accumulation of capital among rural families, who invested some of it into the textile industry. Land values increased, which made such reinvestment lucrative. With sugar and powerlooms, there grew engineering workshops, spinning mills, banks, process-houses, industrial estates, and wholesale markets. The town had an efficient municipality and a reputation for peaceful labour relations. Between 1950 and 1997, the population of Ichalkaranji increased from 27,000 to about 250,000, and the number of those engaged in powerloom weaving and processing from 3,000 to about 140,000. The workers initially came from the surrounding districts in Maharashtra and Karnataka.[6]

From the 1950s, some of the older firms of Surat grew rapidly to become large producers, each with several hundred looms, process-houses, texturizing plants, and in some cases engineering workshops. Developments in process were a major reason for the concentration of manmade fibre-weaving in Surat. Other factors were its cloth markets, cheap electricity, a capital-friendly government, and the absence of unions. Bhiwandi and Surat gained from proximity to Bombay and Ahmedabad, with their huge urban market for fashionable sarees. In Bhiwandi, cloth traders from Bombay invested in powerlooms, especially after the Bombay textile strike in 1982–3. In all these cities, in newly established industrial estates, relatively modern plants weaving cloth came up. Between 1970 and 2000, looms in Bhiwandi increased from 50,000 to more than 100,000. The shift to polyester speeded up. In Bhiwandi in 1985, 60 percent of the production consisted of fine cotton and polyester-cotton shirting and suiting. Saree had all but disappeared. That shift renewed ties between the small town and the city. Most of Bhiwandi's production in manmade fibres was processed in or near Bombay. Bhiwandi's own process-houses in the mid-1980s were still mainly cotton-based.

In Bhiwandi, most pioneering powerloom owners came from families where handloom weaving had been practiced until recently. But in 1985, owners were 'hardly weavers.' In Surat, units, where the owners' family worked, were 'decreasing day by day.'[7] In western India, this process was aided by massive immigration. Certain immigrant groups entered certain types of work. Thus, weavers came from Uttar Pradesh or Andhra Pradesh, thread-joiners from Benares, and boilermen and their assistants in process-shops from Bengal. The capitalists were usually the residents of the town. Being residents meant ownership of rapidly appreciating real estate and therefore easier access to credit.

In Surat and Bhiwandi, the average worker (about 1995) was a young migrant male from the drought-prone interior Maharashtra, or from the overpopulated and poor regions of eastern India. Almost two-thirds of Surat's workers around 1990 were eastern Indians.[8] The first batches of non-local labour were recruited from within the city. They established a channel which the later migrants followed, predominantly as apprentices at loom-sheds. Workers in Bhiwandi were migrants from Andhra Pradesh, Maharashtra, Bihar, and Uttar Pradesh, single males and with little formal education. They lived in the loom-shed or in rented hostels, ate at collective messes, bathed in public taps, and worked 12-hour shifts. The workers led a life of hard work, but with chances of quick upward mobility and of saving money. Their main problem was that the urban environment of Surat and Bhiwandi, both highly congested towns, was unhealthy in the extreme in the 1980s. Slums were built up at the work-site, or at the centre of the town, because long hours made commuting impossible and city transport was bad and expensive. The scarcity of space made living with family impossible. The short-term and opportunistic nature of the contract between employers, workers, and the city made for the underdevelopment of public goods like clean water, clean air, safe food, healthcare, and education for these workers.

Surat developed a rather similar reputation for the poor quality of life it offered to the migrant wage-workers. Jan Breman says that 'brutal' conditions of work and life in the powerlooms persisted 'thanks to state intervention.'[9] The state, in fact, took its hands off from labour regulation. Private investment was a middle-class pursuit in South Gujarat. A significant share of investment in small industries came from the middle-class landowners Anavil Brahmins, rather than merchant communities. They had local political influence. But they were not all wealthy nor capitalists for generations. It would be odd for the politician to think that capital and labour were class enemies in this setup. The political attitude helped investment but left the environment uncared for. Ironically, many migrant workers in Surat came from West Bengal, where Marxist politicians did believe that capital and labour were class enemies, and oppressed capital enough to cause deindustrialization. Bhiwandi too had a bad reputation for the quality of life. But there were exceptions. Ichalakaranji with its relatively cleaner and well-maintained environment and a high level of schooling among powerloom operators represented, by contrast, a cleaner model of wage labour and urban environment. From the mid-1990s, with the entry of large modern factories that employed few workers, and more competition in manmade fibre markets, there was increasing unrest among both capitalists and workers in all these towns of western India.

Powerlooms developed in south India much later than in western India.

South India

In the 1950s, the handloom business was not doing well. Powerloom owners in various parts of the country cited these conditions as the immediate inducement to shift out of handlooms into powerlooms. In Tamil Nadu, the investment wave began from this time. Once again, the handloom root was active, but it was of a different kind of root from western India. As in the west, prosperous members of major weaver castes, Devangas, and Kaikkolars switched to powerlooms. As in the west again, those who did thus switch had a prehistory of participation in long-distance trade in handloom cloth and accumulation of capital. But such people were not alone. Already by then, the agrarian caste of Kongunad, the Gounders, had also entered handloom weaving on quite an extensive scale, mainly as a strategy to supplement unstable returns from agriculture in an area perennially short of water. Almost from the 1950s, Gounder capital and labour began to switch to powerlooms (and a little later, to knitwear in Tiruppur).

Partly because of the participation of farmers, and partly because transportation infrastructure in Tamil Nadu was well developed, the location pattern of Tamil Nadu powerlooms differed from that in western India. The towns here were the main points of trade, whereas production was spread out in rural and small-town clusters around these cores and closely connected with them. Five such clusters were important in 1995: (a) around Coimbatore (Palladam-Tirupur-Somanur-Avinashi), around Erode (Bhavani-Kumarapalayam-Pallipalayam-Chennimalai), around Karur, Salem and nearby, and Rajapalayam-Aruppukottai-Virudunagar towns.

In both Erode and Coimbatore areas, the first powerlooms date back to 1960. In much of this area, the water table is 300–500 feet below the surface and has been falling due to intensive cultivation. Investment in looms was a common way to diversify and secure incomes of farmers who faced water scarcity. Devangas of the region, who seemed to have had greater involvement with long-distance trade, became prominent among the larger powerloom firms, process-shops, and machinery makers. The workers were local, but a rising number came from Kanyakumari, Tirunelveli, Nagapattinam, and Sri Lanka to Kongunad powerlooms. Gounders were farmers with an involvement in the handloom going back to the interwar period. In surveys conducted in the late-1980s, the older generation of Gounder heads of powerloom firms still somewhat straddled agriculture and industry. But the younger people from the same families were more committed to the industry.[10]

The history of Somanur, the most important site from the Coimbatore cluster, was somewhat different from that of the Erode area. The early units here were set up in the 1960s by people who were previously labourers in Bombay mills. Rendered unemployed due to strikes and closures, they returned to their roots in Somanur and started weaving on powerlooms. A similar impetus came from the 1982–3 Bombay textile strike. In both cases, previous contacts with Bombay merchants were helpful, for the product was made mainly on contract with western Indian traders. The first looms may have been bought as scrap from Bombay and reassembled, but increasingly, the looms were new local makes. In the 1990s the industry expanded and offered jobs to migrants from the southern districts of Tamil Nadu.

Notwithstanding the presence of mill labourers and motley groups, the main source of capital in powerlooms was handloom weavers, whether of agrarian or weaver castes. Why did handloom weavers shift to powerlooms? The relatively small difference in the cost of buying a powerloom, the slow speed of the handloom and problems of keeping to delivery schedules, and problems of managing handloom labour, who was often highly skilled and a tough bargainer, reportedly encouraged the switch.[11]

Tamil Nadu began with cotton greys, but from the late-1960s began to diversify into coloured lungies (a wrapped men's garment). The colour stripes, woven on the plain loom, were at first broad and crude. The drop-box loom was introduced in the 1960s. With its local manufacture, usage of the loom spread quickly. The drop-box enabled thinner stripes or more attractive and congested designs. Grey cotton cloth entered a variety of uses: garments for the local market, garments for the export market, fabric for the local market, and fabric for the export market. A great deal of direct export of grey cloth started from the 1980s. For importers in North America, for example, buying Indian cloth in the grey state sometimes made sense because it was relatively cheap, and Indian processing was of poor quality. But a lot of offbeat clothes were exported too in this decade, for example, Jacquard furnishing fabrics from the Karur area, terry-towels from Madurai, gauze cloth from Rajapalayam, and checked shirting to the garment-makers in Erode and Coimbatore clusters. By 1993, the production of fine-quality shirting cloth expanded greatly. Shortly thereafter checked shirting of this kind became fashionable in the Indian market for men's shirts.

Whereas the majority of the older textile mills in western India decayed after 1960, in Tamil Nadu, many older plants modernized themselves. The

Laxmi group of mills were a symbol of Coimbatore's textile-based industrialization. That business notwithstanding, small firms played a more dynamic role. The districts around the town were dotted with spinning mills. Most had started after 1985; some used secondhand machines, were managed by families, and offered short-term jobs. Textile labour was relatively peaceful and well-trained in this area, notwithstanding a large strike that took place in 1997–8. Electricity was expensive but available. The road-rail-port network functioned much better than in northern and eastern India.

The centre of the weaving clusters conducted trade. None more so than Erode. Around 1995, the Erode 'shandy' was one of the largest spot markets in cloth in the world. It was held on Tuesdays and Wednesdays. The clothes came from a circular area of a 30-mile radius centring on Erode. Both wholesale and retail purchases took place. The main products were various types of coloured cloth, usually the cheaper and poorer varieties. Wholesalers who made purchases from this market were from the southern states. The sellers were the powerloom owners. Few merchant firms took part in the spot market.

Merchant firms of the area had cloth made on contract for sale to out-of-state merchants. The out-of-state market was specialized and segmented. Assam and Madhya Pradesh took a lot of towels, the southern markets mainly lungies, eastern India a lot of dhoties, and so on. The local merchants executed orders by putting out. They got the yarn, got it sized, gave them to weavers, received finished goods or greys, and had the grey cloth processed. Nearly all the Erode local merchant firms come from handloom weaving or handloom cloth trading background. The older and the more solidly built houses in the market area dated from the 1920s, the approximate time when the successful handloom entrepreneurs moved from mainly manufacturing to mainly trading. These homes functioned as homes, offices, and warehouses.

Conclusion

Some of the material I draw on to write the chapter came from fieldworks done in 1997–1998. The industry then seemed to be fragmenting. A vast number of generic powerlooms existed side by side with a new and technologically advanced weaving industry, industrial unrest broke out from time to time, textile towns struggled to manage urban growth and pressure on public services. With a few exceptions from south India, the advanced segment had little to do with the history of handloom weaving. Elsewhere, the handloom root was not forgotten completely, but it mattered less to the organization of the business or in predicting entry into it than it did two generations before.

In the 20 years that elapsed since then, these tendencies have become stronger, though I can say that only from impressions and casual conversations.

Table 7.1 Powerlooms in Tamil Nadu

	Tamil Nadu	*India*	*Tamil Nadu's share (%)*
1942	270	15,000	1.8
1948	551		
1959	3,841	45,000	8.5
1972	12,500		
1975	34,000	310,000	11.0
1982-3	93,292	570,800	16.3
1985	100,600	640,000	15.7
1995	233,842	1,365,284	17.1
1997	4–450,000	1,700,000	23–26

Sources: India, *The Fact-Finding Committee (Handlooms and Mills)*, Calcutta: Government Press, 1942, 40; P. Poopathy, 'Economics of Powerloom Industry with special reference to Export Performance and Prospects,' MPhil dissertation of Madras University, 1989; Association of Synthetic Fibre Industry, *Handbook of Statistics 1994–95*, Part I, Mumbai, 1997; Indian Powerloom Federation, 'An Organic Approach to Technical Upgradation and Modernisation of Powerloom Industry in India', Mumbai, no date; my fieldwork done in 1997 and 1998.

The generic powerloom of western and southern India has not disappeared. But it has carried on from crisis to crisis, whereas the better-equipped weaving industry has distanced itself from the former and spread out more. A description of Malegaon published in 1996 already painted a dark picture of a community of powerloom operators sinking in economic and cultural insecurity.[12]

Such was the story of the powerlooms in India after independence. Their phenomenal growth had a lot to do with the decline of handloom weaving after 1947, while at the same time the state tried hard to protect handlooms from powerlooms. Why did the policy fail? To end the book, it would be appropriate to return to the handlooms and see how they fared after independence.

Notes

1 Besides Haynes and me, others have researched and published studies on the powerloom industry. Geert de Neve's work on labour relations in Tamil Nadu powerlooms, and Supriya Roy Chowdhury's writings on the textile industry during a crucial transition in the 1980s are important. While these works discuss their historical origins, a general historical narrative is not their aim. Supriya Roy Chowdhury, 'Political Economy of India's Textile Industry: The Case of Maharashtra, 1984–89,' *Pacific Affairs*, 68(2), 1995, 31–50; Geert De Neve, *The Everyday Politics of Labour: Working Lives in India's Informal Economy*, New Delhi: Social Science Press, 2005.

2 In 1948, the Cotton Textiles (Control) Order introduced a regime, which remained more or less intact until 1985. The motivation behind the policy was, protection

of handlooms, and labour-intensive production of cloth in general. It had five instruments: (a) freeze on mill capacity in weaving, (b) differential excise on cloth, handlooms being exempt, and differential excise on yarn, hank-yarn usable mainly in handlooms being charged at a lower rate than cone-yarn, (c) treatment of units with less than five powerlooms as equivalent of handlooms for tax purposes (in force until 1977, when all powerlooms became tax-equivalent of handlooms excepting lower duty for hand-processed handloom cloth), (d) check on the growth of powerlooms by a scheme of licensing installation, and (e) reservation of some products for handlooms, mainly coarse and coloured sarees.

3 India, *Report of the Textile Enquiry Committee*, New Delhi: Ministry of Commerce and Industry, 1954; India, *Report of the Village and Small-Scale Industries (Second Five-Year Plan Committee)*, New Delhi: Planning Commission, 1955.

4 Bombay, 'Handloom Census,' *Bulletin of the Bureau of Economics and Statistics*, 1(4), 1948.

5 A.B. Rajage, 'The Problems and Prospects of Decentralised Power Industry with respect to Ichalkaranji,' MPhil dissertation of Shivaji University, Kolhapur, no date, 59-A.

6 A.Y. Bedekar, 'A Study of the Powerloom Workers in Ichalkaranji,' MPhil dissertation of Shivaji University, Kolhapur, 1984.

7 MANTRA, Report of Survey, 13.29.

8 'Surat Powerloom Census,' Business Standard, 28.12.82.

9 Jan Breman, *Footloose Labour*, Cambridge: Cambridge University Press, 1996, 212.

10 S. Muthukumar, 'Economic Analysis of Small-Scale Powerloom Industry at Chenimalai in Periyar District,' MPhil dissertation of Bharathiar University, Coimbatore, 1990.

11 K.K. Karuppanam, 'Functioning of the Handloom Industry in Karur,' MPhil dissertation of Bharathiar University, Coimbatore, 1987, 45.

12 Meeta and Rajivlochan, 'The Past in the Present: The Weavers of Malegaon,' *Economic and Political Weekly*, 31(11), 1996, 673–8.

8

HANDLOOM AFTER INDEPENDENCE

This short chapter offers an overview of the post-independence history of handloom weaving until India's economic liberalization in the 1990s. The chapter claims that post-independence policy on the textile crafts built upon a misreading of the dominant tendency in the industry – a consolidation of capitalism – leading to distortions in government intervention and unintended consequences.

Before embarking on that task, a brief recap of the story will be useful.

Revisiting the main arguments

In the eighteenth century, India sold a lot of cloth to the rest of the world. Between 1820 and 1880, India's prominence in the world textile trade declined, as British machine-made yarn and cloth started trading widely. India's decline together with the rise of a cotton textile industry in Britain produced two unfinished scholarly debates. One of these asks how much the British success depended upon capital and knowledge gained from India trade. And the other one asks how badly the Indian economy was hurt due to the decline of its textile industry. In the early twentieth century, nationalist critics of British rule in India claimed that the fall of trade caused misery among textile artisans. Indeed, there was a fall, but the fall was concentrated in the spinning of yarn by hand. Weaving suffered a smaller extent of decline. The declining trend was somehow arrested in the 1880s. Thereafter, the industry started growing (Chapter 1).

This reversal forms the subject of the book. Why did it happen? It goes without saying that it could not and did not happen because either the handloom became a speedier machine or the weavers became steadily poorer. The divergence in loom speed between hand and machine weaving was so great that neither of these two strategies could meet the gap even by a small extent. What, then, is the answer? For an industry that employed several million people, it is hard to claim that there was just one story. This book stresses the most important and consequential story for interpretations of

Indian economic history, also the one that the economic historians might find the most troubling.

The answer according to the book is that the weavers stayed competitive because they possessed skills that machines could not copy exactly, and consumer demand for these skills was strong in the domestic market. Trade and the open economy of the colonial times helped handloom weaving. The railways and political unity integrated distant and isolated markets into larger even national ones. Trade cheapened some key raw materials that were now mass produced and imported, such as cotton yarn, raw silk, dyes, and chemicals. In turn, the ability to access distant but profitable markets and trade opportunities encouraged capital accumulation. The concentration of money led to geographical concentration of the industry into fewer clusters and fewer cities. Weavers from a wide area gravitated to where there were more money and more skills and more complementary services like trade, banks, process houses, and transport links.

Accumulation of money helped artisan-capitalists to try out new technologies. Labour productivity increased. Technological change was at one level easy to implement because most small tools or processes available came from Europe ready-packaged and cheap. However, these were adopted to serve specific purposes connected to cloth quality. That is, weavers adopted them when they felt that by doing so they would be able to deliver quality and diversity of design at an attractive price. For example, wider use of coloured cotton or silk yarn on saree borders, when the dyes and the yarns were imported, happened because the move enabled the weavers to establish brands and variety.

A final stage in this process of endogenous technological change was the powerloom factory. From the frame loom, the idea of a power-driven frame loom was a small step. Weavers replaced handlooms by power-driven looms in products where such a switch was possible. The ground had thus been prepared for what was to become in the next few decades India's largest industry.[1]

The narrative locates the main source of change in the relationship between weaving and the wider economic forces unfolding in India, changes in consumption, integration of markets, and a fall in costs of trade, for examples. It does not see machinery as the driving factor behind everything. That does not mean that competition from machines was unimportant even in the twentieth century when handloom waving had stabilized. Markets and competition were never static but were constantly changing. Consumers did not understand by quality a fixed thing. Machines and factories in India constantly tried to break into the handloom saree business and scored significant success with rayon and printed sarees. Market integration made some weaving traditions fail to establish brands and disappear. Individual weavers, when they could simplify the saree enough, gave up the handloom for the powerloom. In short, survival or growth of handloom weaving did not happen in a protected environment.

The handloom narrative of the book ends in India's independence from British colonial rule in 1947. Between 1950 and 1956, the government of India designed an industrialization strategy. According to the new strategy, the state would lead the process as a regulator and as an investor. The strategy stayed almost intact until the 1980s. What happened to the handlooms in this regime is a rather curious story. It is a curious story because, whereas the new regime made the regeneration of the crafts a major goal, it still served the crafts rather badly. The anomaly stemmed from a crafts policy based on myth rather than facts about handloom weaving.

To see how myth played such a powerful role, we need to go back a little further to the interwar period and study the emerging nationalist discourse on the crafts.

The ideological roots of India's crafts policy

In the interwar period, many people were growing interested in economic development, in the future role of the state in promoting development or industrialization, and in the future of the handicrafts in the developmental or industrial system that was to take shape. Two radically opposing discourses on the future of the Indian crafts emerged from this enterprise.

One of these positions looked at the capitalistic experimentation, urban markets, and innovations then going on inside handloom weaving and allied industries, and which formed the core of this book. In the view of those experts who studied the capitalistic dynamic and contributed to this narrative, these experiments were working but to get more of the same thing, outsiders could help.

They based their writings on the intellectual tradition of crafts studies that had begun with the arts-and-crafts movement of the 1880s and culminated in the production of the craft monographs and the industrial surveys carried out by provincial governments between 1895 and 1910. A little later, a few academics based in Pune's Gokhale Institute of Politics and Economics carried on the intellectual tradition. The founder-director D.R. Gadgil took a keen interest in the subject and encouraged surveys of local towns. One of the master's theses done in this place, in 1936, and later published as a book, talked about factories, capitalists, wage-workers, experiments, and fashions, if in an overly schematic way.[2]

In 1942, a government report, the *Fact-finding Committee: Handlooms and Mills*, revisited the same ground. The making of the report deserves a brief discussion. That tariff protection for textiles and the swadeshi campaign against imports before the move had helped the factory industry in cotton and damaged the handlooms, was understood in policy circles (Chapter 1). In 1942, the Commerce Department of the government commissioned a report to study competition between handlooms and mills. The report could well have been a run-of-the-mill effort, but for the choice of one of India's finest academics of the time, P.J. Thomas (1895–1965, see 'Selected biographies'), as its main writer. Thomas ensured that the report avoided the rhetoric about the crafts completely, whether the Gandhian kind (discussion to follow) that blamed technological modernization for the poverty of the weaver, or the Marxist type that blamed the capitalists for the poverty of the artisan. It became a truly fact-finding enterprise. The interviewees included capitalists, the most articulate section of the industry. With this resource in hand, the report could conclude that the industry had considerable strengths that radiated from the skilled and urban side of the business. That was the last time that the urban handicrafts would figure in mainstream public discourses in a serious way (more on this shift later).

This intellectual tradition offered a rule for engagement to the state and interested outsiders. They should strengthen skill and innovation. Crafts needed science and needed the capitalists who understood and would fund innovation. The fast dyes, Jacquards, dobby, and frame-looms that a section of the industry was using already showed the way for the others. Artisans should show the way to other artisans. Outsiders could not show them how to weave better cloth, but they could sponsor technical schools that would employ skilled weavers who might do that. The town or the city was a natural locus of such activities, for that was where most capitalists were, where the instruments were developed and sold, and the potential market for the most profitable goods was.

The message is best expressed using the words of the Madras and Mysore officer Alfred Chatterton (see 'Selected biographies'): 'The regeneration of Indian industries can only be accomplished by the intelligent application of capital and by bringing to the assistance of the artisans the technical results of modern science.'[3] Capital, science, and skill had already joined hands; this view would want the interdependence to expand and grow stronger. Chatterton articulated the message perhaps most clearly, drawing on a long personal experience of partnerships between the Departments of Industry that he once led and the weaver-capitalists of Salem, Madurai, and other textile towns of South India. Being an engineer himself, his main interest was technology. To write his books and speeches, Chatterton interviewed prominent artisan capitalists and studied their production methods closely. Almost all of his recommendations were derived from such interactions. Many others in the academics and the government followed a similar approach.

From the 1920s, a second discourse on the crafts was beginning to emerge. It built on sentiment more than on scholarship. It built on the belief that colonialism and foreign trade had pushed Indian crafts onto a trajectory of relentless decline and that there was no mechanism internal to the crafts that could stem this decline. They needed help from the state and from the political activists. This idea emerged in the wake of the Indian nationalist movement. M.K. Gandhi, the architect of Indian nationalism in the interwar period, gave it a voice and a clear shape.

The first feature we should note about the second, Gandhian, discourse is that it turned its back on the city. From the 1920s, the Indian nationalists would talk about the village when talking about the crafts. This connection was based on a mythical view of the past. 'In those days,' as one contributor called the past, there was a perfect symbiosis between agriculture, spinning, and weaving. All activities centred in the village. Farmers grew cotton, women in the rich and poor families spun yarn, and weavers wove that yarn, all in the same village. The village crafts were self-reliant and entrepreneurial in meeting the needs of local consumers. 'The villager,' wrote this same propagandist, 'was . . . capitalist and labourer in one person. He was the entrepreneur and expert. . . . The village in India and not the town was the base of the economic structure. The spheres of industry . . . radiated from the villages.'[4] Gandhi went even further. In those days, according to him, 'every portion of the work [on the textile industry] was done by the farming population.'[5]

Where did this image of history come from? The authority that Gandhi and his contemporaries liked to cite was the author-publicist Romesh Chunder Dutt (1848–1909). In his *Economic History of India in the Victorian Age* (1903), Dutt presented a picture of the golden age of the Indian artisan that became a template for the nationalists. Reflecting on the pre-colonial times, Dutt said that '[textile production] was an industry peculiarly suited to Indian village life. There were no great mills and factories; but each woman brought her cotton from the village market, and sold her yarn to the village weaver who supplied merchants and traders with cloth.'[6] Crafts were the 'handmaiden' of agriculture. Dutt had no more evidence to show that the golden age really existed than did the Gandhians. He needed that golden age to claim that British rule had destroyed it.

Then, in the nineteenth century, disaster struck. The colonial policy of free trade and the Industrial Revolution ensured the decline of Indian artisans, a process that Dutt called 'one of the saddest episodes of British rule in India.'[7] Although Dutt held British rule accountable, other writers who accepted that the decline happened saw that it was part of a global process of technological obsolescence. It would be 'misleading to call the Industrial Revolution in England to account for the decadence of our manufactures.'[8] No matter the root, the decline was irreversible, relentless, and externally caused.

A year after independence, in 1948, the Indian National Congress outfit the National Planning Committee deliberated on craft policy. A contributor to the document that came out of the discussion and was to serve as a guide for future policy, declared that 'it is a matter of common knowledge' that before British rule, 40 percent of Indians were industrial, whereas at the end of British rule, 'as a result of the decline of our handicrafts, the disengaged artisans . . . were forced to take to agriculture.'[9] But this decline and fall were much more than just a decline of industry alone, or 'deindustrialization' to use the more modern term (see Chapter 1). Not only was '[t]he tendency of all village industries was . . . towards decline,' but the handicrafts and the village declined together.[10] A whole way of life was becoming lost.

Gandhi now delivered his great message of hope: revive the village. In effect, that would mean recover the old symbiosis between agriculture, spinning, and weaving. In turn, that would mean revive *hand*-spinning of yarn using locally grown cotton. Artisans, after all, had not disappeared, but they were lying low in the countryside. Once the British left the scene, the women should again spin their own yarn from locally grown cotton, and the weavers would weave that yarn. The Gandhians would help them recover the golden age by keeping the memory of hand-spinning alive. Gandhi showed the way by taking up spinning himself (Figure 8.1).

If there was hope for the handloom weavers at all, the hope lay in pushing the city weavers back into the village. The ideal future for handloom weaving was one in which '[m]ore weavers will . . . settle in the villages and not

Figure 8.1 Poster showing Gandhi spinning yarn on a wheel

Source: Historic Collection/Alamy Stock Photo

desert them as they are now doing.'[11] Such a step would inevitably mean a de-skilling of the weaving process. Pushing weavers back to the village and making them weave handspun yarn would amount to the production of thick uncoloured cotton cloth. Making the consumers buy more of it and weavers produce more of it could not be achieved without political propaganda and state regulation.

In the 1930s, the former discourse that stressed the skilling of the handloom weaver was becoming more and more obscure, and the Gandhian discourse that stressed de-skilling of the handloom weaver was rising in popularity. The former was tied to the lower-level provincial bureaucracy and the odd academic. Such people had no political influence at all. The latter was tied to the rising tide of politics. It had a political effect and was gaining traction rapidly. There was not even a contest. The Chattertonian vision died quietly. Sentimental nationalism defeated knowledge.

In the interwar period, M.K. Gandhi became the de facto leader and spokesperson of the political movement for freedom. Nationalist politics until 1920 had taken the form of negotiations and public demand for more Indian representation in running the government. Much of that debate occurred in print. In a country with high illiteracy, few people joined the debate. Gandhi's entry changed politics because he raised issues and made gestures that connected to many people who so far could not take part in politics. One of his gestures was made towards the crafts.

I believe that by bracketing the artisans and the farmers together, Gandhi was trying to create a united platform of resistance and protest against colonial rule. How successful this project was politically is another matter. Intellectually, the problem was that the weavers were already too unequal and differentiated to be united in one platform. The nationalists could carry on this campaign by denying this inequality. In effect, they needed to deny the existence of the strongest part of handloom weaving, which was a commercially successful urban business using an extremely complex technology innovatively for profit. The crafts that Gandhi and his disciples endorsed was simple, weak, traditional, and rural. The most dynamic and competitive part of the handloom weaving industry was neither simple, nor weak, nor traditional, nor rural.

Gandhi was shrewd enough to know that the most successful weavers out there were too skilled to fit either his vision or his political campaign. He, therefore, dismissed skill. His view of craft skill was expressed in this statement: 'the nation has to revise its taste for the thin tawdry and useless muslins. I see no art in weaving muslins, that do not cover but only expose the body.' If the weavers were to receive support, they had better join Gandhi's pet project and weave coarse and thick handspun yarn.[12] The more amateurish the spinner, as most people in Gandhi's milieu were, the uglier would be the cloth and the more successful the mission to de-skill the weaver.

Gandhi's associates, disciples, mouthpieces, and propagandists mechanically repeated these ideas. These disciples were mostly male. The consumers of complex handloom clothes were mostly female. Gandhi's insistence that everyone should wear only clothing made of handspun yarn, consistent with the back-to-the-village sentiment, made for a particularly unattractive and cheerless saree the women in his set were forced to wear. Gandhi's preferred garment for his women followers, therefore, was a drab, unhappy, and misogynist piece of clothing. It was a far cry from the textiles that created the revival of handloom weaving in the previous half a century.

The politically correct saree was not only coarse but white, the colour of widowhood. Many women resented this, but their husbands and fathers ignored them. 'I thought of Gandhiji,' wrote the Malayali poet and writer Kamala Das in her autobiography, 'as a brigand, although I did not speak my mind then. I thought it his diabolic aim to strip the ladies of all their finery so that they became plain and dull. Austerity seemed meaningless.'[13] Gandhi was well aware of the bitterness and resentment the women felt. His message for the women who might want to wear colourful clothing was, 'may they find solace in the music of the spinning wheel.'[14]

In his writings, he loudly praised his few female disciples for their commitment. Invariably these were rich city women with a wardrobe overflowing with silk sarees telling poor village women why the latter should stop wearing the few coloured sarees that they had and buy new white ones. It is anybody's guess how persuasive these rich women were.

It was this bleak and unreal image of crafted textiles that the Indian nationalists chose, after 1950, as the candidate worthy of serious state aid.

Craft policy and weaving: 1950–1990

Inspired by Gandhi's fantasy, or to concede some ground to it, India's socialist leadership after 1947 designed a policy of helping the craft industries. The form of state aid that this policy preferred was subsidization of the coarser and plainer goods and reaching the subsidy to the producer. The merchant and the complex goods were recognized, but these now stood for the exploitation the weavers suffered. Capitalism was made the enemy of the crafts, potentially making them weaker than before. New ministries and departments were set up to channel government money. The preferred institution to handle the money was the cooperative credit and marketing societies to be set up by the state governments. Bureaucrats and ideologues, usually male and with little knowledge of a good saree, implemented this policy. The handlooms' core competence, skill, was undermined, so were the main agents of change, artisan-capitalists, and both suffered attrition.

Where did this policy go wrong? The message of this book is that private enterprise led a positive transformation that reinforced the competitiveness of the industry. In the Gandhian discourse, on the other hand, there was almost no discussion about helping the private enterprise in the handlooms. Their strongest point – innovation, the ability to understand the product enough to know what innovation was needed, and the ability to fund innovation – the state overlooked. The ideological basis of the post-independence handloom policy was based, if not on a swindle, a delusion of which Gandhi was the root.

The new Textile Policy protected handlooms, that is, prohibited mechanized weaving from the production of a wide range of clothes, even from expanding the capacity of production. But the areas protected had no relationship with their comparative advantage. In bordered sarees, the handlooms did not need protection; in plain grey sheets, protection of the handlooms amounted to imposing a tax on the consumer. The power-driven weaving factories, or powerlooms, were formally clubbed with the textile mills, but with the knowledge that many handloom weavers themselves moved into this field often, were in practice left free. The governments of major textile-producing areas, such as Maharashtra and Tamil Nadu, did not enforce restrictions on the powerlooms, as we have seen.

Despite occasional success stories, the general outcome of this package was disastrous. Over the next three decades, it destroyed one of the world's largest cotton textile mill industries. It did not help the handlooms. Cooperatives wasted money, made little profits, became defunct, but stayed alive to make use of government money, became dens of corruption, or where they worked well, represented the interests of capitalists. There was nothing like a partnership between the state and private enterprise, not at least formally. That option was never seriously considered.

Whether because of state aid, its inherent strengths, or a protected market, the handloom number increased for a few decades after independence. A national handloom census in 1987–88 reported nearly four million handlooms working in India, including 2.2 million full-time commercial looms and 1.7 million domestic looms in the north-eastern states. The figure was considerably higher than the estimates in the 1930s surveys. Most such numbers were unreliable. Because government money was channeled through the cooperatives, the latter had an interest in inflating the number of members. Further, these numbers hid many powerloom units.

The percentages are a bit more credible. The four southern states – Tamil Nadu, Karnataka, Kerala, and Andhra Pradesh – had 42 percent of all looms in India. This large area included the older weaving complexes in southern Andhra (mainly Cuddapah district), coastal Andhra (East Godavari, Prakasam, and Guntur), Malabar, the Tamil Nadu towns, northern Karnataka (Bijapur) and parts of Telangana (mainly Karimnagar and Warangal). Outside south India, in Bihar, Uttar Pradesh, West Bengal, and Orissa, handlooms existed in reasonable numbers; the four states included 30 percent of all looms. Elsewhere, in Punjab, handlooms had all but disappeared, and in Maharashtra and Gujarat, powerloom factories had swept the handloom textile towns.

The rise of the powerloom factory was in some sense inevitable. In the major handloom weaving clusters, thanks to the changes described in this book, some moneyed people understood the business well and were willing to go into mass production. Also, in these clusters, the weaving process, the spinning process, and the processing operations worked separately as specialized fields, whereas inside the mills these three were integrated. The enormous size of the mills and their position in the centre of the metropolitan space had made the integration model expensive and uneconomical. The decentralized model was more flexible and, being in smaller towns, less costly. Because the three processes were separated, weaving could now mechanize with a small extra investment.

And yet, because of government regulation, there was little import of technology. The cotton mills were prohibited from modernizing. The powerloom factories, being technically illegal, could not modernize either. Nor did they have enough lobbying power to ask for a license to import machines or get capital from banks. They grew by buying discarded looms or procured looms of local make, but of a vintage that kept their quality poor. One of the world's largest fabric production systems delivered some of the worst-quality fabrics.

In 1985, the policy regime of capacity restrictions and technology embargo formally ended. By then, it had left the cotton mill industry in ruins, a big number of handlooms artificially sustained, and powerloom factories burdened by obsolete looms.

Handloom weaving since 1990

In the 1990s, another round of reforms reduced state aid channelled into the handlooms through the cooperatives. Handicrafts briefly emerged as a leading export. The growing international tourism business stimulated handicraft markets and trade. In the 2000s, within the ministries, talk of rebuilding private-public partnership in the craft industries began. The rethinking was unlikely to revive those handlooms that were destined to fail without subsidy. The new accent was also too export-oriented to matter much to the saree weavers.

Since then, the scope of handloom weaving has narrowed considerably. Although official datasets report over four million still in the business (perhaps on 1.5–2 million looms), the number is suspect as always. The more visible side of handloom production is a set of high-quality goods – mainly bordered sarees – in which the technology still retains a comparative advantage. Increasingly, the best bordered saree became a rich woman's clothing specific to certain occasions. For the more ordinary sorts of sarees, they were completely taken over by powerlooms.

When I published *Artisans and Industrialization* in 1993, serious scholarly work on contemporary handlooms was scarce. Since then, a few studies appeared. One of the more important ones is a book by Kanakalatha Mukund and B. Syama Sundari on Andhra Pradesh weavers as of 2001.

The book advanced three theses.[15] First, weaving declined in the state in the recent decades. Second, the fall concentrated in the state-sponsored cooperative segment. In official perception, capitalist capture of the societies had weakened them; in fact, they had grown organizationally weak and could not withstand the retreat of subsidies. Third, private enterprise thrived in high-quality production lines, where looms had grown, profits had increased, but living conditions of labour did not improve. Another study, by Seemanthini Niranjana, looked at the coastal Andhra handlooms about the same time, and her work revealed the picture of an industry not yet technologically obsolete but struggling to gain market access and overcome institutional deficiencies, including deep structural problems from which the cooperatives suffered.[16] A yet third study with a more specific focus on network ties among weavers in the present times shows that whereas the handloom weavers continue to rely on informal cooperation, the master-weavers among them display unusual characteristics such as high levels of skill, ability to command more resources, and the knowledge of several languages.[17] The capitalist spirit survives, but on a much narrower scale from before.

Even as the range of handloom production has seemingly narrowed, the products where the technology holds its ground have become more skilled and more expensive. This is a niche but not a small or depressed niche. Given India's rapid economic growth and consumerist boom since the 1990s, the niche stays large. The middle class is growing in size and purchasing power. Designed handloom sarees are a visible product on the high street of any major south Indian city. Most international airport terminals in India have a silk saree shop. In the production of the designed saree, handlooms and powerloom weaving retain close bonds. There is constant experimentation on what designs can be woven on powerlooms, and most handloom weaving clusters have both types of technology working side by side. The production of design itself has become an enormously easier activity and far less a preserve of weavers, thanks to computers. Handloom weavers now recruit computer-literate graduates to do a job in a few minutes that would take a senior master-weaver a month to perform a hundred years ago.[18]

As the handlooms seem to be settling to a field where it had long been dominant, powerloom weaving morphed into something else altogether. Most fabric production now takes place in weaving factories that started after India liberalized its trade regime and allowed the import of technology. Technically power-driven, these factories are a generation apart from the traditional powerloom factory. They produce clothes for the ready-made garment industry. The traditional powerlooms have not disappeared. Indeed some that were started with weavers' or handloom merchants' capital have modernized and joined the top-end production system. The rest is too diverse a set to generalize on, as the previous chapter has shown already.

Notes

1 D. Haynes, 'Artisan Cloth-Producers and the Emergence of Powerloom Manufacture in Western India 1920–1950,' *Past and Present*, 172, 2001, 170–98.
2 N.M. Joshi, *Urban Handicrafts of the Bombay-Deccan*, Poona: Gokhale Institute of Politics and Economics, 1936.
3 Alfred Chatterton, *Industrial Evolution in India*, Madras: The Hindu Office, 1912, 209.
4 P.R. Ramachandra Rao, *Decay of Indian Industries*, Bombay: D.B. Taraporevala, 1935, 140, the book was endorsed by Gandhi's mouthpiece J.C. Kumarappa.
5 M.K. Gandhi, *The Wheel of Fortune*, Madras: Ganesh and Co., 1922, 61.
6 Romesh C. Dutt, *The Economic History of India*, vol. 2, London: Kegan Paul, 1903, 388.
7 Cited by Ramachandra Rao, *Decay*, 67. Neither Rao nor Gandhi nor his other disciples seem to have read any one of the craft monographs then available.
8 Ramachandra Rao, *Decay*, 69.
9 Ibid., 68.
10 A.R. Desai, *The Social Background to Indian Nationalism*, Bombay: Popular Prakashan, 1948 (2010 reprint), 86.
11 S.V. Puntambekar and N.S. Varadachari, *Hand-Spinning and Hand-Weaving*, Ahmedabad: All India Spinners Association, 1926, 191.
12 Gandhi, *Wheel of Fortune*, 89.
13 Cited by Dorothy Jones, 'The Eloquent Sari,' *Textile*, 2(1), 2004, 52–63.
14 Gandhi, *Wheel of Fortune*, 55.
15 Kanakalatha Mukund and B. Syama Sundari, *Traditional Industry in the New Market Economy: The Cotton Handlooms of Andhra Pradesh*, New Delhi, Thousand Oaks, CA and London: Sage Publications, 2001.
16 Seemanthini Niranjana, 'Thinking with Handlooms: Perspectives from Andhra Pradesh,' *Economic and Political Weekly*, 39(6), 2004, 553–63.
17 Suresh Bhagavatula, Tom Elfring, Aad van Tilburg, and Gerhard G. van de Bunt, 'How Social and Human Capital Influence Opportunity Recognition and Resource Mobilization in India's Handloom Industry,' *Journal of Business Venturing*, 25(3), 2010, 245–60.
18 Interview of Nalli Kuppuswami Chetti (2014), Chairman, Nalli Silk Saris, Creating Emerging Markets: Oral History Collection, Harvard Business School, available at www.hbs.edu/businesshistory/Documents/emerging-markets-transcripts/ChettiTranscriptWithCoverFinal.pdf (accessed 1 July 2019).

REFERENCES

Amalsad, D.M. (1926), *The Development of the Madras Handkerchief and Lungy and Kaily Industry in the Madras Presidency*, Madras: Government Press.

Anon (1982), 'Surat Powerloom Census,' *Business Standard*, 28 December.

Ashmore, Sonia (2012), *Muslin*, London: V&A Publishing.

Austin, Gareth and Kaoru Sugihara, eds. (2012), *Labour-Intensive Industrialization in Global History*, Abingdon and New York: Routledge.

Baden-Powell, B.H. (1886), 'On Some of the Difficulties of Art Manufactures,' *Journal of Indian Art*, 1(5), 37–9.

Bagchi, A.K. (1970), *Private Investment in India, 1900–1939*, Cambridge: Cambridge University Press.

——— (1976), 'De-Industrialization in India in the Nineteenth Century: Some Theoretical Implications,' *Journal of Development Studies*, 12(2), 135–64.

Baker, C.J. (1984), *An Indian Rural Economy 1880–1955: The Tamilnad Countryside*, New Delhi: Oxford University Press.

Banerjei, N.N. (1899), *Monograph on the Woollen Fabrics of Bengal*, Calcutta: Government Press.

Basu, Shreela and Abhra Basu (2017), *Banglar Terracotta Mandir: Akhyan o Alankaran* (Terracotta Temples of Bengal: Narratives and Illustrations, in Bengali), Calcutta: Sygnet Press.

Bayly, C.A. (1986), 'The Origins of Swadeshi (Home Industry): Cloth and Indian Society, 1700–1930,' in A. Appadurai, ed., *The Social Life of Things*, Cambridge: Cambridge University Press, 285–322.

Bedekar, A.Y. (1984), 'A Study of the Powerloom Workers in Ichalkaranji,' MPhil dissertation of Shivaji University, Kolhapur.

Bengal (1929), *Report on the Survey of Cottage Industries of Bengal*, Calcutta: Department of Industries.

——— (1937), *Report on the Survey of Handloom Weaving Industry in Bengal* (J.M. Ghose), Calcutta: Board of Economic Enquiry.

——— (1940), *Handloom Cotton Weaving Industry in Bengal*, Calcutta: Department of Industries.

Berg, Maxine (1996), 'Women's Consumption and the Industrial Classes of Eighteenth-Century England,' *Journal of Social History*, 30(2), 415–34.

Bhagavatula, Suresh, Tom Elfring, Aad van Tilburg and Gerhard G. van de Bunt (2010), 'How Social and Human Capital Influence Opportunity Recognition and

Resource Mobilization in India's Handloom Industry,' *Journal of Business Venturing*, 25(3), 245–60.

Bharathan, K. (1988), 'Handloom Industry in Tamil Nadu: A Study of Organisational Structure,' PhD dissertation of Madras Institute of Development Studies, Madras.

Birdwood, George C. (1887), *The Industrial Arts of India*, Part 2, London: Chapman and Hall.

Blennerhassett, A. (1898), *A Monograph on the Cotton Fabrics of the Central Provinces*, Nagpur: Government Press.

Bombay (1948), *Report of the Sholapur Handloom Weavers Enquiry Committee*, Bombay: Political and Services Department.

——— (1948), 'Handloom Census,' *Bulletin of the Bureau of Economics and Statistics*, 1(4).

Breman, Jan (1996), *Footloose Labour*, Cambridge: Cambridge University Press.

British Parliamentary Papers (1847), *Cotton (India): A Return of the Quantity of Cotton Wool Exported from the British Possessions in India, in Each Year during Which the Accounts Have Been Kept: Stating the Ports of Shipment, Quantity Shipped, Countries to Which Exported, and Shipment to Each Country*, London: HMSO.

——— (1852–1853), *Calicoes, &c. Return of the Quantity and Value of Calicoes, Muslins, and Cotton Goods and Cotton Yarn Exported from, and Imported Into, India, in Each Year, from 1833 to 1852: Also, Similar Return for the United Kingdom, for the Same Period*, London: HMSO.

Cassels, W.R. (1861), *Cotton: An Account of its Culture in the Bombay Presidency Prepared from Government Records and Other Authentic Sources in Accordance with a Resolution of the Government of India*, Bombay: Government Press.

Census of India (1901a), *Bombay*, Part 1 (Report), Bombay: Government Press.

——— (1901b), *Madras*, Part 1 (Report), Madras: Government Press.

——— (1902), *Punjab, Its Feudatories, and the North-West Frontier Provinces*, Part 1 (Report), Simla: Government Press.

——— (1961a), *District Census Handbook* (Salem District), Madras: Government Press.

——— (1961b), *Handlooms in Madras State*, Vol. 9, Part 11-A, 110, Madras: Government Press.

——— (1961c), *Silk Weaving of Kanchipuram*, Vol. 9, Part 7-A, Handicraft Survey Monograph No. 1, Madras: Government Press.

Central Provinces and Berar (1908–1909), *Report of the Industrial Survey of the Central Provinces and Berar*, Nagpur: Government Press.

Chandra, Bipan (1966), *The Rise and Growth of Economic Nationalism in India*, New Delhi: People's Publishing House.

——— (1991), 'Colonial India: British versus Indian Views of Development,' *Review (Fernand Braudel Center)*, 14(1), 81–167.

Chapman, S.D. (1983), 'David Evans & Co. The Last of the Old London Textile Printers,' *Textile History*, 14(1), 29–56.

Chatterjee, Atul Chandra (1908), *Notes on the Industries of the United Provinces*, Allahabad: Government Press.

Chatterjee, Ruma (1987), 'Cotton Handloom Manufactures of Bengal, 1870–1921,' *Economic and Political Weekly*, 22(25), 988–97.

Chatterton, Alfred (1912), *Industrial Evolution in India*, Madras: The Hindu Office.

——— (1915), *Agricultural and Industrial Problems in India*, Madras: G.A. Natesan and Company.

Chattopadhyay, Raghabendra (1975), 'De-Industrialisation in India Reconsidered,' *Economic and Political Weekly*, 10(12), 523–31.

Choudhury, Suchitra (2015), '"It Was an Imitashon to Be Sure": The Imitation Indian Shawl in Design Reform and Imaginative Fiction,' *Textile History*, 46(2), 189–212.

Clingingsmith, David and Jeffrey Williamson (2008), 'Deindustrialization in 18th and 19th Century India: Mughal Decline, Climate Shocks and British Industrial Ascent,' *Explorations in Economic History*, 45(3), 209–34.

Colebrook, H.T. (1804), *Remarks on the Husbandry and Internal Commerce of Bengal*, Calcutta.

Cookson, H.C. (1885–1886), *Monograph on Silk Industry in the Punjab*, Lahore: Government Press.

Dave, I.R. (1976), *The Saurashtrians of South India*, Rajkot: Publisher not known.

De Neve, Geert (2005), *The Everyday Politics of Labour: Working Lives in India's Informal Economy*, New Delhi: Social Science Press.

Desai, A.R. (1948), *Social Background of Indian Nationalism*, Bombay: Popular Prakashan, 2010 reprint.

Desai, Meghnad (1970), 'Demand for Cotton Textiles in Nineteenth Century India,' *Indian Economic and Social History Review*, 8(4), 337–61.

De Vries, Jan (2008), *The Industrious Revolution: Consumer Behavior and the Household Economy, 1650 to the Present*, Cambridge: Cambridge University Press.

Dewar, F. (1901), *Monograph on the Silk Fabrics of the Central Provinces*, Nagpur: Government Press.

Dutt, Romesh C. (1903), *The Economic History of India*, Vol. 2, London: Kegan Paul.

Edwardes, S.M. (1900), *A Monograph upon the Silk Fabrics of the Bombay Presidency*, Bombay: Government Press.

Enthoven, R.E. (1895), *The Cotton Fabrics of the Bombay Presidency*, Bombay: Government Press.

Fawcett, C.G.H. (1896), *Monograph on Dyes and Dyeing in the Bombay Presidency*, Bombay: Government Press.

Forbes Royle, J. (1851), *On the Culture and Commerce of Cotton in India and Elsewhere*, London: Smith Elder.

Gadgil, D.R. (1928), *The Industrial Evolution of India*, London: Oxford University Press.

Gandhi, M.K. (1922), *The Wheel of Fortune*, Madras: Ganesh and Co., 89.

Garrett, R.V. (1897), *Monograph on Cotton Fabrics of Berar*, Nagpur: Government Press.

Gazetteer (1929), *Mysore (Economic)*, Bangalore: Government Press.

——— (1930), *Mysore*, Mysore: Government Press.

Gazetteer, Bombay Presidency (1884–1886a), *Ahmedabad*, Bombay: Government Press.

——— (1884–1886b), *Belgaum*, Bombay: Government Press.

——— (1884–1886c), *Khandesh District*, Bombay: Government Press.

——— (1884–1886d), *Sholapur District*, Bombay: Government Press.

Gazetteer, Bengal District (1909), *Sambalpur*, Calcutta: Government Press.

——— (1910), *Nadia*, Calcutta: Government Press.

Gazetteer, Madras District (1917), *Salem*, Madras: Government Press.

——— (1918), *Salem District*, Madras: Government Press.

Gazetteer, United Provinces (1909), *Benares*, Allahabad: Government Press.

Guha, Amalendu (1972), 'Raw Cotton of Western India: 1750–1850,' *Indian Economic Social History Review*, 9(1), 1–41.

——— (1989), 'The Decline of India's Cotton Handicrafts: 1800–1905: A Quantitative Macro-Study,' in *Occasional Paper No. 117*, Calcutta: Centre for Studies in Social Sciences.

Guha, Sumit (1985), *The Agrarian Economy of Bombay-Deccan*, New Delhi: Oxford University Press.

——— (1989), 'The Handloom Industry of Central India: 1825–1950,' *Indian Economic and Social History Review*, 26(3), 297–318.

Gupta, G.N. (1909), *Resources of Eastern Bengal and Assam*, Shillong: Government Press.

Habib, Irfan (1985), 'Studying a Colonial Economy: Without Perceiving Colonialism,' *Modern Asian Studies*, 19(3), 355–81.

Hadaway, W.S. (1917), *Cotton Painting and Printing in the Madras Presidency*, Madras: Government Press.

Hadi, S.M. (1896), *Monograph on Dyes and Dyeing in NWFP and Oudh*, Lucknow: Government Press.

Hailey, William Malcolm (1899), *Monograph on the Silk Industry of the Punjab*, Lahore: Government Press.

Hardy, G.S. (1929), *Report on the Import Tariff on Cotton Piecegoods and on External Competition in the Cotton Piecegoods Trade*, Calcutta: Government Press.

Harnetty, Peter (1991), 'Deindustrialization Revisited: The Handloom Weavers of the Central Provinces of India,' *Modern Asian Studies*, 25(4), 455–510.

Harvard Business School (2014), 'Interview of Nalli Kuppuswami Chetti, Chairman, Nalli Silk Saris, Creating Emerging Markets: Oral History Collection,' Harvard Business School, available at www.hbs.edu/businesshistory/Documents/emerging-markets-transcripts/ChettiTranscriptWithCoverFinal.pdf (accessed 1 July 2019).

Havell, E.B. (1905), *Handloom Weaving in India*, Calcutta: Luxmir Bhandar.

Havell, E.B. (1912), *The Basis for Artistic and Industrial Revival in India*, Madras: The Theosophical Society.

Hayami, Akira (2016), *Japan's Industrious Revolution: Economic and Social Transformations in the Early Modern Period*, Tokyo and London: Springer.

Haynes, Douglas E. (1996a), 'The Logic of the Artisan Firm in a Capitalist Economy: Handloom Weavers and Technological Change in Western India, 1880–1947,' in B. Stein and S. Subrahmanyarn, eds., *Institutions and Economic Change in South Asia*, New Delhi: Oxford University Press, 173–205.

——— (1996b), 'Weavers' Capital and the Origins of the Powerlooms: Technological Transformation and Structural Change among Handloom Producers in Western India, 1920–1950,' Association of Asian Studies Meeting, Washington.

——— (1999), 'Market Formation in Khandesh, c. 1820–1930,' *Indian Economic and Social History Review*, 36(3), 275–302.

——— (2001), 'Artisan Cloth-Producers and the Emergence of Powerloom Manufacture in Western India 1920–1950,' *Past and Present*, 172, 170–98.

——— (2012), *Small Town Capitalism in Western India: Artisans, Merchants, and the Making of the Informal Economy, 1870–1960*, Cambridge: Cambridge University Press.

Haynes, Douglas E. and Tirthankar Roy (1999), 'Conceiving Mobility: Weavers' Migration in Precolonial and Colonial India,' *Indian Economic and Social History Review*, 33(1), 35–67.

Heston, Alan (1983), 'National Income,' in Dharma Kumar, ed., *The Cambridge Economic History of India*, Vol. 2, Cambridge: Cambridge University Press, 376–462.

Hobson, E.A. (1887), *Cotton in Berar*, Nagpur: Government Press.

Hoey, William (1880), *A Monograph on Trade and Manufactures in Northern India*, Lucknow: American Methodist Mission Press.

Imperial Gazetteer of India (1908), *Economic*, Oxford: Clarendon Press.

Imperial Gazetteer of India, Provincial Series (1908a), *Bombay*, Bombay: Government Press.

——— (1908b), *Punjab*, Calcutta: Government Press.

——— (1909), *Hyderabad State*, Calcutta: Government Press.

India (1870), *The Berar Gazetteer*, Nagpur: Government Press.

——— (1918), *Indian Industrial Commission*, Report and Minutes of Evidence, Calcutta: Government Press.

——— (1931), *Royal Commission on Labour in India*, Vol. 11, Supplementary, London: HMSO.

——— (1942), *Fact-Finding Committee: Handlooms and Mills*, Calcutta: Government Press.

——— (1954), *Report of the Textile Enquiry Committee*, New Delhi: Ministry of Commerce.

——— (1955), *Report of the Village and Small-Scale Industries* (Second Five-Year Plan Committee), New Delhi: Planning Commission.

——— (1964), *Report of the Powerloom Enquiry Committee*, New Delhi: Ministry of Commerce and Industry.

——— (1965), *Report of the Working Group on Handlooms*, New Delhi: Ministry of Commerce.

Indian Industrial Conference (1906), *Report of the First Indian Industrial Conference* (Benares, 1905), Allahabad.

Indian Tariff Board (1935a), *Oral Evidence Recorded during Enquiry on the Grant of Protection to the Sericultural Industry*, Vols. 2 and 3, Calcutta: Government Press.

——— (1935b), *Written Evidence Recorded during Enquiry on the Grant of Protection to the Sericultural Industry*, Vol. 1, Calcutta: Government Press.

——— (1936), *Report on Woollen Textiles*, Evidence, New Delhi: Government Press.

——— (1940), *Sericultural Industry*, Report and Minutes of Evidence, Calcutta: Government Press.

India, Provincial Banking Enquiry Commission (1929a), *Bengal*, Report and Minutes of Evidence, Calcutta: Government Press.

——— (1929b), *Punjab*, Report and Minutes of Evidence, Lahore: Government Press.

Irwin, John and Margaret Hall (1971), *Indian Painted and Printed Fabrics*, Ahmedabad: Calico Museum.

Jones, Dorothy (2004), 'The Eloquent Sari,' *Textile*, 2(1), 52–63.
Joshi, N.M. (1936), *Urban Handicrafts in the Bombay-Deccan*, Poona: Gokhale Institute of Politics and Economics.
Kakade, R.G. (1947), *A Socio-Economic Survey of Weaving Communities in Sholapur*, Poona: Gokhale Institute of Politics and Economics.
Karuppanam, K.K. (1987), 'Functioning of the Handloom Industry in Karur,' MPhil dissertation, Bharathiar University, Coimbatore.
King, Brenda M. (2005), *Silk and Empire*, Manchester: Manchester University Press.
Latifi, A. (1911), *The Industrial Punjab*, Lahore: Government Press.
Le Fanu, Henry (1883), *A Manual of the Salem District in the Presidency of Madras*, Madras: Government Press.
Logan, F. (1965), 'India's Loss of the British Cotton Market after 1865,' *Journal of Southern History*, 31(1), 40–50.
Lyons, Agnes M.M. (1996), 'The Textile Fabrics of India and Huddersfield Cloth Industry,' *Textile History*, 27(2), 172–94.
Machado, Pedro, Sarah Fee and Gwyn Campbell, eds. (2018), *Textile Trades, Consumer Cultures, and the Material Worlds of the Indian Ocean: An Ocean of Cloth*, London: Palgrave.
Madras (1927), *Preliminary Report on the Survey of Cottage Industries*, district reports (D. Narayana Rao), Madras: Government Press.
——— (1948), *Report of the Court of Enquiry Into Labour Conditions in the Handloom Industry* (B.V. Narayanaswami Naidu), Madras: Government Press.
——— (1954), *Report on the Survey of the Handloom Industry in Madras State*, Madras: Directorate of Statistics.
Mahalanobis, P.C. and D. Bhattacharya (1976), 'Growth of Population in India and Pakistan, 1801–1961,' *Artha Vijnana*, 18, 1–10.
MANTRA (Manmade Textiles Research Association) (1987), *Report of the Survey of Powerloom Weaving at Surat, Gujarat*, Report No. 13, Surat.
Maxwell-Lefroy, H. and E.C. Ansorge (1916–1918), *Report on an Enquiry Into the Silk Industry in India*, Calcutta: Government Press.
McGowan, Abigail (2009), *Crafting the Nation in Colonial India*, New York: Palgrave.
Medlicott, J.G. (1862), *Cotton Handbook of Bengal*, Calcutta: Bengal Printing.
Meeta and Rajivlochan (1996), 'The Past in the Present: The Weavers of Malegaon,' *Economic and Political Weekly*, 31(11), 673–78.
Mines, Mattison (1984), *The Warrior Merchants: Textiles, Trade and Territory in South India*, Cambridge: Cambridge University Press.
Morris, Morris D. (1963), 'Towards a Reinterpretation of Nineteenth Century Indian Economic History,' *Journal of Economic History*, 23(4), 607–18.
Mukharji, Trailokyanath (1888), *Art-Manufactures of India*, Calcutta: Government Press.
Mukherjee, Aditya (2008), 'The Return of the Colonial in Indian Economic History: The Last Phase of Colonialism in India,' *Social Scientist*, 36(3/4), 3–44.
Mukerji, Nitya Gopal (1894), 'Silk Industries of Moorshedabad,' *Journal of Indian Art*, 5, 1–7.
——— (1903), *A Monograph on the Silk Fabrics of Bengal*, Calcutta: Government Press.

Mukund, Kanakalatha and B. Syama Sundari (2001), *Traditional Industry in the New Market Economy: The Cotton Handlooms of Andhra Pradesh*, New Delhi, Thousand Oaks, CA and London: Sage Publications.

Muthukumar, S. (1990), 'Economic Analysis of Small-Scale Powerloom Industry at Chenimalai in Periyar District,' MPhil dissertation of Bharathiar University, Coimbatore.

Naseem Jan, S.F. (1991), 'Growth and Development of Powerloom Industry at Erode (1980–90),' MPhil dissertation, Bharathiar University, Coimbatore.

Nelson, J.H. (1868), *The Madurai Country: A Manual*, Madras: Government Press.

Nicholson, F. and E. Thurston, eds. (c. 1900), *Gazetteer of South India*, Madras: Government Press.

Niranjana, Seemanthini (2004), 'Thinking with Handlooms: Perspectives from Andhra Pradesh,' *Economic and Political Weekly*, 39(6), 553–63.

Parikh, Indira, Pulin K. Garg and Indu Menon (1992), *Women Weavers*, New Delhi: South Asia Books.

Parthasarathi, Prasannan (1998), 'Rethinking Wages and Competitiveness in the 18th Century: Britain and South India,' *Past and Present*, 158, 79–109.

Patel, Raoji B. (1906), 'Handloom Weaving in India,' in Proceedings of the Industrial Conference at Baroda, Madras, 83–92.

Patel, S.J. (1952), *Agricultural Labourers in Modern India and Pakistan*, Bombay: Current.

Prakash, Om (1976), 'Bullion for Goods: International Trade and the Economy of Early Eighteenth Century Bengal,' *Indian Economic and Social History Review*, 13(2), 159–86.

Puntambekar, S.V. and N.S. Varadachari (1926), *Hand-Spinning and Hand-Weaving*, Ahmedabad: All India Spinners Association.

Rajage, A.B. (no date), 'The Problems and Prospects of Decentralised Power Industry with Respect to Ichalkaranji,' MPhil dissertation of Shivaji University, Kolhapur.

Ramachandra Rao, P.R. (1935), *Decay of Indian Industries*, Bombay: D.B. Taraporevala.

Ranga, N.G. (1930), *The Economics of Handlooms*, Bombay: Taraporevala.

Ray, Indrajit (2009), 'Identifying the Woes of the Cotton Textile Industry in Bengal: Tales of the Nineteenth Century,' *Economic History Review*, 62(4), 857–92.

——— (2015), 'The Myth and Reality of Deindustrialisation in Early Modern India,' in Latika Chaudhary, Bishnupriya Gupta, Tirthankar Roy and Anand V. Swamy, eds., *A New Economic History of Colonial India*, London: Routledge, 52–66.

Riello, Giorgio (2013), *Cotton: The Fabric That Made the Modern World*, Cambridge: Cambridge University Press.

Riello, Giorgio and Prasannan Parthasarathi, eds. (2008), *The Spinning World: A Global History of Cotton Textiles, 1200–1850*, Oxford: Oxford University Press.

Riello, Giorgio and Tirthankar Roy, eds. (2009), *How India Clothed the World*, Leiden: Brill.

Robson, R. (1957), *The Cotton Industry in Britain*, London: Macmillan.

Roy, Tirthankar (1988), 'Size and Structure of Handloom Weaving in the Mid-1930s,' *Indian Economic and Social History Review*, 25(1), 1–24.

——— (1993), *Artisans and Industrialization: Indian Weaving in The Twentieth Century*, New Delhi: Oxford University Press.

——— (1997), 'Capitalism and Community: A Study of the Madurai Sourashtras,' *Indian Economic and Social History Review*, 34(4), 437–65.

——— (2002a), 'Acceptance of Innovations in Early Twentieth Century Indian Weaving,' *Economic History Review*, 55(4), 507–32.

——— (2002b), 'Madras Handkerchiefs in the Interwar Period,' *Indian Economic and Social History Review*, 39(2–3), 285–300.

——— (2003), 'Changes in Wool Production and Usage in Colonial India,' *Modern Asian Studies*, 37(2), 257–86.

——— (2007), 'Out of Tradition: Master Artisans and Economic Change in Colonial India,' *Journal of Asian Studies*, 66(4), 963–91.

——— (2011), *The Economic History of India 1857–1947*, Third Ed., New Delhi: Oxford University Press.

——— (2012), 'Consumption of Cotton Cloth in India, 1795–1940,' *Australian Economic History Review*, 52(1), 61–84.

——— (2013), *Economic History of Early Modern India*, London: Routledge.

——— (2017), *Company of Kinsmen: Enterprise and Community in South Asia 1600–1950*, New Delhi: Oxford University Press.

——— (2018), 'Karkhana,' in Kate Fleet et al., eds., *The Encyclopaedia of Islam Three*, Leiden: Brill, 143–6.

Roy Chowdhury, Supriya (1995), 'Political Economy of India's Textile Industry: The Case of Maharashtra, 1984–89,' *Pacific Affairs*, 68(2), 31–50.

Sambamurthy, V. (1948), 'Cottage Industries versus Industrialisation,' in *Rural and Cottage Industries*, Bombay: Vora and Co., 96–102.

Samman, H.F. (1904), 'The Cotton Fabrics of Assam,' *Journal of Indian Art*, 10, 21–4.

Sastry, K.R.R. (1925), *South Indian Gilds*, Madras: Indian Publishing House.

Sattaur, Jennifer (2012), 'Thinking Objectively: An Overview of "Thing Theory" in Victorian Studies,' *Victorian Literature and Culture*, 40(1), 347–57.

Saunders, A.J. (1920–1922), 'The Sourashtra Community in Madurai, South India,' mimeo prepared at American College, Madurai.

Sharma, Kaamya (2019), 'The Orientalisation of the Sari – Sartorial Praxis and Womanhood in Colonial and Post-Colonial India,' *South Asia: Journal of South Asian Studies*, 42(2), 219–36.

Singh, Manjit (1990), *The Political Economy of Unorganised Industry: A Study of the Labour Process*, New Delhi: Sage Publications.

Sivasubramonian, S. (2000), *National Income of India in the Twentieth Century*, New Delhi: Oxford University Press.

Specker, Konrad (1989), 'Madras Handlooms in the Nineteenth Century,' *Indian Economic and Social History Review*, 26(2), 131–66.

Srinivasa Raghavaiyangar, S. (1892), *Memorandum on the Progress of the Madras Presidency during the Last Forty Years of British Administration*, Madras: Government Press.

Swallow, Deborah (1999), 'The India Museum and the British Indian Textile Trade in the Late Nineteenth Century,' *Textile History*, 30(1), 29–45.

Swaminathan, Padmini (1992), 'Technical Education and Industrial Development in Madras Presidency: Illusions of a Policy in the Making,' *Economic and Political Weekly*, 27(30), 1611–22.

Talboys Wheeler, J. (1862), *Hand-Book to the Cotton Cultivation in the Madras Presidency*, Madras: Higginbotham.

Tarlo, Emma (1996), *Clothing Matters: Dress and Its Symbolism in Modern India*, Chicago: University of Chicago Press.

Telang, S.V. (1932), *Report on Handloom Weaving Industry in the Bombay Presidency*, Bombay: Government Press.

Thomas, P.J. and B. Natarajan (1936), 'Economic Depression in the Madras Presidency (1825–54),' *Economic History Review*, 7(1), 67–75.

Thorner, Daniel (1962), '"Deindustrialization" in India, 1881–1931,' in D. Thorner and A. Thorner, eds., *Land and Labour in India*, New York: Asia.

Thurston, Edgar (1897), *Monograph on the Cotton Fabric Industry of the Madras Presidency*, Madras: Government Press.

——— (1909), *Tribes and Castes of Southern India*, Madras: Government Press.

Trivedi, A.B. (1949), *Post-War Gujarat*, Bombay: Bhagirathi Press.

Twomey, M.J. (1983), 'Employment in Nineteenth Century Indian Textiles,' *Explorations in Economic History*, 20(1), 37–57.

United Provinces (1924), *Report on the Industrial Survey of the United Provinces*, Allahabad: Government Press.

Venkatraman, K.S. (1936), *Handloom Industry in the Madras Presidency*, Madras: The Diocesan Press.

——— (1936–1937), 'The Economic Condition of Handloom Weavers,' *Journal of the University of Bombay*, 5, 75–104.

Vicziany, Marika (1979), 'The De-Industrialisation of India in the Nineteenth Century: A Methodological Critique of Amiya Kumar Bagchi,' *Indian Economic and Social History Review*, 16(2), 105–46.

Wielenga, Karuna Dietrich (2016), 'Repertoires of Resistance: The Handloom Weavers of South India, c.1800–1960,' *International Review of Social History*, 61(4), 423–58.

Williamson, Jeffrey G. (2013), *Trade and Poverty*, Cambridge, MA: MIT Press.

Yanagisawa, Haruka (1993), 'The Handloom Industry and Its Market Structure: The Case of the Madras Presidency in the First Half of the Twentieth Century,' *Indian Economic and Social History Review*, 30(1), 1–27.

Yusuf Ali, A. (1900), *A Monograph on Silk Fabrics Produced in the North Western Provinces and Oudh*, Allahabad: Government Press.

SELECTED BIOGRAPHIES

Previous chapters mention individuals who had a significant influence on the discourse that the crafts were commercially viable, that they should have a place in India's economic modernization, and they contained a knowledge base that was potentially valuable. Inspired by that ideology, they wrote influential works, reports, and led documentation projects. This section presents short biographies of some of the more well-known members of that set.

Birdwood, Sir George (1832–1917): Curator, civil servant, writer. Born in Belgaum and trained as a doctor, Birdwood taught botany and medicine at Grant Medical College, Bombay, in his early life. Later he was involved in the management of museums, and his work in this field was appreciated enough to earn him the title of Sheriff of Bombay. After a period of semi-retirement due to poor health, Birdwood worked for the India Office in London and as a curator in museums in London. Birdwood published profusely on the botany, raw materials, and handicrafts of India, including *The Industrial Arts of India* (1880). During his time as a special assistant in the revenue and statistical department of the India Office (1879–1905), Birdwood published various collections of the East India Company records, including *The Register of Letters of the Governor and Company of Merchants of London Trading into the East Indies, 1600–1610* in 1893. The *Industrial Arts of India* is a systematic description of the skilled handicrafts of his time, and a classic resource for studies of the subject. Source: Oxford Dictionary of National Biography, online resource.

Chatterjee, Sir Atul Chandra (1874–1955): Civil servant, writer. Joined United Province's service after passing the Indian Civil Service examination (1897). Ten years later, produced *Notes on the Industries of the United Provinces*, a classic resource on the subject. Later served as a member of the Viceroy's Council, President of the International Labour Organization, Adviser to the Secretary of State for India, and as Indian High Commissioner in London. Source: *Samsad Bangali Charitabhidhan*

(Samsad Biographical Dictionary of the Bengalis), Calcutta: Sahitya Samsad, 1976, 10.

Chatterton, Sir Alfred (1866/1867–1958): Engineer, industrial adviser, writer. Trained as an engineer and a fellow of the Imperial College, Chatterton joined the Indian Educational Service and was Professor of Engineering, Madras (1888–1900). In 1908, he became Director of Industries, Madras, and in 1912, Director of Industries and Commerce in Mysore. A prolific writer, Chatterton campaigned that many types of crafts were skilled enough and sound enough as businesses to survive machines, but they needed to consult engineers to improve the quality of their tools. Source: Grace's Guide, online resource. Chatterton was a member of the Indian Industrial Commission between 1916 and 1918; Controller of the Indian Munitions Board in 1917, and an adviser to the Tata Industrial Bank in Bombay. His publications include 'Notes on Chrome Tanning in Madras' (1906), *The Industrial Evolution in India* (1912), *Agricultural and Industrial Problems in India* (1915), and 'The Industrial Progress of the Mysore State' (1925).

Forbes Watson, John (1827–1892): Born in a farming family of Aberdeenshire, trained as a surgeon, joined Indian service and was a lecturer in physiology in Grant Medical College, Bombay. From 1857, he succeeded John Forbes Royle as Director of India Museum in London and was appointed an adviser to the India Office on Indian products. Forbes Watson produced many short articles as part of his job. The project 'Textile Manufactures of India,' commissioned about 1860 'to consist, as originally designed, of 1000 specimens and 240 coloured plates supplying an almost exhaustive series of examples of the high art textile decoration for which India is famous,' turned out to be his most challenging commission. The project was abandoned in 1879, after the production of 16 volumes. Source: 'Synopsis of Dr. Forbes Watson's Life and Work,' *Journal of Indian Art*, 3, 1890, 25–32.

Gadgil, D.R. (1901–1971): Gadgil was a policy advisor for the latter half of his working life. He started as an economic historian. His first major published work, a Cambridge thesis, was 'a sketch of the economic history of India' (Preface to *Industrial Evolution of India*, London: Oxford University Press, 1924). Two chapters in the book, 'the country artisan' and 'the organization of urban industry' expressed the view that a worthwhile economic history of India would need to engage with the artisans rather than dismiss them as a relic. Gadgil could encourage and commission research to follow up this idea thanks to his directorship of India's premier social science research institute in the 1930s and 1940s. Students and associates in Gokhale Institute of Politics and Economics (Pune) produced works on the urban handicrafts of western Maharashtra, including very useful studies of handloom weaving in Sholapur, which figures prominently in this book.

Gandhi, Mohandas Karamchand (1869–1948): Leader of the Indian independence movement against British colonial rule. Gandhi claimed that the future of an independent India was not industrialization, but an agrarian, village-led economy. Gandhi called for Indian people to take up hand-spinning (see khadi) and encouraged the boycott of textiles imported from Britain to India.

Havell, Ernest B. (1861–1934): Artist and art teacher. Havell was Principal of the Madras School of Industrial Arts between 1884 and 1892, and of the Government School of Art in Calcutta between 1896 and 1906, where he worked with the Indian painter Abanindranath Tagore. He was also a keeper of the Government Art Gallery (1896–1906). Havell pioneered the Indianization of art school curriculum and popularized Indian traditional and modern art in the West. Advocacy of skilled crafts was a part of this mission. At times, Havell's campaign for Indian art took on a militant aspect, which endeared him to the Indian nationalists and distanced him from other India-enthusiasts. Havell co-founded the India Society in June 1910. The Society was formed in response to a remark upon Havell's lecture at the Royal Society of the Arts by George Birdwood, who claimed that India had no fine art tradition of its own. The India Society held many significant exhibitions and promoted publications, including Rabindranath Tagore's *Gitanjali* (1912), and Havell's own *Handbook of Indian Art* (1920). Source: Oxford Dictionary of National Biography, online resource.

Mukharji, Trailokyanath (1847–1919): Writer and curator. After completion of school, Trailokyanth left home in 1865 unable to bear the poverty of his family home. He settled in Orissa and started writing in Oriya, befriended William Hunter (1840–1900), a Bengal officer and author of the classic study *The Annals of Rural Bengal* (1868). Hunter inducted him into government service. Mukharji served as Curator of the Indian Museum in Calcutta from 1886 to 1896, organized exhibits for the Calcutta International Exhibition and the Amsterdam Exhibition of 1883, and for the Colonial and Indian Exhibition of 1887 and the Glasgow International Exhibition of 1888. The product of these activities was *Art-manufactures of India* (1888), a major resource for this book. In later life, Trailokyanath earned fame by writing fantastic and humorous tales in Bengali, a genre then rare if not unknown. Mukharji remains the most significant exponent of that genre in the Bengali literature. Mukharji's English travel writing, *A Visit to Europe* (1889), was popular in Britain as well as India. His Bengali writings include the compilation of the first Bengali language encyclopaedia, *Bangla Bishwokosh* (volume 1, with Rangalal Mukhopadhyay). Source: *Samsad Bangali Charitabhidhan* (Samsad Biographical Dictionary of the Bengalis), Calcutta: Sahitya Samsad, 1976, 257.

Mukerji, Nitya Gopal (b. and d. not available): Silk technologist, writer. Author of *Saral Krishi Bigyan* (Agricultural science simplified, in Bengali, 1904) and *Resham Bigyan* (Science of silk, Bengali, 1908), was selected by a government scheme to learn silk making in Padua, Montpelier, and in Paris, possibly in 1885–1890. One of his tasks was to find out how Louis Pasteur had succeeded in controlling the pebrine disease of the silkworm in France and Italy. The disease caused considerable damage in Bengal. On return, Mukerji served the Government of Bengal as Deputy Collector and Scientific Instructor. During his tenure, he wrote a remarkable study in English of the silk-weaving industry of Bengal (1897) in the monographs series (see the glossary entry 'monographs'). He resigned from the job due to disagreements with his superiors, the exact reasons for the disagreements are not known. Sources: *Samsad Bangali Charitabhidhan* (Samsad Biographical Dictionary of the Bengalis), Calcutta: Sahitya Samsad, 1976, 196; Thomas Wardle, 'On Sericulture and Silk Weaving in Kashmir and India,' *Journal of Indian Art*, 13, 1910, 108–12.

Ranga, N.G. (1900–1995): Politician, academic, writer. Born in a peasant family of Nidubrolu, Andhra Pradesh, Ranga earned a degree from Oxford and took a teaching job in economics in Madras in 1926. Soon after, he joined the nationalist movement as a follower of Gandhi. After independence, he briefly moved away from the National Congress, which then subscribed to Jawaharlal Nehru's socialism, and moved closer to economic liberalism that the Swatantra Party represented. He was a founder of the party. After the party's decline in the 1970s, Ranga rejoined Congress and was elected from the Guntur parliamentary constituency for over a decade in the 1980s. Despite the time he spent in national politics, Ranga did not wield much power in either the Congress or the Swatantra Party. However, he was respected, not least because of his credentials as an academic. His *Economics of Handlooms* (1930), the reprint of the Oxford thesis, is a chaotically written, descriptive, yet evidence-based study of weaving in a region otherwise poorly served by scholarship. Its somewhat pessimistic tone may reflect Ranga's Gandhian leanings.

Tagore, Rabindranath (1861–1941) (*see also* Sriniketan): Rabindranath Tagore was a Bengali poet, Nobel laureate and educationist. He is most well known for his contributions to Bengali literature and music and his role in the Indian nationalist movement. In 1922, with Leonard Elmhirst, Tagore established the Institute of Rural Reconstruction in a place renamed as Sriniketan ('sree' in Bengali is not exactly translatable, elegance, fortune, and beauty capture some of the nuances; 'niketan' means abode). The Sriniketan school tried to create and impart a modern scientific knowledge-base that could be applied to the everyday problems of peasants and artisans. The school was an expression of Tagore's educational philosophy that human freedom was attained through an education that made its recipients realize their full potentials, and that British colonial school education, a rootless mix of western and Indian contents, fell short of this ideal. His school in Santiniketan (literally the abode of peace) was an earlier expression of this philosophy. Sriniketan was a more practice-based model. Elmhirst (1893–1974), a British agronomist, initially assisted him in the project, and later became his friend and associate. Source: Uma Das Gupta, *Rabindranath Tagore: A Biography*, New Delhi: Oxford University Press, 2004.

Theagaraya Chetty, Sir P. (Pitti) (1852–1925): Lawyer, industrialist, politician, and publicist, Theagaraya Chetty was born in a Devanga family of handloom weavers. Late in life, he became famous as a leader of the non-Brahmin movement of Tamil Nadu. Around 1900, however, he was well known to the industrial administration of the Madras government as a leading textile producer and merchant. Through collaborated effort, the government and Theagaraya Chetty campaigned effectively among weavers for the adoption of several improved tools, including the fly-shuttle slay.

Thomas, P. (Parakunnel) J. (1895–1965): Academic and adviser. Despite the huge symbolic role of the crafts in Indian nationalism (see Chapter 8) and India's dominance in the textile trade in the early modern times, not many Indian academics before 1970 moved into the systematic historical study of artisanal textiles. Thomas was an exception. A Syrian Catholic from Kottayam area in Kerala, Thomas studied economics and went to Oxford for research. His B.Litt thesis led to books and articles on the trade in Indian 'calicos' in Europe, calico (derived from Calicut in coastal Malabar) meant a white cotton cloth popular as an Indian export. The work, *Mercantilism and the East India Trade* (London: P.S. King, 1926) is still widely cited. His doctoral thesis was a history of public finance of British India (London: Humphrey Milford, 1939), again, a book that stood the test of time. An academic in the 1930s, Thomas joined the government after 1947 and was elected to the legislature. His relevance for this book rests on a landmark study, Report of the *Fact-finding Committee: Handlooms and Mills* (1942) that he supervised, possibly wrote (see Chapters 1 and 8). The report was a remarkable document not only because it processed a huge quantity of novel information and statistical data on the handloom industry, but also offered an analytical narrative on the handloom weaving industry, which was quite historical in outlook. Thomas also published several works on the history of the Syrian Catholics of South India, and the apostle Saint Thomas.

Thurston, Edgar (1855–1935): Doctor and curator. Superintendent of Madras Government Museum and lecturer in anatomy at the Madras Medical College, Thurston was a prolific contributor to the *Journal of Indian Art* on many types of artisan industries of southern India, most importantly cotton and silk weaving. His contributions to the Ethnographic Surveys of India, or Tribes and Caste reports, are better known to scholars. Less known is the overlap between his writings on south Indian livelihoods and the Tribes and Caste essays, which contain rich descriptions of the work people do to earn a living.

Yusuf Ali, Abdullah (1872–1953): Civil servant and writer. Hailing from a Bohra business family of Bombay, Yusuf Ali studied English literature in Bombay, studied law in England, and joined Indian Civil Service in 1895. His career, colourful personal life, maverick political views (he supported Britain in its battle against the Ottoman Empire during World War I), and scholarly accomplishments (his translation of the Quran is considered the most authentic by many scholars of Islam) obscured one of his other achievements, a 160-page book on the silk-weaving industry in the United Provinces, published in 1900. His biographer in the Oxford Dictionary of National Biography does not mention this work, and a biographical book notes its cultural symbolism but not its significance as a textile history resource. The silk book, like Nitya Gopal Mukerji's counterpart work on Bengal (see Mukerji), was based on the compilation of novel information (see 'monographs' in Glossary). (Source: M.A. Sherif, *Searching for Solace: A Biography of Abdullah Yusuf Ali, Interpreter of the Qur'an*, Kuala Lumpur: Islamic Book Trust, 1994.)

GLOSSARY

Baluchari saree: Silk sarees traditionally produced in the towns of Murshidabad and Bishnupur in Bengal, characterized by depictions of mythological scenes on the *pallu* (end) of the saree.

Benares saree: Sarees traditionally woven from silk and gold thread or jari in the city of Varanasi, or Benares, characterized by Mughal-inspired floral and foliate motifs.

Bombay-Deccan: Districts of the Bombay Presidency on the Deccan plateau. The larger districts with a significant handloom association include Sholapur, Bijapur, and Belgaum.

Chiffon: A plain woven, lightweight fabric of fine twisted silk or nylon yarn.

Chikan: A style of fine white embroidery on white muslin or cotton which is produced primarily in Lucknow.

Chintz: Woodblock printed and glazed fabrics originally imported to Europe from India. The original Hindi word of which chintz is a derivative is chhit or drop, in practice printed.

Crepe: A plain woven, transparent fabric of highly twisted raw silk, rayon or wool, and embossed to have a crisp, wrinkled surface.

Devanga: A south Indian caste who traditionally followed the occupation of weaving. Around 1900, Devangas in Tamil Nadu traced their origin either to Andhra Pradesh or Karnataka. P. Theagaraya Chetty (see 'Selected biographies') was a prominent member of the caste who left a mark on the history of weaving in south India.

Dharmavaram saree: Originally woven in the town of Dharmavarm, in the Anantapur District of Andhra Pradesh. These sarees are woven from mulberry silk and gold or silver thread and carry two-tone colouring.

Dhoti: A garment, primarily worn by men, which is made from a single piece of fabric wrapped around the hips and between the legs.

Dobby: As a fabric, woven on a dobby loom, which is characterized by its raised texture and geometric pattern. As an instrument, an attachment to create such designs.

Draw-boy harness: The shaft on a dobby loom which controls a set of threads. Raising or lowering several harnesses at one time gives a variety of gaps between the warp-threads for the shuttle containing the weft thread to be thrown. The name is originally derived from the draw-boys, who manually operated the device by pulling on draw threads, and whose job was later mechanized. The Jacquard made some of the functions of a draw-boy obsolete.

Drop-box: Box containing shuttles with threads in various colours, used in figure-weaving looms.

Dupatta: A women's scarf-like piece of material, traditionally worn as a part of the salwar-kameez, and draped across the chest and/or head.

Fact-finding Committee report, 1942: One of the most valuable sources on textile history until the mid-twentieth century (see Thomas, P.J. in the 'Selected biographies').

Gauze: Thin, almost transparent fabric made of silk, linen, or cotton.

Ghaghra: A long, embroidered, gathered skirt originating from western India.

Hat: A village market.

Ilkal saree: Originally woven in the town of Ilkal in the Bijapur district of Bombay province (now Balgakot district of Karnataka state). These sarees are distinguished by their silk pallu (border of the loose end of the saree) which are woven separately and then attached to the main body of the saree.

Jacquard: Named after Joseph Marie Jacquard (1752–1834), the Jacquard attachment, invented around 1804–5, controls individual warp threads on a loom by using punch cards, allowing for the weaving of intricate patterns.

Jamdani: A brightly patterned, sheer cotton fabric. Dhaka in Bangladesh (Bengal before 1947) and Tanda in Uttar Pradesh were known for jamdani weaving.

Julaha: Muslim handloom weavers of northern and eastern India.

Kaikolar: A traditional weaving community from southern India, established primarily in the state of Tamil Nadu, but also in some parts of Kerala, Andhra Pradesh, Karnataka, and northern Sri Lanka.

Kalamkari: Kalam means pen. Kalamkari refers to the process of using a bamboo pen to draw designs onto textiles. A few towns on the south-eastern coast and near it, like Kalahasti, were once very famous for this type of work.

Kanchipuram saree: Saree made in the town of Kanchipuram in the state of Tamil Nadu. One of the more successful saree brands of the twentieth century; to the consumers Kanchipuram stands for traditional floral and other motifs applied on unusual colour combinations between the border, the loose end, and the body of a saree.

Khaddar *see* **khadi.**

Khadi: Cloth which is woven from cotton yarn that is made by hand, using a spinning wheel. Khadi was popularised by Gandhi, who used it as a symbol for Indian economic independence, through the rejection of the purchasing of industrialized fabrics which were produced in Britain and sold to Indian consumers.

Kinkhab (kamkhwab): Translating loosely to dream-work (khwaab in Hindi is dream), kinkhab refers to brocade with heavy use of gold and silver threads. Kinkhab sarees are often extensions of a jari or metal-thread-making industry.

Kongunad: A region of western Tamil Nadu, one of the earliest territorial divisions within the region and part of the Madras Presidency during British rule. Districts here, Coimbatore, Erode, Salem, Namakkal, Karur, and Tirupur, contain a concentrated hub of textile and apparel production, some of which had an association with handloom weaving until recently.

Koshti: A weaving caste of mainly western and central India.

Kumbakonam saree: Silk sarees originally produced in the town of Kumbakonam in Tamil Nadu. Later became a trade brand not necessarily made in this town.

Kurta: Loose shirt worn primarily by men.

Labbai: A community, mainly based in Tamil Nadu, known as traders, including textiles and leather.

Lehenga: Long, full, embroidered skirt worn usually for special occasions.

Madras Handkerchiefs: A two-and-a-half to three-yard square piece of coloured cotton cloth made for exports. A product that evolved out of, and outlived, eighteenth-century Indo-European, India-Africa and intra-Asian trades in Indian textiles; until the 1990s, Madras handkerchiefs remained a major cotton handloom export from south India, with its main market in coastal Nigeria. In 1993, it formed in value about 10 percent of handloom apparel exports; handlooms formed 7 percent of India's textile exports.

Madras-Deccan: Districts of the Madras Presidency on the Deccan plateau. In the book, the region is also referred to as southern Andhra districts. The main districts were Anantapur, Kurnool, Bellary and Cuddapah.

Mahajan: Literally 'great people' in Sanskrit, mahajan in economic history sources from Bengal would refer to the generic capitalist, very often, moneylenders.

Masulipatnam: A port city in the Krishna district of the Indian state of Andhra Pradesh. A major trading and manufacturing town in the seventeenth century.

Momin: Muslim weavers of North and West India, concentrated in the eastern districts of Uttar Pradesh (or United Provinces in the colonial times), also known as Ansaris in north India.

Monographs: Around 1880, the government of India announced a desire to document Indian crafts. Promoting commerce in Indian goods was one of the aims, another one was to revive the crafts. Edward Buck (1838–1916), the Secretary of the Revenue and Agriculture Department, played a prominent role in the documentation enterprise. He started the *Journal of Indian Art*, 17 issues of which were published between 1886 and 1916. The journal published a series of surveys of artisanal industries in the provinces and became a catalyst in the semi-official discourses on the craft policy in this time. The provincial governments then followed up the enterprise with a series of sponsored works. Most of these were published both in the *Journal*, and as books, but some were published only as books. These were called monographs. The monographs were of varying quality and content. The best ones not only wrote reports and collected facts about an industry but also made use of the photographic representation of objects pioneered in India by William Griggs (1831–1911), also associated with the *Journal of Indian Art*. The list of authors on the textile studies includes S.M. Edwardes (an Assistant Collector, Bombay), N.N. Banerjei (Assistant Director of Land Records and Agriculture, Bengal), Edgar Thurston (see entry in 'Selected biographies'), Abdullah Yusuf Ali (see entry) and Nitya Gopal Mukerji (see entry).

Muslin: Cotton fabric in a plain weave using very fine yarn. The degree of fineness for a cloth to qualify as muslin varies.

Padmasali: A Hindu caste from the states of Telangana, Andhra Pradesh, Maharashtra, Karnataka, and Tamil Nadu. The Padmashalis are traditionally weavers.

Paithani saree: Traditionally woven in the town of Paithan, near Aurangabad in Maharashtra, the Paithani saree is made of silk and gold or silver thread. Paithani saree now is said to be influenced by Buddhist motifs in its designs, due to Paithan's closeness to the Buddhist Ajanta caves.

Paj: A form of soft silk.

Patan: *see* Patola.

Patola saree: The name derives from Patan, a town in northern Gujarat. A double *ikat* woven saree from Patan, usually from silk. Ikat is a broad type of design making, that involves dyeing the threads by the tying method.

Phulkari: Literally 'flower work,' an embroidery technique from the Punjab region.

Pochampally saree: Traditionally woven in Pochampally, near the eastern border of Hyderabad town in the state of Telangana. The sarees use both ikat technique (see Patola) as well as geometric patterns.

Rayon: Fabric made from fibres of regenerated cellulose derived from plant and wood, also referred to as viscose or artificial silk.

Sahukar: A generic term for moneylender or capitalist.

Salwar: Baggy trousers which are gathered at the ankles, worn as part of salwar-kameez.

Saree: An Indian woman's garment comprised of a piece of cloth which is draped around the body.

Shandy: The Tamil counterpart of hat (see hat). Derived from the Tamil shanthai, meaning market.

Sourashtra, Saurashtra: A region of Gujarat. In this book, a Hindu community of south India who speaks a language distinct from local dialects, who trace their origin to the Saurashtra region, and whose main occupation was handloom weaving until the early-twentieth century.

Sriniketan: *see* Tagore, Rabindranath 'Selected biographies.'

Surat: A port city in Gujarat, famous for its production of silk and rayon textiles, objects of gold and silver, and more recently, diamonds.

Swadeshi: Derived from Sanskrit, 'swa' meaning self or own, and 'desh' meaning land, was a primarily economic movement within the larger movement for Indian independence. The swadeshi movement aimed to boycott British products and instead revive Indian products and production processes.

Take-up motion: A loom attachment or system that withdraws the cloth from the weaving area of a loom, thus making sure the fabric has an even texture.

Tanjore saree: Handloom saree originally woven in the town of Tanjore in the state of Tamil Nadu, characterized by motifs derived from Tanjore paintings.

Warp: Lengthwise threads on a loom, usually twisted harder than a weft thread.

Weft: Threads which are interlaced at right angles to the warp threads on a loom.

NOTE: Those interested in reading detailed works on many of the cloth types that are described in this list, their provenance, and the technology involved in their making are directed to two works, one of them in Bengali, that were also consulted in the preparation of the Glossary. These are: Rosemary Crill, *The Fabric of India*, London: V and A Publishing, 2015; Syamali Das, *Bharater Oitiyyamoy Bastrasilpa: Atita theke Bartaman* [India's Textile Heritage: From the Past to the Present], Kolkata: Shree Book Agency, 2018.

INDEX

Note: Page numbers in *italic* indicate a *figure* and page numbers in **bold** indicate a **table** on the corresponding page

For Product Safety Concerns and Information please contact our EU
representative GPSR@taylorandfrancis.com
Taylor & Francis Verlag GmbH, Kaufingerstraße 24, 80331 München, Germany

www.ingramcontent.com/pod-product-compliance
Lightning Source LLC
LaVergne TN
LVHW011132300926
849160LV00008B/614
9781032175164